DISCLOSED POETICS

Manchester University Press

ANGELAKIHUMANITIES

editors
Charlie Blake
Pelagia Goulimari
Timothy S. Murphy
Robert Smith

general editor
Gerard Greenway

Angelaki Humanities publishes works which address and probe broad and compelling issues in the theoretical humanities. The series favours path-breaking thought, promotes unjustly neglected figures, and grapples with established concerns. It believes in the possibility of blending, without compromise, the rigorous, the well-crafted, and the inventive. The series seeks to host ambitious writing from around the world.

Angelaki Humanities is the associated book series of
angelaki – journal of the theoretical humanities.

Already published

The question of literature: the place of the literary in contemporary theory
Elizabeth Beaumont Bissell

Postmodernism. What moment?
Pelagia Goulimari (ed.)

Absolutely postcolonial: writing between the singular and the specific
Peter Hallward

Late modernist poetics: from Pound to Prynne
Anthony Mellors

The new Bergson
John Mullarkey (ed.)

Subversive Spinoza: (un)contemporary variations
Timothy S. Murphy (ed.)

ANGELAKIHUMANITIES

DISCLOSED POETICS
Beyond landscape and lyricism

John Kinsella

Manchester University Press
Manchester and New York

distributed exclusively in the USA by Palgrave

Copyright © John Kinsella 2007

The right of John Kinsella to be identified as the author of this work has been asserted by him in accordance with the Copyright, Designs and Patents Act 1988.

Published by Manchester University Press
Oxford Road, Manchester M13 9NR, UK
and Room 400, 175 Fifth Avenue, New York, NY 10010, USA
www.manchesteruniversitypress.co.uk

Distributed in the United States exclusively by
Palgrave Macmillan, 175 Fifth Avenue,
New York, NY 10010, USA

Distributed in Canada exclusively by
UBC Press, University of British Columbia, 2029 West Mall,
Vancouver, BC, Canada V6T 1Z2

British Library Cataloguing-in-Publication Data is available

Library of Congress Cataloging-in-Publication Data is available

ISBN 978 0 7190 9560 3 paperback

First published by Manchester University Press in hardback 2007

This paperback edition first published 2014

The publisher has no responsibility for the persistence or accuracy of URLs for any external or third-party internet websites referred to in this book, and does not guarantee that any content on such websites is, or will remain, accurate or appropriate.

Printed by Lightning Source

CONTENTS

List of illustrations	*page* vii
Acknowledgements	ix
Preface	xi

I **Pastoral, landscape, place ...**	1
Definitions of pastoral?	1
Can there be a radical 'western' pastoral?	4
Parrotology (on the necessity of parrots in poetry)	16
Landscape poetry?	30
The dark side of the beach: undisclosed poetics	36

II **Spatial lyricism**	47
A new lyricism: some early thoughts on linguistic disobedience	47
Olivetti Lettera 32	74
Distortions – on questioning the primacy of the accented syllable: notes on alternative spatialities for poetic rhythm	78
Line breaks and back-draft: not a defence of a poem	93
Line breaks coda	101
The search for the new idea, the unique? Against poetics?	102
On *Graphology*	110

III **Manifestoes**	113
Anthologising the nation	113
Notes towards netdeath and the loss of page style: working 'off the page'?	119
Consensus	124
The group, linguistic innovation, and international regionalism: prelude to the preparation of a group manifesto	128

Intensivism 137
Hyperpoetics and the curvature of subsets 140
Treatise on rooms and windows 144

IV **Ageing, loss, recidivism ...** 161
Domine, refugium ... 161
Graphol-age-ia poetica: ageing as confrontation or avoidance of death 168
A loss of poetics 183
Poetics recidivous and the de-poetics of lightning, herbicides, and pesticides 199
Afterword to *The New Arcadia* 221

V **Appendices** 226
From Marcus Clarke's 'Preface' to the *Poems* of Adam Lindsay Gordon, 1880/1893 226
Windows 228
Imitation Spatialogue (Sublime) 230
Letter from Graham Nerlich 234

Bibliography 240

ILLUSTRATIONS

1 North Window 1   *page* 158

2 North Window 2   158

3 North Window 3   158

4 South Window   158

All photographs taken by John Kinsella.

ACKNOWLEDGEMENTS

I'd like to thank the many journals and conferences that have supported sections of this work in various drafts. Special thanks are due to Andrew Taylor, Gerard Greenway and my partner, Tracy (Ryan) Kinsella. Also, I would like to extend special thanks to Dennis Haskell, Glen Phillips, Marjorie Perloff, Brian Worsfold and Maria Vidal at the English Department at the University of Lleida; the editors and readers at *Angelaki, Artful Dodge, The Australian Book Review, Colorado Review, The Commonwealth Review, Island Magazine, The Literary Review, Meanjin, Poetry Review, Salzburg Review, Southerly*; Kenyon College in Ohio, Churchill College at Cambridge University, the Landscape and Language Centre at Edith Cowan University; Bill Louden for being generally interested and supportive; Manchester University Press, Matthew Frost and the press's readers; and many others. I would also like to acknowledge and thank those I have chatted with about various issues discussed in this book.

PREFACE: BEYOND LANDSCAPE AND LYRICISM

This is not a defence of poetry – in fact, in many ways which I hope will become evident, I feel that poetry is indefensible! However, it is a questioning of what drives a personal poetics to become so inclusive that it is a vehicle for personal ethics, politics, a record of one's own life and relationships from such a singular point of view, and a generator for digesting the massive amount of information one absorbs in day-to-day life. Though an admirer of the Parnassians and later the French Symbolists, and a translator of Rimbaud, I cannot place art above anything outside itself.

As I said in my autobiographical work *Auto*: 'My name is John Kinsella, I make poems' (2001, p. 60). That's what I do because I have done it since childhood, it's what I do because it's how I know best to express myself, because I feel impelled, and because it's the infrastructure to a broader life. In thinking about how I write, I have found myself searching many familiar areas, with the most commonplace being as necessary as the most esoteric. Ploughing a field on Wheatlands when I was eighteen is every bit as important to me as first reading Deleuze and Guattari, and being a vegan as essential as enjoying the poetry of Shelley. In my adult life, the teaching of poetry has become inseparable from my poetics: I teach what and how I have learnt so others can learn for themselves. I am interested in offering approaches and processes, not end results. The unfinished intrigues me.

There are a number of specific threads running through this Poetics, the strongest being issues of what constitutes place, and why and how we write about it. Be it a pastoral construct as means of controlling an environment (and its population), or the body as text, or a radical envi-

Preface

ronmentalism (to resist the pastoral imposition), all are entangled together and none gains primacy. Landscape is part of time, and the lyric is a representational grounding of time. The singing of a poem, the speaking of a poem, the rhythm and intonation of a poem, are also inseparable. This is a work that out of its disparate parts suggests a synthesis is possible, even desirable, but recognises the decay, pollution, and destruction of not only natural environments but the markers of place itself. The poem becomes 'place' when the survey markers and gridworks of landscape are overlaid and re-signified with the survey markers and gridworks of text. The poem is either complicit with or resistant to the status quo, the state-sanctioned version of literature that feeds a stultifying nationalist and hierarchical agenda: this is an issue that drives my poetry and poetics. When it is resolved, the poetry will stop, from me at least.

The language deployed in this work is as varied and variable as my poetry, and is intended to be a mirror for and a mirror from that creative work. It is not an analysis, but a stretching out of the poetic line. It is commentary, but interactive commentary. It is a conversation between text, reader, place, and poet. This ranges from an exploration of pastoral in a general sense, through to the case-specific: to a personal poetics vis-à-vis ideas of nation; to pedagogical issues in writing and the compilation of manifestoes; to how one might textually map landscape; and, probably fundamentally, to the relationship of the autobiographical self to the production of the poem.

PASTORAL, LANDSCAPE, PLACE ...

Definitions of pastoral?

Can 'pastoral' as both a super-rarefied genre-form and a historical political vehicle – of a problematic variety – have any relevance in the age of factory farming, consciousness of land destruction, cloning, genetic modification, pesticides, herbicides, the citification of the rural, and the de-landing and disenfranchisement of indigenous communities (nomadic, agrarian, civic, urban, etc.)? Traditionally, pastoral worked as a vehicle of empowerment for the educated classes through the idyllicising and most often romanticising of the rural world. There was a huge gap between the rural workers portrayed and the manner of their presentation.

One possible turning point in this approach was Wordsworth's 'Michael' (1800/1984, pp. 224–236), in which a consciousness of the collapse of the idyll found expression as part of popular poetic and dramatic culture in English. Earlier, the Elizabethan court wits could invest their Italian-inherited pastorals with ironic relief, and utilise an arcadia as a playground for aristocratic or land-owning sensibilities, but ultimately they stayed firmly grounded in the hierarchies of control – of the divine right, the order of relations that played with the pagan hierarchy of Gods and humans, and the ladder of authority that entailed using this as a vehicle for Christian hierarchies. The goatherd or shepherd or rural worker in general could transcend his place on that ladder through lyrical skills – specifically oral (singing) – or shows of strength. And in the Greek and Roman worlds, these usually turned out to indicate some noble lineage that had been lost or obscured through fate – usually pollution or hubris. Ironically, instead of distancing pastoral from modernity, such a world-view increases its relevance to modernity. Just look at the way the company Monsanto sells plant genetic-modification technology – the so-called benefits of this technology are sold to the broader population insofar as they are said to make food production more efficient, and this is as relevant to the urban consumer as it is to those living in the country. To the farmer, it is sold as a cheaper and more reliable means of producing food – that is, it will increase their profits. Ultimately, the company sells its technology in a universal and egalitarian way, as a means of improving the 'pastoral', when in fact it is establishing a hierarchy in which the company actually benefits, over both farmer and consumer (the farmer is then obliged to buy the chemicals, seed stock, and so on, that the biotechnology requires; the consumer faces uncertain risk to health, etc. – as does the environment).

Traditional pastorals were basically not read or heard by the 'kind' of characters they purported to be about, whereas contemporary 'pastoral'/ 'anti-pastoral' writers expect that their work might be read by all who can read the language in which they write. It's the paranoia of the poet that far fewer people will ever read a poem than might be hoped for. Can contemporary pastoral poems speak to rural workers, to farmers, to those who make the pesticides? Maybe; maybe not. It depends on intent and reception. Does audience define pastoral? Do the educated Greeks enjoying Theocritus, or the Romans reading Virgil, constitute the idea of pastoral audience?

A poet like the rustic John Clare, who might be seen as more of a nature poet than a pastoral poet, is nonetheless appealing to a pastoral readership in terms of publishing demographics, but he actually came out of the place, felt angered by enclosure, and in the process wrote a subtextual anti-pastoral, sometimes an overt one. The pastoral is not really about nature, except insofar as it is about landscape, the mediation of nature through human interference and control. A critical language is deployed to discuss these issues, which in a sense becomes part of the pastoral construct itself, so that pastoral is about the language of presentation as much as about the language of place. Terms like 'pathetic fallacy' become in this context a self-conscious critique of the anthropomorphising of place and nature, yet pathetic fallacy is itself one of the weapons of pastoral.

For pastoral has been military, despite claims of serenity and peace. The masque performed in the seventeenth-century English country mansion is a violence against workers and might be seen, in Marxist terms, as a strategy of class warfare by the bourgeoisie or ruling classes. But this is where the pastoral has grown and changed in the twentieth century. Post- Eliot's *The Waste Land* (1922; Eliot 1990), just to cite one obvious example – or maybe just post- the first world war – a brutal awareness, a trauma in the relationship between language and place, have meant a re-evaluation of what constitutes the idyll. Of course, people will always try to use the construct to configure some sweeter alternative, and that is as much the case in poetry now as it ever was. However, there are many more pollutants involved, and a lot more meta-critical awareness of the absurdity of idyllicising anything at all. The configuration of the bucolic in terms of the weekend getaway, the vacation, or the desensitising of urban consumerism has to be taken into consideration.

One must be aware of the 'new pastorals' of the vacant block and city-fringe wastelands, the most 'legitimate' of urban pastoral constructs equipped with their quota of gardeners, and the worked allotment, in which the small urban farmer grows his or her own vegetables. Ironically, the cemetery too is a scene of pastoral, or conveyance and maintenance of pastoral relationships between the sanctity of the providing earth and its keeper. The earth accepts the body and is enriched by it; the keepers of the cemeteries become 'goatherds' and 'shepherds' just as unreal as those in the literarily and culturally mediated world of Theocritus.

Pastoral has always been about the tensions within morality, and a moral guidebook for behaviour. Hesiod's *Works and Days* (ca. 750 BC–675 BC/1999) presents the right things in the right order, as they should be. The cemetery, often with nationalistic as well as religious symbolism (segregation, apportioning), does exactly that. The pastoral should also be thought of in terms of its social and spiritual evocation, for the two are inseparable. The protection of the flock is seen as a noble thing, but the flock is being preserved only for human use: at best, shearing; at worst, eating. So works the priest or rabbi or imam, the social worker or the teacher – guidance becomes a form of social and spiritual control.

Pastoral is a vehicle not only for general social and spiritual evocation, but for the linguistic dynamism of the language in its regional context as well – of all languages. In the specific case of Australia and Australian language, pastoral is twofold – a construct to recreate European, specifically English, rural power-structures, the reconfiguring of 'home' in an alien landscape. Such language-usage comes out of a politics of oppression and degradation of indigeneity. A new pastoral must come out of this that re-examines what constitutes the rural space and how that is mediated.

Another concern is gender – is the pastoral a patriarchal tool? Its traditions certainly suggest so, but some of the most interesting and challenging pastoral poetry being written in English today is by women. In short, the modern pastoral should be about challenging conventions – an engagement with the 'traditional', yes, but also with the innovative. It has always been political, and has remained so. The pastoral of orbital roads, railway tunnels, the window box, the back garden – all are part of it. But it is, possibly most significantly, a process for comparison – of producers, fetishisers and consumers, of destruction and profit, of the gaps and similarities in the way cultures discuss their use of space, of the use of nature and a concern for environmental preservation. The rights of animals – wild and domesticated, free and farmed – are pivotal.

Pastoral belongs in the realm of the gesture – of the meeting-point between drama and lyric, inseparable as they are. But it is the silences and absences that need exploring as much as anything else. The pastoral is about how land and the people within the land are marked – where the signs of authenticity and belonging are imposed or laid. The presentation of a pastoral drama in the court of Elizabeth I was a costly and complex act, mixing rural-estate realism (*in situ*) with decoration and allusion. So one would be in the park and be in Arcadia as well. Allusions to contemporary political issues, to social concerns, were often comically played out. And perhaps that is something that also marks the radical pastoral of our time – the humour is dark and ironic, but still there. In some pastoral, it was always like this, especially in the history of the anti-masque. So what we have is a lineage of the radical combined with the safe, the constant. The seasonal cycle, love, marriage, and death.

The problem now is that even the seasons are dramatically changing, and doubt plays a major part in the construct of pastoral. Nothing can be taken for granted. Once again we see that paranoia of form and intent. In reading contemporary pastoral we are looking for ways of interpreting the sign – of place, presence, and spirit. A crisis is often invoked, but redressed. Closure is always an issue. Players in the field might be ciphers, but there is an awareness of this; perhaps there always was, certainly in the 'western tradition'. The challenge to this by indigenous peoples is the key to the radical redressive pastoral, and one with which all those interested in the genre should concern themselves. Multi-sensed, the cornucopia may be full of rot and doubt, but it is still there in the complete array of colours and living for presentation!

Can there be a radical 'western' pastoral?

In his *Rambler* essays 36 and 37, written in 1750, Samuel Johnson insists on the rural nature of the pastoral, considers the legitimacy of the Golden Age rules of pastoral, the (mis)interpretations of modern critics, and challenges those poets who would take their explorations beyond the soil of the farm. In particular, he challenges 'piscatory' poetry, the poem substituting the sea for the land, pointing out among other weaknesses that the sea has not the variety of the land, and therefore has less subject range.

Johnson says:

> But pastoral subjects have been often, like others, taken into the hands of those that were not qualified to adorn them, men to whom the face of nature was so little known that they have drawn it only after their own imagination, and changed or distorted her features, that their portraits might appear something more than servile copies from their predecessors. (1750/2000, p. 191)

If the pastoral as a model is already at least a degree of separation from reality, we might agree that those who adorn the model are even further away. Johnson also confirms that the ancient lineage of the pastoral model derives from the rural space being the origin of human society, and that this space is part of our primal experience. But we might add that those poets writing literally in the rural space have little intention of leaving their poems there.

Whether it is Theocritus staged in Alexandria, or Virgil consumed in Rome, the country feeds the city, feeds the town, or feeds the house. Pastoral has always been about a sense of removal from the place of work, and the manipulation of the rustic voice is standard. The pastoral is fundamentally the city's idea of the country. To place 'sophisticated' language about 'philosophical' issues in the mouths of goatherds or fishermen (to continue with the sea pastoral) is on the same line of separation as the linguistic transference of real speech into 'written speech', of the dialect into the pastoral Doric.

The pastoral's insistence on rules of engagement with the rural world is part of the control mechanism that tames the 'natural', and orders labour and its benefits. Like all literary conventions, the pastoral is a mirror to the monopolising of comfort, power, control. Dr Johnson insists on the rural content of the pastoral, but he misses the core component: it is an order of relationships between the natural, the farmed, and those who benefit mostly from this. The city feeds off the country, so the city benefits mostly from the pastoral. The place of labour has to be made aesthetic, to be given a beauty, to cover up the truth of hardship. That labour has divisions within itself: of ethnicity, of religion, of local reputation. The radical pastoral considers the model to be constantly altering, for relationships within that model to be shifting.

The idyllicism of the pastoral juxtaposed to the loss of alternative idylls becomes a mirror of oppression, and potentially liberation. The Native American poet (of Creek, Scottish, and Irish ancestry) Janet McAdams (2000) explores pastoral tropes in the context of identity, gender, landscape/nature (totemic, visceral), and issues of oppression and power. She does not necessarily write a pastoral poetry, but she is writing around it in a confrontational way that asks if reconciliations are possible. Landscape and the 'rural' are usually asides, but still a component of her image-making (see her poem 'The Island of Lost Luggage' [2000, p. 13] and, more directly, her poem 'Ghost Ranch' [in *Tri-Quarterly*, 2003, pp. 188–189]). This is a highly political poetry. The new radicalising pastoral poetry is not always identifiable as such.

As anyone who has had anything to do with farming will tell you, it is hard work and open to disaster. And disasters do not always find resolution. The pastoral as a genre is about closure; radicalised pastoral is about suggesting the only closure there is is uncomfortable, and very likely death. Where the pastoral is a model of fetishised nature, radical pastoral is identifying the nature of these fetishes.

Radical pastoral declares that what might be seen as idyllic in the country in conventional pastoral is really reflective of a corruption of nature, that modern (in the least) farming and rural living lead to the destruction of the environment (erosion, salinity, dust bowls, poisoning), are exploitative of the non-human, and are very often part of an exploitation of the working poor.

In his second article on pastoral, Johnson says:

> Pastoral, being the *representation of an action or passion by its effects upon a country life* [Virgil], has nothing peculiar but its confinement to rural imagery, without which it ceases to be pastoral. This is its true characteristic, and this it cannot lose by any dignity of sentiment, or beauty of diction. (1750/2000, p. 196)

Johnson is arguing here that the 'elevated' (the Pollio of Virgil) is as pastoral as anything that is seemingly rustic.[†] And here Johnson is surprisingly post-modern: rural imagery is the pastoral, even if the

---

[†] Johnson is succinct and to the point in recognising the falsities of debate over the nature of rural voices in pastoral poems – over the sophistication of the shepherd and goatherd in the Golden Age. He pertinently and interestingly notes: 'Pastoral admits of all ranks of persons, because persons of all ranks inhabit the country. It excludes not, therefore, on account of the characters necessary to be introduced, any elevation of delicacy of sentiment; those ideas only are improper which, not owing their original to rural objects, are not pastoral' (1750/2000, p. 195). Characteristically, Johnson is both expansive and reductive at once.

argument is not for specifically rural purposes. Where he is possibly wrong is in the notion that rural content is necessary for a poem to be called pastoral.

Pastoral, to my mind, is actually about an order of relationships between poet and song, text and singers, the expectation of what is real by an audience and what the reality actually is. It is a simulacrum in the first place, and a model can be established based upon the rural, that seems to have little actually to do with the rural. Pastoral began because the taming and farming of the natural was one perceived 'beginning' of social ordering, of social control through systems designed to increase safety, comfort, and wealth. I would argue that this system can apply as readily to an urban space, as much as the farm, or the sea for that matter.

To create a radical pastoral, we need an awareness that on one hand the adornment of the rural material is secondary, as Johnson noted in these essays, and, further down the track, that the rural material does not have to be literally present for it to be pastoral. However, the aim of radical pastoral is surely to highlight (even rectify: it is a machine for change) abuses of the non-human 'natural', of inequalities and injustices in hierarchical interactions.

Technically, this might be achieved by hybridising the conventional pastoral voice or form with a more innovative paratactic non-lyrical technique. Here we may consider Steve McCaffery's 'Some Versions of Pastoral' (2003, pp. 50–56) with the title's deceptive suggestion of Empsonian counterpointing, with its play on the class of word, image, and participants in the genre of pastoral, and its reliance on a knowledge of critical analysis of pastoral and literary convention, from the most obvious and most popular (the shepherd), through to the more elusive language play. It thrives on dramatic irony:

> Go figure it
>
> the bearded man in a cup
>
> ending it not until now
>
> in a shroud-snow with the sheep
>
> occurring in
>
> the shepherds

In many radical pastoral poems, nature is cybernetically fused with aspects of the urban, and a symbiosis forms textually in which social issues are put forward through discrepancy. It seems that this is part-way towards a realisation of radical pastoral, for until the natural world itself is separated from human fatalism, its own agencies respected, the hierarchy is just shifting ground. So the truly radical pastoral is conscious of the ironies of its own literary production. The very paper it is printed on is a loss for nature, is part of a control of nature. Publishing poetry is a form of farming.

Andrew Duncan's poem 'At Camden Lock' is a radicalising poem that makes use of pastoral tropes. It is not bucolic; it is absorptive and comparative. It takes allegory and removes the Gods, makes chemical the Golden Age. Through the use of animals (specifically non-'farm' animals), and a noted absence of the natural, in talking of the lock, Duncan creates an anti-pastoral. Its concern is human, and the lock becomes analogous to the consuming machine of the social system/s, but the welfare of animals and issues of the planet's health are a distant second to this. The poem is an inversion of the biblical Noah's Ark story, with an irony playing on the idea of religious 'pastoral' care, of destiny, of servitude. It is a 'Godless' challenge. What would have made it a radical pastoral is for these concerns to have been evident as well:

> Among penguins and marmots, a row of monkeys
> Of a dozen species, I saw each one
> Fiddle with the lock or the bolt,
> Imitating human fingers.
> Every control gate has a fastening.
> They go through what acts are possible without a forest.
> I make a mental model of this special geometry.
> Symbols unlatching edge of pattern cycles.
>
> (2001, p. 76)

The question of the lyrical or unified self is pivotal here. Like Khlebnikov's use of the 'I' (1997), it is fluid, an indeterminate. It is both a historically observant and registering I, but also a more general mythologising I. The unified self is both sincere and ironised. When we think about conventional pastoral, we may note a removal of the lyrical self through the dramatis personae: the poet mediates self through the singer, or the idea of the rural or Golden Age authority figure. Even when georgically suggesting what is good, what is the ordered and productive way of doing things, the voice is attributed to the farmers rather than the poet (the poet–farmer becomes the farmer, then the poet). Virgil writes in Book I of *Georgics*,

> Much service does he do the land who with the mattock breaks up the sluggish clods, and drags over it hurdles of osier; nor is it without reward that golden Ceres looks on him from Olympian heights. Much service, too, does he who turns his plough and again breaks crosswise through the ridges which he raised when first he cut the plain, ever at his post to discipline the ground, and give his orders to the fields. (37 to 30 BC/1999, p. 105)

Australia still prides itself on having lived off the wool of the sheep's back, the myth of the bushman, and the rural/vast interior feeding the cities on the coastline. Australian poets either writing out of the rural space or utilising these myths of the rural space have long used the pastoral poem or pastoral ideal ironically, as a vehicle to challenge authority. Few are completely radical, but an awareness of both the expansiveness and the limitations of the genre is clearly evident. Probably the best known meta-textual poem, written by a man who had little to do with the country but saw it as part of the Australian condition, was John Forbes's 'Speed, a Pastoral'. A classic of literary misdirection, of allegory with serious consequences, it is a poem about literary conventions, popular culture, and the irony of the unsuitability of European literary traditions in Australia, and of the anachronistic terrors usurped by more modern horrors. The satire displaces the pastoral mode:

> it's fun to take speed
> & stay up all night
> not writing those reams of poetry
> just thinking about is bad for you
>
> (2001, p. 111)

The poem has nothing bucolic about it, and even in Johnson's more flexible version, it would not pass as pastoral on any level. But it clearly is, because the poem's title impels us to engage with it through pastoral tradition, and the poem posits relationships between literary authority figures who have explored pastoral (Keats, Flaubert), and those who follow in the romantic swirl ... Michael Dransfield, Australian poet, is believed to have died of complications relating to a heroin overdose (this is argued):

> you know Dransfield's line, that once you become a junkie
> you'll never want to be anything else?
>   well, I think he died too soon,
> as if he thought drugs were an old-fashioned teacher
> & he was the teacher's pet, who just put up his hand

> & said quietly, 'Sir, sir'
> & heroin let him leave the room.
>
> (p. 111)

The old-fashioned teacher might well be the literary convention of the pastoral ...

This is anti-pastoral, but not radical pastoral. Yet radical pastoral does exist in Australian poetry. One proponent of it is the vegan animal-rights activist Coral Hull. Her poems often reverse the vivisection of the rural by scrutinising it to the point of revelation: accusation and condemnation are frequently the result, and Hull has been criticised for being too blatant. Hull's project, however, is not to be polite, but to challenge the polite conventions of song exchange, to show that a beauty in which animals and environment are degraded is no beauty at all. The poet treads a fine line between didacticism and evocation, as we might consider in her prose poem, 'November 3rd, 1997, Murder Scenario':

> I am going to replace the subject of 'cow' with 'child', in order to reply to your statement/question that: 'it's better to wear the skin off a dead child than to go and kill a child yourself.' First of all being a children's rights activist, this statement is offensive to me. Why? Because I think that the use of the word 'better' somehow condones the former ... (Hull and Kinsella 2000, p. 66)

Whether one believes the poem should evoke or tell, or do both, there is no question that the radical pastoral seems to challenge the norms of pastoral telling, of pastoral singing, and pastoral convention, in addition to challenging the terms of its own production. So it is 'po-mo' in its self-knowledge, but only because an argument needs to be defensible if it is to do real work in the community. The radical pastoral poet wants radical change.

Some have conjectured that an end-game is being played out in pastoral poetry and drama, that a radical or radicalised pastoral has evolved as a way of challenging traditional and even modern versions of the pastoral. This would involve a complete undoing of what it is to be pastoral through an exploration and dismantling of familiar pastoral materials – building blocks, tropes, and modes of presentation and representation.

To overturn the inheritance of the pastoral, it is necessary to enter the body of the pastoral itself. Instead of writing from outside the rural space, one needs to write within. Instead of enjoying the fruits of the rural which feed the pastoral, one should step outside the systems of exploitation that fuel the idyll. The clearing of native vegetation; the abuse of animals; the poisoning of land, water, and air; the fundamentals of controlling nature, of exploiting it for the short-term benefit of humans (which ultimately turns out to be harmful to humans in any case), become textual.

This is a case not merely of political and ethical diatribe, but of changing the linguistic co-ordinates within the poem: a linguistic disobedience, possibly, but certainly a challenge to language's representational power. Language is fluid and unstable, and the realities of 'pastoralist' thinking are very results-orientated, very empirical. The tension here, the nature of this discrepancy, is where radical pastoral is located. The radical pastoral poem does not tell us what to do or think; it is an active undoing of the tradition. It is indirect non-violent action, as effective as, or hopefully more effective than, 'locking on' to machinery that is about to destroy an environment.

As a poet involved in challenging pastoral tradition, and more relevantly, as a vegan anarchist pacifist who spends most of his life in rural areas, I feel an obligation to overturn the language of exploitation and disempowerment that has characterised the pastoral. Be it in the appropriation of the goatherd or shepherd in the pastoral eclogue, or the neatly controlled terraces of the *Georgics*, the pastoral has always been an idyllicised representation of the rural world, most often for the allegorical delectation of urban or town audiences. As we discover in Williams (1973) and others, even the country house becomes a stage in which the antics of the rural working folk are hierarchised and placed within a power structure for the amusement of the gentry.

There are many poets writing of the rural world or the forest or the bush – the mediated natural environments and farming communities – who challenge the status quo, who undermine it linguistically or thematically, but few if any who seek to demolish all that builds the power structures in the first place. It could be argued that mere participation in the pastoral prevents a true challenging of its codes.

One who comes close to that challenge in the scientific specificity of his grammar is Peter Larkin, who writes in *Terrain Seed Scarcity*:

> To be insufficiently with what is given to us is to be detached from it: it may be a token by which to experience the unbrokenness of roots (along a specifically historic etiolation) through and towards a common landscape. (2001, pp. xi–xii)

The idea of creating the pastoral through the absent, and a pastoral absence in nature, is both to reaffirm the independence of nature from human agency, and to lay claim to nature. A spiritual hierarchy is observable here that is not radical, but the integrity of nature as thing-in-itself is, as a thing not to be fetishised. The systems are independent, and co-dependent:

> Or unforesting discretion of tree-cover. Not to infill horizon but shallower row when shadow goes downwood. Spent lengthward, there was always a doom of frittered vestment one wile less than desertion. (2001, p. 57)

More common is a pastoralisation of poetry in which other political issues are played out on the stage of the rural, without any highlighting or awareness or possibly even a conscious negation of the exploiting of the natural world that takes place in these spaces. The creation of mythologies, or authentications of presence, and/or the challenging of social and ethnic inequalities, take precedence; or the natural or rural environment is used symbolically as part of this discourse.

The poetry of 'major' cultural space poets such as Derek Walcott, Seamus Heaney, and Les Murray, might be seen to work in these ways. The idea of the bard, or the voice of a people highly localised in a particular physical environment that then becomes the amplifier for greater human concerns, is what allows the poets to becomes generically representative, and absorbable by larger audiences. In a variety of senses, each of these poets relies on pastoral mythologies, and certainly methodologies. By an implication of participation (through living in a place or recalling a place), they connect directly with the heritage of altering that place. They become voices for the powerless, and yet simultaneously part of the power structure – the classic pastoral generator.

Poets who are more apparently radical, such as Lisa Robertson from Canada and, say, Lisa Jarnot from the USA, work through pastoral textuality, gendering and challenging the political inconsistencies of the genre, yet still remaining knowledgeably complicit. Their role-playing may be different, but it is still, as they might agree, a form of role-playing within the genre. In the early 1870s in France, Arthur Rimbaud, a poet highly adept at taking poetic tropes and role-playing them into something new and generative, consciously bent the pastoral to his mission to derange the senses, or to escape the power structures of the matriarchal home. His absent-soldier father is the symbol of both oppression and liberty, and instead of the clear lines of movement of traditional pastoral, there is a contradiction between the liberation of the Arcadian space and its confinement. In Rimbaud's poem 'Le Dormeur du val' ('The Sleeper in the Valley') (1870/1997, p. 105) the pastoral idyll is made aesthetically pleasing and terrible at once, with

Pastoral, landscape, place

the young soldier shot dead, his body now one with nature, though stunningly at odds with it.

In the pastoral tradition, the anthropomorphising of nature renders nature more compliant, safer: the wilds across the *cordon sanitaire* are made controllable. A beauty is created from the inability to reconcile this tension:

> Le Dormeur du val (The Sleeper in the Valley)
>
> It is a richly green hole where a river sings
> Hooking silver tatters – fantastical and bright –
> To the grass; where the sun shines down from the swelling
> Mountain; it is a small valley frothing with light.
>
> A young soldier sleeps with open mouth and bare head,
> The nape of his neck bathing in the cool blue stain
> Of watercress: stretched out in grass, beneath the clouds,
> Pallid in his green bed where the light falls as rain.
>
> Feet amongst the gladioli, he sleeps. Smiling
> The smile of a sickly infant, gently napping.
> Nature, you must cradle him warmly: he is cold.
>
> No scents or smells disturb his nose, make it tremble;
> He sleeps under the sun, one hand resting tranquil
> On his chest. He has two red holes in his right side.
> (October 70) [my translation]

The peacefulness, even idyllicism, of the poem – the feet of the dead soldier are even in the gladioli – is evoked through the synthesis created by colour: 'green hole'/'silver tatters'/'cool blue'/'green bed', and even the 'red holes'. This use of colour blends all the elements into the one picture of nature; there is a pastoralisation of the Christ-death image through the evocation of simultaneously the stigmata and the spear-thrust, as it is diffused into the scene. Thus this is a poem of displacements, with the pastoral mode gently but decisively shifted.

The history of the pastoral is full of turning points, but nonetheless remains a continuous line. In this context, perhaps Wordsworth's 'Michael' (1800/1984, pp. 224–236) with its acknowledgement of the collapse of the idyll, is not as dramatic a turning point as some critics would have us believe, or as I have myself at times argued. If we extend this model of pastoral templating: of poems without bucolic content (which 'Michael' is almost entirely made up of), but coming out of the pastoral modus operandi, we will find increasingly 'anti-pastoral' work moving towards radical expressions of the pastoral. In a sense, this is to be expected in the western poetic inheritance, as so much relies on the pastoral experience.

Consciousness of the abuse of the environment for the sake of human gain and human power-play is the key. That is why the Forbes poem considered earlier is only partly radical; it does not seek to rectify the ironies and contradictions of the bucolic. It shows an implicit awareness that the irony exists, and this is used to make social and cultural comment, but it does not venture anywhere near the rights of the land or of animals.

The same might be observed of one of the most investigative of contemporary 'pastoral' poets, Lisa Robertson. Her poems are pure investigations of genre, though at the same time incorporating other genre tropes. Once again, she takes the sense of the pastoral, and ironises. She includes aspects of the bucolic, and dismantles from within: a feminist and gender-deconstructive agenda. Her pastoral is gender-radical, even radical in its upturning of convention, but not radical in its challenging of the usurping of natural agency by humans. Possibly, the only way the latter can achieved is by going the Coral Hull path to extending personal radicalism to poetic radicalism: the body of the poem is the body of oneself. *L'écriture féminine* (Cixous, 1994) made literal is the body writing the poem, the poem written in the body, a literature of action.

At the back of her book *XEclogue*, Robertson records:

> *XEclogue* has had many houseguests. Eighteenth century poet, traveller, and political critic Lady Mary Wortley Montagu wrote a series of privately distributed satirical poems called 'City Eclogues', these were my introduction to their genre. Frank O'Hara and Virgil extended its horizon. Throughout *XEclogue*, the shorter, italicised songs of roaring boys mistranslate the anonymous Latin of the *Pervigilium Veneris*, fourth century A.D. songs to Venus ... (1993, pages not numbered)

The mention of the mistranslation is part of the language of slippage that revolutionises genre. The book begins with 'How pastoral: a prologue': 'I needed a genre for the times that I go phantom ...'. This masterpiece of dissemination and movement of the self – its interaction and separation from the voice, the lyrical self, and expectations of narrative – is the radicalisation of the maleness of pastoral tradition, starting from the satires of Montagu, themselves departures from the bucolic. From 'Eclogue Two: Beauty':

> I'm loquacious or raucous, swanning for the fun of it
> But I'd sooner tear the subtle moss from under poplars
> Than he should put a note of love into her golden mouth:
> I'll nudge the queer sorrow her barbarity merits. (not numbered)

The syntactical and gender plays work against the 'natural', and the equation of nature and the feminine is exploded. But the suffering of the land, of animals, is secondary to the irony as thing-in-itself, and gender concerns of the piece per genre readings.

So where do we find the radical pastoral? What about the death of a fox on the vacant lot, the churchyard being pesticided, graveyard losing more and more of its bush periphery, sports ground so saturated in herbicide and pesticide sprays that it glows. Window-box pastorals of the city are not a revolution, but a realigning. We have to think tangentially – the genre is played out, ironised, but still deeply entrenched. The pastoral has been invested with threat, can even be malevolent ('Michael' again), but in the end it is tamed by a lack of radical instruction and incitement to action. Closure is its preservation and ineffectiveness. It lacks the sublime.

Pastoral is the contrary of sublime, and issues of a radical sublime are a key to the new radical pastoral. The beauty-horror of a polluted sky emanating a sickly red sunset, the exquisite crystalline salt formations resulting from clearing and degradation of land in the Western Australian wheatbelt; standing on the edge of something horribly beautiful, the majesty of good replaced by the trauma of damage, and the thrill of wasted spaces. As the basis of image-making, and as a symbolism, these serve the poet's purposes as well.

Traditionally, the sublime has little dramatic place in the pastoral; though place may evoke the sublime, it is usually about calming and quelling confrontations: the message of the competition, of competitiveness is resolution, the good order of the poem reflecting the good order of the universe. More recently, a poet like Lisa Jarnot has merged the sublime and the pastoral, to edge towards something radical, though still linguistically 'trapped' in battling the conventions of literary inheritance. The Hungarian poet Miklós Radnóti, writing in the 1930s and early 1940s, recently re-translated by George Gömöri and Clive Wilmer (2003), wrestled with the classical harmonisation of the pastoral, the modernist renderings of pastoral, and the pastoral in the face of terror.

The pastoral is the quiet model the state relies on: the Nazis (especially Hitler, and also Goering with his Polish hunting forests) relied on the notion of an Arcadia, of the bucolic, to fuel their purist and racist views of humanity. The hierarchical good order of the pastoral suits nationalising systems well. The Nazis incarcerated and shot Radnóti, who was a Hungarian Jew. In his brilliant 'Seventh Eclogue', where the song competition or song exchange has become a conversation by the persona from within to without the poem, Radnóti does something socially more radical than any other pastoral poet (though he was not only a pastoral poet). The poem shows the suffering of the human inextricably linked to the sufferings of nature: in the poem as fog, or night, or 'like a caterpillar inching my way across paper' (p. 75), and not loudly or in specific rural activity.

The suggestion and evocation of human loss and human needs *are* nature, and that is where this poems transcends. The Johnsonian equation is threadbare, but this is certainly a pastoral, and a pastoral more than adornment or a conversation with literary convention. Trauma and terror are universal. As poetry, it is enough:

> You see? As dark comes on, the barracks and the grim oak fence,
> Girded with barbed-wire, dissolve: night soaks them up.
> Slowly the eye relinquishes the bounds of our captivity
> And the mind, only the mind, can tell how taut the wire is.
>
> (p. 75)

The translators point out that 'Seventh Eclogue' was written in the prison camp near the copper mines at Bor in Serbia (p. 17). Pastoral displays a country place in its absence: in this great poem there is a ghosting of pastoral, a ghosting of lost place. It is a pastoral of absence, a gesture of pastoral hidden by the mountains, the horror of internment, 'the end plunged into obscurity, and miracles' (p. 75).

Parrotology (on the necessity of parrots in poetry)

Order: Psittaciformes
Family: Psittacidae

> The parrots, the only family in the order, are a large group of small to moderately large birds found in the warmer parts of the world, especially Australia, New Guinea and South America. Their bill is strong and hooked, and short legs have two toes directed forwards and two back. (Storr and Johnstone 2001, p. 146)

In Australia, the parrot family includes lorikeets, rosellas, budgerigars, cockatiels, cockatoos, galahs, and corellas ...

Driving with my daughter just outside the wheatbelt town of York, we came across a 28 parrot that had just been struck by a car. I scooped it up in a cloth and my daughter held it on the back seat until we could get home and house it. Having been bitten numerous times over my life by those 'strong and hooked' beaks, I warned her to be wary. But the parrot – a splay of emerald, turquoise, black and yellow feathers – was too dazed to bite, and clearly had a broken wing. Though we've always called these beautiful birds '28s', technically they are a ring-necked parrot, and possibly even the Port Lincoln variety of ring-necked. The demarcation lines between varieties are hazy. The local 'nickname' matters as local names do. We eventually handed the injured bird over to the town's 'bird lady', who later let me know that it had died due to massive brain damage. My daughter doesn't know it died. She said it was the closest she'd ever come to something so 'amazing'. I left it at that.

Despising nation and patriotism and jingoism as I do, I guess I baulk a little when I hear that 'parrots' are clichés or over-used symbols of Australia – particularly the Australian outback. I have a personal history of parrotology, a deep respect for all their varieties, and a fascination for their manifestations in literature, particularly poetry.

For me, a parrot isn't simply a parrot. In the thrust forward to make of Australian poetry something more cosmopolitan, internationalist, and sophisticated, there's a little throwing of the baby out with the bath water. Arguments of literary maturity are very much the old cultural cringe stuff reformed as residue, a bit like the cherishing of remnant bushland when all else is cleared down to salinity. The parrot becomes a transitional object in this nation-child's shift from 'linguistic acquisition' (to echo something Bill Grono said regarding our toddler recently) to linguistic confidence and exploration.

Arguably, this exploration of linguistic possibilities in poetry – searching for new ways of expressing confidence in identity – is parallel to, or maybe even an extension of, the narratives of exploration that 'opened up' land for 'settler' use, and sought to reset the co-ordinates (namings, markings, topography, and explication) of place, with the aim of creating 'guilt-free' occupation/presence. It might well be, disturbingly, a new form of colonisation ...

In the Australian issue of the stalwart British poetry journal *Agenda*, out after I completed the first draft of this essay, the critic Martin Dodsworth says:

> Whilst it *[Australia]* was coming out from under the shadow of Empire it is understandable that its poetry should have sought to reinforce a fragile national identity. But things are different now; there is a new confidence, identity is no longer the issue that it was, and poets can if they wish go easy on the kangaroos and the wallabies, the parrots and the rosellas. (2005, p. 169)

This is fascinating in a number of ways. Every new migrant, if not those who have resided here a long time, wrestles with identity on arriving in Australia. Many indigenous commentators would argue that the loss of indigenous languages constitutes a consistent loss of identity on that (paramount) level alone, and those concerned with the destruction of the land would argue that identity-loss is inseparable from this loss. And so the list can be continued. Dodsworth's point, to give it credit, is not so much that to be 'confident' one has to go into a denial of, say, references to native fauna, but that to write outside such signifiers allows for a maturity and freedom.

My question is, why? Surely any signifier can be used in a clichéd manner – not only the name of a bird or animal, but of a building, piece of art, or shopping mall. In fact, any word or phrase or line in a poem, used without attention to the range of readings outside one's own immediate purpose, would be impoverished.

Don't get me wrong, I actually value skilfully arranged clichés in poetry – as long as the clichés are doing work on (or deconstructing) their own existence in the poem. Robert L. Mitchell's use of the expression 'renovation of clichés' when talking about the nature and aspects of 'poetic voice' (in the poetry of Charles Cros) is particularly appropriate in considering the reinvigoration and energising of clichéd language. To renovate is both to renew and reinvigorate; the reader's desire to enter the familiar yet also be surprised is the marketing tactic employed from selling neo-colonial houses through to contemporary takes on the sonnet:

> By poetic voice, I mean those stylistic devices or traits which are particularly characteristic of a poet's writing and which reveal certain marked tendencies through their idiosyncratic usage. These elements may range from choice of words (the predominance of a particular part of speech, a predilection for the abstract or concrete, the use of neologism, the renovation of clichés, or borrowings from other languages, to name a few possibilities) to the use of particular types of images, to noticeable idiosyncrasies regarding syntax, rhythm, structure, rhyme, and versification. (Mitchell, 1976, p. 16)

Parrots for me are always 'renovated' – an addictively necessary part of a poetics. They are the source of beauty in my aesthetics. I am probably an irrelevancy to theirs, but who knows? Anthropocentrically, William Hogarth noted:

> The shapes and colours of plants, flowers, leaves, the paintings in butterflies wings, shells, &c. seem of little other intended use, than that of entertaining the eye with the pleasure of variety. (1997, p. 27)

And this is often what's observed of parrots: their infinitude, their beauty. The range of their colourings is a constant pleasure, but not much thought is given to why that myriad of difference exists. There are biological and geographical answers, obviously evolutionary and creationist answers. But in the moment of poetic contact, it's the array of colours combined with the uniqueness of movement that captures the poet.

I share with the poet Dorothy Porter an interest in the rare or extinct night parrot – it is (or was) not a particularly colourful parrot. Its sublimity is in its discretion, its vulnerability, its solitude. Porter wrote a book of poetry entitled *The Night Parrot*, and I (coincidentally) wrote one entitled *Night Parrots*. The ground dwelling, the strange cry, habitation in arid Australia, and probable extinction make it vulnerable to the interiorities of the poet. Though we 'deploy' the parrot in very different ways, the parrot becomes an alter ego, a conscience, counterpoint, antagonist, most-often indifferent companion, of address. In Porter's work this is more literal – the bird is a 'character' in the internalised dialogue with a shifting persona – whereas in mine it is most often absent. From Porter's 'Trial Separation':

> it's the dry season
>   the night parrot
>   is starving
> and won't mate
>   can't nest
> and finds my water
>   bitter,
> we're fighting ...
>   (Hampton and Llewellyn, ed., 1988, p. 245)

Characteristic of Porter's poetry in general is the play between the casual, familiar language and a razor-edged intensity. Her night parrot is no mere empty signifier.

I do understand why the *Australian Book Review* should gratefully observe that the 'wonted parrots' were strangely silent when they ran their inaugural poetry competition. What they note, of course, is the familiar trope – like the gum tree or kangaroo – that becomes signifier for a larger, more generalised discourse of national identity. It's the cover-all, the cliché. We might also add to this the metaphoric investment of the familiar with emotional predictability: the beauty of the bird becomes a sign for a complexity that is not really there. It is not difficult to list reasons why the 'parrot' is perceived as a cliché in Australian poetry, but it does lead one to ask a few questions.

For example, how many anthologised Australian poems are about parrots, or even include parrots? How and when did they become figurative currency? Why the joy at not encountering them? First, we'd have to consider the demographics and cultural values of the judges. Are they urban people for whom the parrot is a bland representation of the rural other – an expected trope that denies variety in all its guises? Is the parrot the Anglo-Celtic displacement of indigeneity, a kind of legitimising or reterritorialising of the sign? The rendering of the Derridean monster into something acceptable? The event de-fanged, or de-beaked? By way of distraction, let's think of Australian parrots as version of the hippogriff.

We might ask of the cultural density and liberality of the city – real or desired – is everything therein *not parrot*? Interestingly, 'pissed as a parrot' applies as much to parrots in the north of Queensland consuming fermented fruit as to rainbow lorikeets dining on the fermented nectar of *schotia brachypetala* in the Sydney Botanical Gardens, so drunk they featured in the *Sydney Morning Herald* (Macey 2004) and wire pick-ups in newspapers around the world. In the gardens, beneath the drunken parrots, families of diverse spiritual beliefs, politics, social attitudes, ethnicities, and cultural practices look up and take note. Some might be embarrassed, some make jokes at the expense of the parrots, some feel pity, even empathy. The parrot as symbol of nation falls off its perch ...

Chris Mansell's 'Definition Poem: Pissed as a Parrot' (interestingly only a few pages before Dorothy Porter's parrot poems in *The Penguin Book of Australian Women Poets*) is a poem of word slippage – 'If the sheep's fly-blown it's a rosella'. It is also a poem that implicitly satirises an aspect of pseudo-cultural identity (Australian drinking behaviour) at the same time as affectionately laying claim to it. The following lines add to the plethora of claims for the origin of the expression, ironised doubly in the polite colonial occasion (tea taking) and the cringe of scientific (and cultural) validation (Sydney University):

> But I went to afternoon tea
> in the School of Chemistry at the University of Sydney
> at 4pm on Thursday 6 November
> and there, Dr A. R. Lacey, physical chemist, MSc PhD,
> informed me, in his capacity as a true blue,
> down to earth, dinky-di, grass roots Aussie that
> when working on his horse stud in Wingecarribee Shire
> he had observed that Gang Gang cockatoos
> fall with paralytic suddenness
> from the branches of Hawthorn bushes
> after ingesting the berries ...
> (Hampton and Llewellyn, ed., 1988, p. 237)

In this larrikin lampooning, Mansell manages multi-directional satire while, in essence, not writing about parrots at all. Official culture, she suggests, diverts attention from the full story.

The parrot is of the city as much as of the country – where diversity and flock sizes are rapidly diminishing as tree hollows and other nesting spaces vanish with the clearing of land, with pesticide and herbicide dulling colour and hearts, and where teenagers take pot-shots with more ruthless efficiency than one can imagine, with 22s. I love parrots because I once, before I became a vegan, killed them ...

I lived for a while in an apartment opposite the Perth Zoo – an ambivalent interaction from a vegan perspective. I loved being near the animals, but not where and how they were kept. It made me angry. A vast flock of lorikeets gathered in the Moreton Bay fig trees around South Perth near the zoo, close to the river, attracted by the abundant fruit-bearing trees. Rainbow lorikeets are not native to Perth, and this healthy flock was mostly the result of ten birds let loose near the University of Western Australia in the 1960s. They are considered public enemy number one in Perth now, and their appearance in a celebratory or any poem other than one of damnation, would be considered treason by farmers (waiting outside the city limits for the onslaught), the agricultural department, and suburban gardeners. Here's part of a report on them by Babs and Bert Wells of CALM, Western Australia:

> At present there do not appear to be any effective control measures for rainbow lorikeets. Shooting provides only temporary relief and lorikeets are unresponsive to a variety of scaring devices.
>
> Under the Agriculture and Related Resources Protection Act 1976, administered by the Department of Agriculture, rainbow lorikeets are declared pests of agriculture in the south-west land division excluding the Perth metropolitan area.
>
> They are listed as 'acclimatised fauna' under provisions of the Wildlife Conservation Act 1950, administered by the Department of Conservation and Land Management. Rainbow lorikeets can be shot or live-trapped on private land in accordance with an open season notice in place under the Wildlife Conservation Act 1950 without the need to obtain a damage licence from the Department of Conservation and Land Management. (2002)

What is generally agreed is that the lorikeets have become part of an artificial environment (the city), replete with 'exotic' eucalypts and palms that attract and encourage these birds. I have heard many local poems refer to them as positive symbols – of lively colour, of life as opposed to the 'deathly' pollution or detritus of city life. This is, in most cases, classic separation of the signified and signifier. Few people, including poets, bother to identify birds, animals, or plants, and they become for people simply ciphers – points of comparison in the quick-fix simile.

It's easy to see why parrots in Australian poems get the bad reputation. But there is a double irony here – the bird's 'non-belonging' becomes metaphor for colonisation on an obvious level, but also, since they are declared vermin, for their status in 'uncaring' Australian society. Pragmatics leads to a defensive military language of vermin and control (much like that deployed against refugees). In the way that we read texts against their intended meaning, so the general 'parrot' in a Perth poem shocks with implication. The benign becomes the aggressively challenging (and here was I thinking I was just writing about nature being nice and the human made being soul-less ...). The simpler the apparent usage, the less defined the noun, the stronger the signs of disturbance.

It's fascinating to consider the near-absence of parrots, galahs, and cockatoos in Dorothy Hewett's poetry, coming as she did from a parrot-heavy region. They are there, but rarely. Her poems refer to many birds – especially crows and magpies – but not many parrots. In 'Memoirs of a Protestant Girlhood', we read 'black cockatoos massed shrieking in the sky', with the cockatoos taking on their familiar guise as mass and threat seen so often in colonial Australian poetry.

Individuated cockatoos are to be found imprisoned in 'Zoo Story', 'the white cockatoos parody our babble' ... The caged birds do not babble; it is the humans that do. In their alienation, the birds are given the choice of refusal, of denial of the human. In the first case we have them speaking to the persona out of nature, in the second, mocking the persona (the 'we') because they are out of nature. Around Wickepin, where Hewett grew up, parrots, as mentioned above, are prevalent – pink and grey galahs, ring-necked parrots, and other species. In the reconstruction of her childhood they have been made largely absent – either because they lack the starkness of her symbolism and recall, or because this absence is a declaration of some denial, hiddenness, lack, or deletion. Rosellas appear in *The Alice Poems*:

> rosellas flush out behind her
> in the branches naked fledglings
> lift up their beaks for worms.

(1995, p. 213)

and there is a 28 parrot that bites Alice to the bone and then dies:

> the parrot joined them
> flat on its back claws in the air.
> (1995, p. 218)

– this is reminiscent of her fellow Western Australian Randolph Stow, and also of Sidney Nolan's painting. The appearance of these parrots and their life–death 'attack' on Alice's 'instress', her resistance to expectation ('Bitch bitch ...') and compliance, their reappearance later when time is wound back and they live again, are part and parcel of the cathartic symbolism Hewett reserved for these birds. The cliché of the parrots is reinvested so pathologically that the self-myth is transferred, transfigured, and resurrected in them. The general absence of parrots in Hewett's poetry is not accidental ... When they do appear, they are hyper-real and come loaded with portent and death.

The parrot (oh, a rosella is a type of parrot), the wallaby, or the kangaroo (the latter two are closely related), even deployed as clichés, should never be written off. Let's take a look at a few uses of 'parrots' in colonial Australian poetry. Here's the opening of Richard Whately's 'There is a Place in Distant Seas':

> There is a place in distant seas
> Full of contrarieties:
> There, beasts have mallards' bills and legs,
> Have spurs like cocks, like hens lay eggs.
> There parrots walk upon the ground,
> And grass upon the trees is found ...
> (Kinsella, ed., forthcoming)

This is a trope of early encounter. We also see, for example, the issue of 'contrarieties' in Barron Field's 'The Kangaroo'. This is the reconfiguring of expectation per experience, the search for a language of contradiction in this light to express and describe creatively (and scientifically, for that matter) what is being seen to oneself, one's fellow participants in the new experience, and those 'back home' who only have their immediate environment and other artefacts and observations from empire-building to compare with and help build the picture.

Parrots *had* been seen and collected by the British from other parts of the globe before they were encountered in Australia, of course, but to Whately and the audience of his time, the parrots in the new colonies warranted mention of specific behavioural (as well as visual) characteristics that set them apart. Here, there is as much fascination as pride, and a lexicographical registering of language-shift: finding different coordinates for the description of the world as it is (never as it seems). Furthermore, not uncommonly, these parrots become symbols of the pleasure-pain of the grotesque, that particularly Australian perversion of the sublime that has the majestic moment tainted with depression, loss, or potential cataclysm. Here are a couple of lines from Charles Harpur's 'A Storm in the Mountains':

> The duskness thickens! With despairing cry
> From shattering boughs the rain-drenched parrots fly!
> (Kinsella, ed., forthcoming)

The lines almost collapse under the weight of themselves, and these are no bright and frivolous 'parrotic' symbols at work. With the destruction of habitat, it amazes me that in poetry parrots persist in text as if they had been unassailed. The urbanite, noting the 'renegade' flocks of parrots appearing in cities around Australia, might well take this to mean excess and a lushness of the symbolic – not so out in the wheatbelt. Flocks of certain parrots, galahs, and cockatoos thrive until culled, but others are extinct or on the verge of extinction. Where I am now, the destruction of wandoo habitat has meant a lack of nesting places (hollowed branches and trunks) . . .

The refutation of 'parrots' – the sign or signifier 'parrot', or simply the visual representation of 'parrot' in a poem – goes hand in hand with the denial of participation and agency within the aesthetic. Because parrots are not made (yet) by humans, because they are seemingly no more than poetically receptive to mimesis and reproduction or recounting in the text (they don't answer back despite their ability to 'mimic' human speech), they are beyond sympathy. They mimic aspects of the human but cannot be appreciated as participating in the poem-text. Here is what Descartes has to say about parrots in *Discourse on Method* in 1637:

> For it is really remarkable that there are no men so dull and stupid, including even idiots, who are not capable of putting together different words and of creating out of them a conversation through which they make their thoughts known; by contrast, there is no other animal, no matter how perfect and how successful it might be, which can do anything like that. And this inability does not come about from a lack of organs. For we see that magpies and parrots can emit words, as we can, but nonetheless cannot talk like us, that is to say, giving evidence that they are thinking about what they are uttering; whereas, men who are

born deaf and dumb are deprived of organs which other people use to speak – just as much as or more than the animals – but they have a habit of inventing on their own some signs by which they can make themselves understood to those who, being usually with them, have the spare time to learn their language.

And this point attests not merely to the fact that animals have less reason than men, but also to the fact that they have none at all.

Bearing Descartes's words in mind, let's consider Colin Allen's comment in 'Animal Consciousness':

> A common refrain in response to such arguments is that, in situations of partial information, 'absence of evidence is not evidence of absence'. Descartes dismissed parrots vocalizing human words because he thought it was merely meaningless repetition. This judgement may have been appropriate for the few parrots he encountered, but it was not based on a systematic, scientific investigation of the capacities of parrots. Nowadays many would argue that Pepperberg's study of the African Grey parrot 'Alex' (Pepperberg 1999) should lay the Cartesian prejudice to rest. This study, along with several on the acquisition of a degree of linguistic competence by chimpanzees and bonobos (e.g., Gardner et al. 1989; Savage-Rumbaugh 1996) would seem to undermine Descartes' assertions about lack of conversational language use and general reasoning abilities in animals. (2004)

I argue that the appearance of the 'parrot' in Australian poetry is an essential and reasoned phenomenon, on the grounds that the birds themselves actively inculcate themselves into the imagination of those who encounter them on a variety of levels; that they are monitors (like frogs) of the health of an ecosystem and therefore political and environmental symbols; that they have a symbolic function in the imagination of contradiction – damnation and deliverance – and that though deployed as nationalist jingoistic icons or default positions (easy observation like 'gum trees'), they are equally used iconoclastically.

In a sense, the arguments (and experiments) of 'animal consciousness' are as elitist and insulting as Descartes's summations, but the hierarchising of ability does serve to show that human sense of faculty and facility is judgemental and limited. The parrot in the poem is no less valuable than the person in the poem – both are ultimately textual and symbolic. They are not really there, no matter how 'touching' the text. A sophisticated liberated poetry might just as well do away with people. The bird that 'mimics' does so because of human interaction – forced or (rarely) circumstantial. It involves itself in the language.

A little personal history of writing parrots. I have written a lot of bird poems – referring to birds from around the world, from the various places I have lived in, whether watching a cardinal in mid-Ohio or a blackbird in Cambridge, England. I suppose one has to get out from beneath the shadow of nature to really come of age – something I doubt I will ever do! I spend a lot of my non-poetry time writing and lecturing on environmental and political issues, so it is not surprising they should become a prime focus of my creative work.

Parrots – especially Western Australian wheatbelt parrots – are more than symbolic or textually easy; they are part of my life's experience. Up until the end of my teenage years, I shot them as often as I could. Sometimes I trapped them for our aviaries, but most often I killed them and left them where they dropped. I have seen boxes and boxes of parrot carcasses, and once even a box of 28 parrot heads, at country rubbish tips. It is easy when those around you declare them 'vermin', and as much as you admire and are fascinated by them, there's a frisson in destroying the beautiful. Thankfully, I eventually ended my role in their destruction.

Writing about parrots becomes an act of atonement – though it does not make what I did any less horrific, it does declare not only a recognition of wrong-doing, but also a hope that words might make others reflect. On motorbikes with my cousins near York, I would race 28 parrots – they have a penchant for a fast undulating flight alongside vehicles travelling on narrow roads – sideswiping wandoo and salmon gums, a few feet above the gravel, accelerating as fast as the bike.

As symbol, parrots become the destruction not only of beauty in nature (and all, to my mind, is beautiful in nature), but of the 'beauty' in oneself. They are contradictory symbols, and always disport themselves against nation, against settler culture, against bigotry. I guess I have loaded them right up, and I am not alone in this. Many contemporary Australian poets 'deploy' parrots out of direct experience and observation, but also reflectively against the 'parrot cliché'. A modern 'parrot poem' by Peter Skrzynecki, 'To this day', from *There, Behind the Lids* (1970), brilliantly takes the stilled retrospective moment invested with the silence of listening, and recounting, and divests the clichéd bird of all – 'mostly' – but the colours. The colours of a parrot are what most people recall, along with the shriek, or squawk, or call. The parrot – ostensibly non-threatening – is loud, bright, defiant. The still moment is lit up by the colour alone. A reminder of presence in landscape, a vestigial consciousness of dreamtime agency haunts non-indigenous parrot poetry.

Skrzynecki was once termed a 'migrant' poet, a strange liminal term that owes its origins to shifts in population following the Second World

War, but is obviously applicable to non-indigenous Australians generally. Consciousness of newness in a place is countermanded by fatuous claims of First-Fleet authenticity, and the parrot as totemic representative of the pre-migrant and the synaesthesic touch-point, spark for the migrant's symbiosis and imagining of the place s/he works and lives in, is dynamic. Whether in dreamtime mythology the red of a particular parrot's wing is the result or cause of fire, or the red fires an awareness of intertextuality within the articulation of place, the presence of the parrot becomes a metamorphic and transitional figure – a reminder and a prompt.

> My father came in much later, carrying some
> Of the potatoes he'd dug up in the late afternoon;
> Took off his hat, wiped the dirt from around his eyes;
> Rolled a smoke and told us about the bird he saw:
>
> Remembering the colours, mostly, that was all –
> Of the small, green and blue parrot that alighted
> On a nearby clump of wattle as he sat there
> Scraping the mud and grass from his gum boots:
> Remained there as he stood up, reached over
> And threw a handful of sunflower seeds into the tree.
>
> (Skrzynecki, 1970)

In trying to chart the usage and repetition of specific words or phrases in poems – why, say, 'parrot' works cumulatively across different poets' works as it does – I have started using Set Theory as a method of discussing the collecting of words in lines and stanzas in poems. Russell's Paradox is the key, I feel – it basically led to the progression from a naive set theory to Axiomatic Set Theory. This from the wonderfully morphic and mutating contradictions of the web-based 'Wikipedia, the free encyclopedia':

> Russell's paradox (also known as Russell's antinomy) is a paradox discovered by Bertrand Russell in 1901 which shows that the naive set theory of Cantor and Frege is contradictory. Consider the set M to be 'The set of all sets that do not contain themselves as members'. Formally: A is an element of M if and only if A is not an element of A.
>
> $M = \{A \mid A \notin A\}$.
>
> In Cantor's system, M is a well-defined set (disputed …). Does M contain itself? If it does, it is not a member of M according to the definition. On the other hand, if we assume that M does not contain itself, then

it has to be a member of M, again according to the very definition of M. Therefore, the statements 'M is a member of M' and 'M is not a member of M' both lead to Russell's paradox ... (Wikipedia 2005)

Parrotology finds its apotheosis in the paradox. The pervasive presence of parrots in all aspects of Australian life (from television to tomato sauce bottles), means that it is necessarily part of any set associated with 'nation'. It is part of the schema, part of the contents. If we deny the parrot its presence in the poem, then it permeates subtextually. Parrots shadow Australian poetry – or poems written in or out of Australia. I have argued before that Australian pastoral poetry is what so much urban Australian poetry defines itself against – so pervasive are the notions of the 'outback', 'the bush', and 'the farm'. So it is with symbols and signifiers such as 'parrots', 'kangaroos', and 'gum trees' – they are more than part of the place, and their inclusion in a poem does not necessarily mean jingoism. Avoidance becomes a fear as much as anything else – brilliant birds that can terrify with their call; that can mimic what we say. They are reminders of our own failings, our own mortality. As Ouyang Yu's translation of 'An Imperial Palace Poem' by Zhu Qingyu (Tang Dynasty) shows,

> lonely flowers behind the closed palace door
> beautiful women stand side by side in a jaded verandah
> they would love to talk about what's going on in the palace
> but dare not say a word before the parrots
>
> (2005)

this apprehension is timeless and geographically wide-ranging. For Ouyang Yu, a Chinese-Australian who grew up in China, the presence of parrots is polymorphous. There is a wonderfully ironic inflection of the brooding fear in mainstream Australia that the primacy of the English language will be challenged – do the parrots hear in Chinese or English translation, so to speak ...?! Ouyang Yu says of this poem that 'imperial concubines [are] in fear of being informed against by the parrots, parrots being imperial police informants!' (2005). This evokes the idea of the wariness of parrots in poetry as a general fear of surveillance; their absence a delusion of freedom (from Empire, the colonial state)?

In the early 2000s, I wrote a poem called 'White Cockatoos' – the generalised local name given to corellas. White cockatoos – or 'cockies' – are not endemic to this region. White cockatoos are supposedly only found in the Kimberley region in Western Australia, though widespread in the eastern states. The misnomer is of particular interest given that rogue aviary-escapee white cockatoos have in fact been forming colonies just outside Perth. Supposedly, they have not reached the wheatbelt.

In fact, they have – I have regularly seen two or three white cockatoos in large flocks of corellas, themselves considered 'pests' around here and culled yearly (including being shot in the town and on the local school oval!). I emailed an authority on birds recently, who, after confirming he felt corellas should be culled, professed to be very interested in my observations. Realising it would mean more culling, I remained silent.

The reconfiguring of the 'actual' (according to scientific nomenclature), the overlaying of indigenous naming with more recent 'Western' namings, and the nicknaming of a 'pest' bird as one that would be considered even more of a 'pest' ... Degrees of separation take us to both confidence and insecurity about belonging. The paradoxical familiarity and loathing of the species (especially when they eat crops and fruit) make them part of a conversation even when they are absent: a kind of semi-benign threat that at worst can given you the disease psittacosis or tear your finger, or terrify you with their other-worldly, othering cry, a step closer to death; or at best make you feel good about the glory of the day. Here is that paradoxical poem:

> White Cockatoos
>
> Spectres inverting sunlit
> paddocks after late rain
> field into quadrature out
>
> of blind-spots, raucous
> it's said, like broken glass
> in a nature reserve
>
> but that's no comparison;
> cowslip orchids' yellow parameters
> curl like tin, or cowslip orchids'
>
> yellow parameters reflect clusters
> of white feathers from canopies
> of wandoos or sheaths of flight,
>
> down in deep green crops
> ready to turn when rains are gone,
> beaks turned back toward
>
> whereabouts unknown,
> but almost certain to appear,
> at least as atmosphere.
>
> (Kinsella, 2005a, p. 56)

When I was driving back from the city recently, a flight of white-tailed black cockatoos flew out of the jarrah over the road, screeching. Uncle Jack used to say that along with glistening gum leaves and a ring around the moon, they meant bad weather was coming. We have just had the driest July in 120 years and the downbursts of rain of the last forty-eight hours are a massive relief. The clichés of the Australian bush line up like the planets, making science of superstition.

Landscape poetry?

The Dyott Range, near York, in the central wheatbelt of Western Australia, has been heavily weathered – its eroded remains reach a high point at approx 1500 feet (457 metres) above sea level with Mount Bakewell, known among indigenous locals as Walwalinj. It is the main topographical feature of the region in which my family live. It is the centre of my poetry, certainly over recent years. It is also the 'burning reminder' that nothing in this 'landscape' can be taken for granted, and none of it can be owned. Many indigenous Australians talk of the land owning them, rather than them owning the land, and this should be a universal truth. Some talk of themselves as custodians entrusted with a responsibility for the land's physical and spiritual health.* Non-indigenous Australians have, generally, paid scant regard to this truth. Yet no text that has come out of the land, or is a response to the land, can be separated from the land itself, and from the implications of colonisation and occupation.

One of the most famous documents in Australian literature is Marcus Clarke's preface to the poetry of Adam Lindsay Gordon (1880/1893). There he seeks to define the mood of the Australian landscape from the European (especially British) Australian perspective:

> What is the dominant note of Australian scenery? That which is the dominant note of Edgar Allan Poe's poetry – Weird Melancholy. A poem like 'L'Allegro' could never be written by an Australian. It is too airy, too sweet, too freshly happy. The Australian mountain forests are funereal, secret, stern. Their solitude is desolation. They seem to stifle, in their black gorges, a story of sullen despair. No tender sentiment is nourished in their shade. In other lands the dying year is mourned, the falling leaves drop lightly on his bier. In the Australian forests no leaves fall. The savage winds shout among the rock clefts. From the melancholy gums strips of white bark hang and rustle ...

---

* More frequently in recent times, the expression 'traditional owners' is, in fact, being used by some indigenous people.

... In Australia alone is to be found the Grotesque, the Weird, the strange scribblings of Nature learning how to write. Some see no beauty in our trees without shade, our flowers without perfume, our birds who cannot fly, and our beasts who have not yet learned to walk on all fours. But the dweller in the wilderness acknowledges the subtle charm of this fantastic land of monstrosities. He becomes familiar with the beauty of loneliness. Whispered to by the myriad tongues of the wilderness, he learns the language of the barren and the uncouth, and can read the hieroglyphics of haggard gum-trees, blown into odd shapes, distorted with fierce hot winds, or cramped with cold nights, when the Southern Cross freezes in a cloudless sky of icy blue. The phantasmagoria of that wild dreamland termed the Bush interprets itself...

[A fuller quotation from this document is included in the Appendix.]

This othering and fear of the unknown, fused with a Victorian occultism, resonates throughout the Australian literature of the late nineteenth century, and indeed earlier and later. But this is not the bush I recognise, and it is not just a matter of time having passed. Many still view the Australian forests and deserts as places of the 'other', where the rules of the Clarke geo-psychology come into play. The forests are where people grow dope and murderers dispose of their victims; the desert is the place you drive into and perish, to be found six months later a few miles from your car (even the radiator drained for water).

Clarke's view, of course, is not as simple as a mere case of othering. His is a complex and 'rhizomic' piece of writing in which he is almost literally establishing a visceral relationship with the sublimity of a unique landscape. Ironically from a contemporary point of view, while seeking to cathect the landscape 'alien' to a European sensibility, Clarke is actually increasing the othering through his diminution of indigeneity.

Recently, as part of an anthology of Western Australian writing I was preparing, I came across a volume entitled *The Lure of the Golden West* by Thomas Sidney Groser, Late Honorary Secretary and Senior Brother of the Brotherhood of S. Boniface, Western Australia. Published in 1927, but recording experiences from the turn of the twentieth century, Brother Groser's text contains the following observation:

There is scarcely a more lovely picture imaginable than a West Australian Bush in the Springtime. Pink is perhaps the prevailing colour – certainly where the 'everlasting' predominates. But flowers of every other colour of the rainbow are there – white daisies; pale blue leschenaultia; red, blue and cream orchids; scarlet and yellow kangaroo paws growing to three feet in height on slender stems; purple and mauve heather; golden buttercups and wattle – to mention but a few. The rich green undergrowth of Spring-time, and the evergreen and flowering eucalyptus trees, form a rich setting for this glowing pageantry of colour. The indigenous trees of Australia never, perceptibly, lose their foliage.

Marcus Clarke, a prominent and familiar writer of the Antipodes, alludes in his books to some peculiarities of Australian scenery. But he writes of the Eastern States, and knew nought, apparently, of the glorious South-west. His pictures are often weird and fantastic in the extreme. They contain very much that is true, but very much on the other hand that is totally inapplicable to many parts of the Continent. (Groser, 1927, p. 216)

Brother Groser then quotes Clarke's piece exactly as in the Appendix and adds:

In all that is fantastic, weird and melancholy, to my mind, this picture of Marcus Clarke's, itself, takes some beating. But then, it must be remembered, it is a word painting for the preface of a volume of poems whose author was melancholy in the extreme. It was a melancholia which was responsible for Gordon's premature and self-inflicted death. But though temperamentally unstrung, Gordon put his soul into his writings, and justly won for himself an enviable reputation as a true songster. He possessed a keen sense for manliness and natural beauty. Between his poems and Marcus Clarke's Preface to them, there is as much difference as between chalk and cheese. Yet despite this criticism of the weird pen-painting above, after making due allowances for the peculiarities of Eastern conditions, there is a great deal in it that is true and applicable to certain parts of Australia. (p. 219)

The disclaimer built into the last lines is interesting. I also look to a disclaimer, but for a different political reason. For me, the problem is not in the recognition of the weird, the melancholic, the grotesque, but in the application of those to an othering of indigeneity. The weird, the melancholic and the grotesque are aspects in my personal seeing that I cherish, and search out – realising that such values are those of my experience and disposition translated into my interaction with the land. I can also see Brother Groser's bright flowers, but for me they are a beauty tainted by the horrific history of colonisation and displacement.

Critics have consistently remarked on my work that it is too concerned with death, and that in it (even) death has become so prevalent that it is not the 'mysteries' of death itself that are explored but the basic recognition of its necessary presence. This is, in part, true. Death is a constant around which life is measured. In a colonial environment (and colonisation can be 'post' only in discourse, not in reality – recolonisation is how indigenous presence is continually suppressed, 'assimilated', denied, or controlled), death has been written into the process of dispossession. Furthermore, the rural spaces I have spent much of my life in have been devastated by European farming practices – the destruction of the topsoil and the removal of trees and scrub (that would normally keep the water table down and prevent salinity leaching up to the surface), have led to widespread salt. Now here is the paradox – salt is a terrible thing, and yet it is also a natural part of the environment. But through abuse of place, it has spread and replaced the scrub that once kept it at bay.

Salt occurs a lot in my poetry. Its negative side is obvious, but more subtle is its beauty – a crystalline kingdom of apparent nothingness, it becomes a stage for a theatre of absurdity, a different kind of poetic language. I write loss and destruction, lovingly. I write people whose viewpoints are very different to my own, who politically oppose me as I oppose them, but I celebrate the difference. Out of the destruction comes something fresh and vital. For me, poetry is a sublime thing, but also gritty and angry. It can do something. It is awareness and the blood flowing through veins. It is the unseen stream below the surface sought by the diviner and found to be running salt.

The gendering of place also fascinates me. Groser alludes to the maleness of Adam Lindsay Gordon's way of seeing – 'He possessed a keen sense for manliness and natural beauty' (1927, p. 219). For me, gender is among other things a complex and interchangeable way of seeing the land. The use of maleness or femaleness or hermaphroditism in my poetry is meant to show how mobile our interaction with place is. Every difference in ourselves vis-à-vis community will change the way we experience the land. Women in my poems often use a 'masculine' language as a way of destabilising the patriarchy, and a character like 'doll boy' (Kinsella, 2003, p. 80) ironises the feminisation attributed to his gayness by the 'blokes' of the community. For a small Western Australian wheatbelt community, gender identity locates itself on every level of casual or official interaction.

I am interested in re-examining the same events and places over and over again – at different times, under different circumstances. I am interested in the interstices of the macro and the micro, of the twig and the tree. I am equally fascinated by the way things that do not seem to fit create their own language of belonging. On my desk at the moment is a photograph, taken by my mother, that shows a section of mud and stone wall – the remnants of a house destroyed near Meckering during the massive earthquake that ripped apart the fault line in the late 1960s. My cousins spent that night in their station wagon as the family farm shifted, wells lost water, and gullies opened into small canyons. The birds and other animals went silent, the weather patterns temporarily altered. What is unusual about this piece of red mud and grey granite wall, open to the 'pure' blue sky, is the V of plaster that still adorns it. It is decorated around the top of the wall with a *trompe l'oeil* cornice of neo-Etruscan arch frescoes. The plaster-work probably comes from the early twentieth century, and would have been part of a large federation-style bedroom or parlour. It is an anachronism inside a modern intrusion. The ironies fold in on themselves. These ironies drive my poetry, like the fence-post hacked out of the magnificent wandoo, the sheep entangled in barbed wire. As a vegan, I am appalled by the mistreatment and use of farm animals, but these things are intrinsically part of my poetry – sometimes presented with political sympathy, at other times in a matter-of-fact, that's-how-it-is manner. The metaphors take over, and the slippage is where the poem locates itself.

Because I have lived largely in the UK and USA since 1996, the dominant features of landscape for me become points of focus from afar. Another point of reference is the Needlings, which looks down over what remains of my uncle's and aunt's farm, once part of a massive 'settler' property. I have described or conveyed the Needlings in a poem ('Inland', 1998c, p. 138) as a stone theodolite. It measures distances in reverse – that old and wise adage, the further we move away, the closer we get. Landscape is the appropriate word for me, as it is about human mediation of the environment.

My work is an anti-pastoral, as I have often indicated, attempting to tackle the contradictions and uncertainties, with an ecologically inclined politics, but also an eye to 'how it is'. Language is another landscape, and where these two planes meet is where abstraction and, I feel, enrichment, come into their own form of focus. My mother's property is at the base of Mount Bakewell, and my bedroom there looks out onto an ancient extinct volcano. The bushland atop it is the only 'alpine' environment in the wheatbelt, and is the home of a very rare species of orchid – unique, they say – as well as other plants, and probably animals. That is at the peak, the irony being that government communications equipment leads to the summit being semi-protected by nature reservation laws, while the base and a good deal of the slopes of the mountain are leased farmland, destroyed by cropping and stock.

Bats fly down from the mountain at night, and during the day, in very warm weather, paragliders take off, sometimes illegally, from the mount. Take-offs are permitted from private property, but not from reserve/Crown land on the summit. From the workshed behind the house I record all flights that cross my eyesight. I transpose into my journals, and onto paper via a manual typewriter. A wagtail flies into the shed, bobs out again; '28' parrots drop fruits from York gums and a flock of pink-and-grey galahs swerves into view with the setting sun, purple on the 'purple mountain', as a mid-nineteenth-century poet described it (Brockman, 1870 on, forthcoming re-publication). It is a place of immense spiritual significance to the indigenous people of the area (see pp. 74–75).

I am making connections with landscape in mid-Ohio, but I cannot do this in the same way that I can in the place of my childhood memories. A hybrid landscape arises – a composite world in which deciduous black walnuts cross-pollinate with salmon gums. A red tanager and a cardinal morph with elegant parrots, and the ironies of living among seas of genetically modified corn do not escape me. But I *am* connecting, because land is land, and its codes, though so different, are based on the same speech. This 'benign' exploration is exciting, stimulating, and fraught with potential disaster. The benign can become the intrusive, the possessive. But that is also the case where I come from. I retreat to language, a language of poetry obsessed with the real, with observation, but digressing into the abstractions of a hybridised world that becomes its own place.

Apart from a love of the land, I am fascinated by the way stories are told and observations presented. I teach poetics and literary theory, always grounded in praxis, in examples. Gérard Genette's (1980) ideas of duration in narrative, the relationship between the 'time of the tale' and 'the time of its telling', serve my need to revisit place and circumstance from different angles. The shortest event might take the longest time to tell, the longest event the shortest in the telling. Many of the events portrayed in my poetry – if not all – have a concrete set of references, but they also generate their own internal references and timescale. The story exists independently of its telling. I stick photographs over my walls and recreate the places I am not in. There is no nostalgia for them; I do not miss them, they are just a fact. They are there, painful as well as rewarding. They are ingrained.

My brother's sheep dog, Shep, stares away from the camera. He has heard something – possibly the fox that was barking in the scrub near the mountain. It is evening: *that* time. The fox, like the dog and the photographer, are late-comers to the place. They know no other, though, no matter how far they wander. There is an ongoing thirst for reconciliation. Dry for years... a few tufts of blond grass edge the gravel pit. The warped claws of a massive York gum, uprooted by a storm years back, grasp at the ochre. It is singed at the top, and split – now lying semi-horizontal. Twisted up. A lightning strike. As a child I was struck by lightning – thrown off my feet. My auntie says my eyes stuck out on stalks, and ever since then I've looked and looked and looked. (I will return to this motif further on, as it is pivotal to my aesthetics.) I can see the ant on the chip of rose quartz, I listen for the creatures that burrow away from the heat. The dugite suns itself, confident.

One of the storylines I keep rolling through my imagination is the story of the map. I collect map grids of the Avon Valley – my home place. Aerial and field data; scale 1:50 000; horizontal data; vertical data; contours; depressions; trigonometrical station (Mount Bakewell, Needlings ...); stream perennial; stream, intermittent, stream mainly dry; telegraph line; waterhole or soak; clay plain; flood plain; creek or brook; tank or small dam; spring; sealed road; unmade road ... The smothering of another people's or other peoples' tracks, their dreaming, their 'songlines'. 'Dunmore', 'Avonside'. The destructive, delusive overlay. 'Note: The representation on this map of any road or track is not necessarily evidence of public right of way' (York, Sheet 2234–11). Between Cold Harbour Road and Station Road a number of creeks begin. It is a place of sources and ends, and reclamations.

The dark side of the beach: undisclosed poetics

The iconography of the Australian beach has become a tool of nationalism and tourist boards – the two being inseparable. The myth of the bronzed (white) Aussie has merged with 'lifestyle' freedoms of antipodean living, counterpoint to the imagined greater pressures and regulations of, say, Europe and America. In terms of colonialist Australia, the beach is much more: it is the point of access, the place where the colonisation begins, where the overwhelming oceans yield their reward. The voyages of exploration and discovery find their endgame. It is not coincidental that the overturning of what is now termed *terra nullius* in the Mabo case began with an examination of continuous occupation of a beach/shoreline-related space in the Murray Islands. There is an implied necessity that the symbolic point of entry should be the point of recognition, of undoing.

Australians are called a coastal people – much emphasis is placed on the proportion of the population 'clinging to the coastline'. This serves the national purpose well: the vast unknown of inner Australia works as the attracting and repelling magnet in a dialogue between centre and coast. A model of movement is suggested. We move in from the point of entry, the coast. On this model, the interior might be allowed to be indigenous if no mineral wealth is found, but the coasts are claimed by the colonisers.

In Australia, you learn to swim early. Australians generally pride themselves on their national swimming heritage. I could swim early, though I was never a swimming athlete. I was a pragmatic and practical swimmer – could do whatever I needed to do, and did not think about when I did it. It was not an aesthetic, or a style; it was a function. When attending a physical education session on Back Beach for Geraldton High School, I took the jibes of my teacher and certain schoolmates for not being he-man enough – I was just beginning my growth spurt and was not the biggest boy on the block. Shortly after, I found myself pulling one of the big youths from a rip, and basically saving him from drowning. It was not because of strength or skill, but because of a knowledge of conditions that came from swimming at the beach day after day, week after week, in all circumstances. The ocean was large and potentially dangerous, and I defined myself against that threat. Then later, almost twenty years ago, in a depressive alcoholic and substance-induced stupor in which the world did not seem to add up, I walked into the sea one night with the intention of being consumed by it. I remember quoting from Wallace Stevens's 'The Idea of Order at Key West' (1982, pp. 128–130):

> She sang beyond the genius of the sea.
> The water never formed to mind or voice,
> Like a body wholly body, fluttering
> Its empty sleeves; and yet its mimic motion
> Made constant cry, caused constantly a cry,
> That was not ours although we understood,
> Inhuman, of the veritable ocean.
>
> (p. 128)

These lines were important, but none more important than the first sentence of the next stanza: 'The sea was not a mask.' For me, the sea represented the stripping away of lies and untruths, of the social discrepancies that drove me so strongly against being part of a society that had no respect for nature. I wanted literally to become part of nature. It was not sexual, but a negation of sexuality. And the sea would make me genderless. I was told by hospital staff at Fremantle Hospital that a fisherman pulled me unconscious and fully clothed (what does this mean regarding gender?) from the ocean and called an ambulance. I was saved by mouth-to-mouth – I united with one whom as a vegan I was most at odds with.

For me, the ocean became a symbol of reconciling opposites. A friend of mine who stayed with me in the wheatbelt, when I was farm-sitting twenty years ago, would walk with me through the retreating sea of stubble, and would be amazed by the oceanic immensity of the paddocks, the vista. He was eventually to drown himself in the Swan River. I wrote my elegiac volume of poetry *Full Fathom Five* (1993) in the light of this loss. Subtextually, it is really a book about rivers and oceans without shores, without beaches, in the same way that an earlier volume of mine, *Night Parrots* (1989), was about deserts as endless beaches without oceans, without water. The title poem of *Full Fathom Five* is based on the Jackson Pollock painting of that name – a painting whose precise mass and size is measured by the size of the canvas, the weight of paint and objects inserted into the paint, as well as by the specific measurement of the title, but whose depth and size are measureless, weight unknowable. You drown in that painting, and if there is an aesthetic at work in that volume, it is one in which beauty is unknowable, if desirable. It is potentially found in the face of the drowned, or in, say, the 'wheatbelt gothic', as much as in traditional notions of beauty– issues raised by Pollock's precursors, as well as by Pollock himself and my poem. At the beginning of the poem I quote Shakespeare from *The Tempest* and James Joyce from *Ulysses*:

> Full fathom five thy father lies;
>   Of his bones are coral made;
> Those are pearls that were his eyes.
>   Nothing of him that doth fade
> But doth suffer a sea change
>   Into something rich and strange.
>   *The Tempest*, Act 1, Scene ii. Shakespeare (1977, p. 21)

> Five fathoms out there. Full fathom five thy father lies. At once he said. Found drowned. High water at Dublin bar. Driving before it a loose drift of rubble, fanshoals of fishes, silly shells. A corpse rising saltwhite from the undertow, bobbing landward, a pace a pace a porpoise. There he is. Hook it quick. Sunk though he be beneath the watery floor. We have him. Easy now. (*Ulysses*, James Joyce, 1961, p. 50)

The tension between certainty and the unknown are electric in these quotes. They resolve, or suggest closure, through the symmetry and rhythms of the language, but in meaning they cannot be entirely resolved. It is chaos theory at work, and it is the uncertainty that I find attractive; the risk, the calm masking the terror. For me, the beach has always been a place of uncertainty.

I enjoyed visiting the beach as a child, later lived by it in Geraldton, and in a vicarious kind of way in Fremantle, but it was inland I looked. Geraldton was a nexus point in this sense – the rural and coastal meeting, with palpable friction. I like the dry spaces, the unrelieved spaces with their hidden and precarious water sources. And when there is water in the wheatbelt, I hope against the odds that it is fresh water. What has so angered me and found expression in my poetry is the tragedy of polluting and disturbing these water sources with clearing and its resultant salinity, with chemical fertilisation run-off, with levelling-out of river-beds.

The sea, the ocean – vaster and already saline – became for me a symbol of resistance, desirably alien to human endeavour. It could not be completely got around – or dredged. Sadly, this is merely symbolic, since the oceans suffer as much as any other part of the bio-system. And in the same way that I realised the damage done by shooting birds and animals in the country, damage I had personally inflicted on the environment I feel so closely attached to, I developed an awareness regarding my killing fish and other creatures in the ocean.

Apart from fishing throughout my childhood – just another form of hunting – I used those pernicious instruments of destruction, the gidgee and spear gun. I plundered reefs around Geraldton and Drummonds Cove, I watched as injured fish swam off. I was stung by a cobbler on a Geraldton beach and thought my life had ended. The pain was so excruciating I threatened to do the near-impossible: shoot my foot off with an air-rifle, the only weapon at hand. There is a bizarre symmetry to this – a symbol of one kind of death dressed up as play, and the indirect symbol of another kind of death-play: fishing. The cold-blooded are as sentient as the warm-blooded.

Geraldton was also the scene of the worst race-violence I have witnessed. Most weekends, white teenagers would fight Yamatji teenagers on Front Beach. These were staged but brutal conflicts through which the town's race violence would be ritualised. The beach worked both as 'occupied zone' and point of reiterated dispossession. Beaches are liminal spaces always contested – nothing alienates people more than restricted beach access, especially the private beach. As a child going to my mother's childhood playground, Coogee Beach, I would cross the barbed wire and walk along the munitions high-risk beach. Not far, because the military line literally drawn in the sand was ominous and we knew it would have consequences, legally or physically. But still, we resisted it.

'Drowning in Wheat' (2003, p. 64) was written about a farm near Mullewa, not very far from Geraldton. My rural poems are full of seas of wheat – a not uncommon literary description – and vehicles that traverse those waters like boats, using the mariner's tools of navigation. One of the earliest sea images I used in my 'outback' poetry was that of calenture, in a series of 'Lasseter' poems I wrote (1998, pp. 88–102). The loss of points of reference, or, through connecting with indigenous Australians, a new set of co-ordinates, displacing Biblical prophecy with a visionary appropriation, was calenture – the phenomenon of sailors seeing green fields for the sea, stepping out and drowning. For me, the most solid ground is deceptive and a delusion, and the paddocks of Wheatlands farm were a type of calenture. Furthermore, the salinity that devastated the district from excessive clearing was evidence of the oceanic, and the salt waste like some endless tidal flat. The most common salt birds are waders around there – avocets and stilts. It all fits.

As a teenager, I spent time on 'access' holidays with my father at Karratha. The tidal flats of Karratha instilled a displaced notion of beach in me. The beach was an overwhelming presence, but an antithesis of the sandy and regular beaches of the south-west. The water vanished, and walking out, one would sink to the knees in a thick silty mud that stuck ferociously. This was an anti-beach that cleaned nothing away.

But the thin beaches of the Canning River were more my haunt than the beaches of even the Indian Ocean. These too were irregular, never quite satisfying beaches. Did they deserve the name beaches at all? Between brackish salt water and grassed banks with pressured stands of paperbarks, suffering from the wash of speedboats, they nonetheless glowed with white sand. Down towards Bullcreek, the sand shifted with swamp, and mud ate at the beaches. Washed white bivalves cushioned underfoot, while anglers hunted the waters for kingfish. They had their own brutality. We swam in the algae-ridden water, and baked in the midday sun, photosensitising our skins, priming them for skin cancers later in life. In England, as she cut three skin cancers from my face, a doctor told me not to return to the summers of Australia. A kind of exile by exposure.

The fenland beaches of Cambridgeshire. Wisbech, Waterbeach, or further east, the shores of the Broads. A language was lost when the Dutch drainage engineers showed the English the way to isolate and leave the fen people high and dry. Inland waterways, shorelines. So, writing the pastoral of the fens, beaches were my silent reference point. Difference and distance clarify. The draining of the land effectively desexualised, and made less threatening, the landscape. Its fluidity, its abjection was dried out.

A witnessing of nakedness on the beach can facilitate early sexual experience. In the Western Australian sandhills, naked people wandered, looking at other naked people sunning themselves on the beach. Geraldton, Sunset Beach. Behind naturism a series of exploitations might operate. The question of personal freedom, the liberty of the body, and the intrusion of the gaze. The voyeur and the 'without hang-up' grind uncomfortably; the stories that could be told. That are processed and analysed in my books *Genre* (1997a) and *Grappling Eros* (1998a). One night in Geraldton, lost with mates drinking in the sandhills, I saw 'he-men' shed their clothes and run about naked, bottles of green ginger wine swinging. They threatened me with a beating if I revealed what they had done.

The beach is a queer place, of 'ambivalent sexuality'. The pruderies and paranoias seem to lower themselves – on the surface, literally. People can get away with looking, with having 'a perve', without necessarily being called a pervert. The gaze takes on different meanings, is deployed in different ways. There is an illusion, or delusion, of things being more available. Casual sex might be possible, despite the usual prohibitions. The beach becomes the place where taboos might be broken.

The beach can be duplicitous, though: a place where you might get away with admiring the sculptural physique of a well-formed body, but where the Charles Atlas kicking-sand-in-the-face brings its tyranny regardless, and despite our being encouraged to accept all body types in the cooling space of the beach. The beach, especially the nudist beach, presents an anonymity, an opportunistic tableau. Occasional sex, vicarious interactions, go hand-in-hand with genuine sunbathing – though separation of the two is problematic.

Prospect and refuge collide on the duned beach. The vastness of the ocean offset by the hiddenness, the surprise of stumbling across the sunbather, the watcher, in the hills. The fragility of the dunes, the susceptibility to erosion and damage, are resisted. All fences are crossed, lines broken – the open beach is viewed from a place of seclusion. The open and the closed are simultaneously enjoyed.

When I left university I lived for a time in a flat in Cottesloe, with a full view of the sea. It was not a great time in my life, and I would sit at my window staring out at the ocean – at ships coming in, small pleasure craft in the local waters. I watched one burn to the waterline one day, watched the sea rescue in full swing. It was bizarre, surreal. Time was slowed down, even stood still. I felt the hopelessness of an inability to help, and yet it also seemed unreal.

The events outside my window were a surreal drama in which I had little role. Even seagulls lost agency, controlled by an immensity indifferent to their personal plight. The sea was not the nurturing womb, it was the unknown, with its fate, its indifference. The disaster seemed to be unresolvable, but language was persistent in exploring this damage. The image never goes away for me – I brace other images against the certainty of its doubt, the doubt of survival, of damage.

There is an inherent contradiction in this imagistic memory of disaster: it is part of something greater than itself, but it is the separated, disconnected moment. A moment that is inexpressible, that is the dead seagull plunging past the window. It is a moment in a continuum, as Maurice Blanchot might note, it is part of a sentence. The rescue craft will reach it, but the disaster is self-contained. In *The Writing of the Disaster*, Blanchot says:

> If someone pronounces this word, the *disaster*, we feel that it is not a word, not the name of anything; indeed, we feel that there never is a separate, nominal, predominant name, but always an entire complex or simple sentence, where the infinitude of language – of language in its unfinished history and its unclosed system – seeks to let itself be taken in hand by a sequence of verbs, and yet seeks at the same time, in the never resolved tension between noun and verb, to fall, as if immobilized, outside language – without, however, ceasing to belong to it. (1995, pp. 74–75)

The rugged coastline of the south-west has always enticed me, as fraught with disaster as it has been, and remains. I enjoy the precariousness, the risk. The king or freak wave is a fact, and caution is necessary, but the unpredictable is also the figurative. The power of the southern ocean, straight through to the Antarctic; just ocean out beyond Eclipse Island. The Gap at Albany has been a focus for me, a through-the-eye-of-the-needle, since I was a small child. I knew someone who jumped in there and survived. I saw a tourist gradually being pulled in by a camera that swung from his neck, perched on the side opposite the lookout, extended too far in search of the dramatic shot as the ocean smashed against the ancient granite. He was pulled back by the feet just in time.

The beaches on the Torndirrup peninsula are semi-protected by rocks and headlands. Young children can swim at Frenchman's Bay. When the whales were dragged in not far away the sharks would gather and tear at the carcasses. Albany, more than anywhere else in the state, is a place of occupation and entry. The brilliant white beaches become the carpets over which the explorers and military and colonists made their way. It is on the wilder beaches of the south-west that I have picked up massive sheets of plastic, ropes, oil, and other garbage that romantics might call flotsam and jetsam, but which is simply pollution. As the oceans die, the beaches display the death, but always evoke poetry.

In my research for a forthcoming novel, *Post-Colonial*, I speculate that the poet Arthur Rimbaud visited the Cocos Keeling atoll in the Indian Ocean and its beaches on his journey or escape from Batavia back to France. Charles Darwin formulated his theory of coral reef formation while visiting the Cocos Atoll (1846). Across those sands the dreaded Setan (Bunce, 1988, p. 115) calls to those in boats, calls them into the sea, to drown, to be dragged into the dunes on South Island.

On the beaches sheltered by coral reef on the Sumatran side of the islands, rubber thong pressings littered the beaches. Prison Island was just beach and coral and a few palms. On the same side the heavy breakers crushed the coral and the beaches tore your feet apart. I hid on the islands, hid from myself. The beaches were mixed blessings. People surfed off the quarantine station, a place of duplicity where trade was done in ostrich chicks. To protect Australia, the quarantine is twisted and refugees are quarantined in the no-man's-land of territorial 'two-wayed-ness'. Australia bought the islands from the Clunies-Ross family in the mid-1970s for five million dollars – this country makes use of the islands, but also use of their distance as denial. They should be independent – the Cocos Malay people deserve a say over all their beaches.

I often wonder who 'owns' the beaches of Perth.* The people's 'representatives' in federal or state or local government? The people themselves? Who has the rights, the custodianship? Some fifteen years ago, I came to live in the limestone cave behind Bathers Beach in Fremantle. From there I watched the coming and goings of bathers and recreationalists, depressives and those bursting with joy, doing their exercises, excited by the body. The officials came, the lovers hand-in-hand. Microcosm on microcosm. But I felt alienated from this beach – I belonged there no more than I belong in the wheatlands of Western Australia. I feel close to the latter, but the voices that come out of the land speak a language I do not know. I have to respect them. And I have to respect the same but different voices on the shoreline. At that time, I was struggling for self-respect, as much as anything else.

---

* On 19 September 2006, in the case of Bennell v. State of Western Australia, in the Federal Court, Justice Wilcox recognised Nyungar people's Native Title over the Perth region. The state immediately moved to appeal against this decision. Native Title is not the same as ownership.

For someone more interested in wheatfields, why this place in Fremantle? Fremantle was where those embroiled in the antithesis of the city found a way out. Port towns are liminal spaces as well, where the coming and going are tangible, where people who do not fit tend to gather. I moved into the cave one night after wandering the streets. Others shared the space as well, and a drug-using community existed around this small space next to the whale tunnel, under Arthur's Head, below and just south of the Round House.

There is a quote on a plaque by Bathers Bay that represents two of my frustrations: the killing-place of the whaling station, and the American occupation of the ports by their weapons of mass destruction. I was a regular in the Fremantle lock-up for my vociferous protesting against their presence, nuclear and non-nuclear. The quote comes from Herman Melville's *Moby Dick*: 'That great American on the other Side of the sphere, Australia, was given to the intelligent world by whale-men.' I notice that with assertive irony, the land rights flag is at least flown from Arthur's Head alongside the state flag and other flags. You can see the old whaling sea-wall still, and now South Mole reaches out to shelter the harbour on the other side.

The strange thing about living unwashed in this cave was that I rarely walked the few metres down to the sea, a sea hidden by much more scrub then than now. Each day the police came by and cleared me off, but they did not arrest me. By that stage, many people other than family had cut me off because my life had got out of control. However, I had a series of remarkable if brief conversations with the potter Joan Campbell, whose studio was not far from the cave. The old stone building resisted and embraced the sea, and I recall her large earthen pots reminded me of antiquities wrested from the depths. She was wary of me at first – dreadlocks, spouting poetry, and probably crazy. I remember her saying to her assistant, 'It's okay, it's that poet.'

Those memories – as brief as they are, are recorded, if that is the right word for the ambiguities and errors of poetry, in a poetic sequence I wrote while there: 'Dissertation on a Dysfunctional Personality' (1995a, p. 109). It was winter when I was there, and I often burnt rubbish and stuff from around the port to keep warm – the smoke ingraining the porous limestone, inverting the process of petrification – roots growing up and not down. McKenzie Wark has noted that we no longer have roots, but aerials (1994, p. xiv). By that thin stretch of beach I listened to the gentle, sometimes harsher, waves of the bay and thought of York gums and jam trees.

I visited the cave again recently – it is much the same, though parts of the cliff face have been bricked for 'safety'. It is neater, cleaner. Somebody still frequents it – the detritus of street living is there. The thing that made me angriest, and also did back then, was the Roundhouse. I used to think that sleeping near it and the whale tunnels were ways of absorbing the hate of colonisation, accepting that I was part of its brutality. The Roundhouse, the first gaol in Western Australia, with its legacy of death and torment, only exists today because a Harbourmaster decided it was a good windbreak for his house. For indigenous people, it was a living hell, as was Rottnest. Places of Westralian identity, of making a history.

The Roundhouse is a panopticon – a prison in which each cell can be viewed, under surveillance from the centre – they all look in on a well, a source of life. The irony permeates the solid walls. Michel Foucault, in *Discipline & Punish: The Birth of the Prison*, wrote of the Utilitarian philosopher Jeremy Bentham's idea for the ideal prison:

> Hence the major effect of the Panopticon: to induce in the inmate a state of conscious and permanent visibility that assures the automatic functioning of power. So to arrange things that the surveillance is permanent in its effects, even if it is discontinuous in its action; that the perfection of power should tend to render its actual exercise unnecessary; that this architectural apparatus should be a machine for creating and sustaining a power relation independent of the person who exercises it; in short, that the inmates should be caught up in a power situation of which they are themselves the bearers. (1977, p. 201)

and:

> The Panopticon is a machine for dissociating the see/being seen dyad: in the peripheric ring, one is totally seen, without ever seeing; in the central tower, one sees everything without ever being seen. (1977, pp. 201–202)

The roundhouse is an anomaly in the panopticon sense: the inverted central viewing position, the fact that the windowless cells 'look out' on the beach, the sea – on vast spaces of unavailable escape. The building itself is a beacon, a point of reference on the shoreline, and yet there was no visibility from within for the prisoner, and no escape. People have committed suicide in that building in recent years. It is history as persecution, a history of deprivation, of a dialectic in which colonial materialism triumphs. It should be removed, or turned into a memorial to those who suffered within its walls, the land dedicated to the indigenous spirits that are present. In the cave, I thought these things. I wrote poems in my head, and some actually on paper. Trying to be outside society yet vestigially remain attached to it, you and your writing tend to become self-absorbed – hunger and isolation are great tools of the self.

The dark side of the beach might be found in perceiving it as an edge: an edge that might be broached, or an edge that might be used to ward off strangers. The language of invasion with its 'securing the beach', 'beach heads', 'amphibious landings', seeks to utilise the beach to secure land, to make it concrete. The beach, however, is not concrete – with shifting tides and the work of the weather it is an in-between space, a liminal zone. It is a place where sea creatures lay eggs, where crabs bunker down for the day. It has its own rules. It can also symbolise an inability to look inward, a hope for bounties from elsewhere, as in Dorothy Hewett's cutting poem of Australian coastal clinging, 'Coastwatchers':

> they don't look inland
> but creep to the edge of the sea
> and huddle
> eyes scanning the horizon of loss
> they wait for the cargo
>
> (1995, p. 344)

And it can symbolise external conflict and death, the threat from other shores, and a threat that comes from behind the shore as well, as part of the human condition when religious faith is lost. Matthew Arnold wrote in 'Dover Beach':

> Listen! you hear the grating roar
> Of pebbles which the waves draw back, and fling,
> At their return, up the high stand,
> Begin, and cease, and then again begin,
> With tremulous cadence slow, and bring
> The eternal note of sadness in.
>
> (1969, pp. 210–212)

In recent years in Australia, an appalling fear of 'invasion' from sea by refugee vessels has driven a xenophobic and anti-humanitarian government policy towards refugees. The beach becomes militarised, the refugees seen as breaching the border. The beach becomes a symbol of Australian insularity. It is like living in a cave and being consumed by your own dysfunctions, incapable of accepting the beauty of the oceans – its comings and goings.

II

SPATIAL LYRICISM

A new lyricism: some early thoughts on linguistic disobedience
originally addressed to Marjorie Perloff

Part 1
The lyric is the basis of all my poetry, but its signature is blurred and reconstituted. I consider myself a linguistic lyricist, a 'new lyricist', or a lyrical hybridiser. A deconstructive lyricist. As to the question of the unified self, I have been many people in my life – I remember them all, though the memories are tenuous. I think an ethics and a politics binds these selves together – though I am probably wrong. The error in the line is where 'truth' lies. Metaphors are mistakes, metonyms associations that the arbiters of language would like us to believe are there. The arbiters of language: those who would control an environment. All arbiters of language? Sense exists in the non-word, in the guttural gesture; in expression and emptiness. Poetry is not expression. It is a halfway house, it is where words mutate and degenerate, rehabilitate and regenerate. Words are never the same after the poem, though. Poetry is not about sameness, even though the same refrain might come again and again, echo through the literature.

Use the pain. Write with it. This is bad as advice, though it might be appropriate to evoke a reaction against itself. The anxiety of influence (Bloom, 1973/1997) resonates because patriarchy has created the environment for the reception of poetic texts – the Oedipal struggle is written not only in what a poem says, but in the actual techniques traditionally used to express it. The private poetry of women may bear many exceptions to this, but the male control over publishing, in western tradition at least, has meant a hierarchy of form. Poetry as an emotional pamphleteering. As a placebo. The difficulty for the lyric in conveying 'emotional' content is that it cannot be effective if the material is not carefully controlled. The looser this control, the less we can accept the genuineness of the emotions. Anti-war poetry in particular relies on the credibility of the emotional distress in the face of war's horror. Does Leon Gellert say what we think he says in 'If You Were Here'? Or is he displacing, insofar as this poem is actually an extended metaphor for the isolation and dislocation of war?

> If You Were Here
> (Overlooking the Valley of the Nile)
>
> If you were here
> These long grey fields of space
> So quaint and yet so drear,
> Stagnant with age, yet green with corn and palms,
> Would have new grace.
> Could I but hear your voice and feel your arms
> The glory of the Egypt dawn would seem
> More grand, more clear;
> An ecstasy unrivalled in the wildest dream,
> If you were here.
>   January, 1915 (1917, p. 31)

If we were not aware that this was written during the First World War, it might strike us as being a poem primarily about absence and aloneness in the exoticised environment, when in fact behind it is the weight of a war of such scale that it was altering the very way the poet perceived his relationship to place, history and language itself.

Poets 'hate' poets; or perhaps it is more relevant to say that each poem written displaces another. In the case of Gellert's poems of war, there is both a critique of war and a celebration of comradeship that are unique to their time, and in many ways they work against earlier poems with a sense of noblesse oblige.

Regardless of time and place, at the core of the poem is the object–subject relation. The tree is in the window, through the window the tree – the unified self says it with certainty. Parataxis, enjambment. The window tree limbs loosely I see wood glassly. Line length, metrics and breath. Neat definitions. The line rolls on and on, written in sand. It blows away shortly after implying completion. It can neither begin nor end, being perfect in conception but decaying as it is written, inscribed. Plato would have a field day. We do not want poets in this organisation.

I believe my work moves through the many nuanced layers of the 'lyrical I/non-lyrical I' construct. I often use sequences: within the sequence a textual dialogue is created. Even the narrative destabilises itself through alternative relationships being set up between different sections, chapter, occasions, events. Numbered, asterisks, roman numerals: different languages. Annotations work in a similar way: dialogues within texts, within the frame of the page, across frames, between different surfaces. All poems are part of a larger project. A greater sequence of language usage. Nothing exists as a thing-in-itself. Efforts to disconnect create new connections. I write an anti-pastoral; an eruption of urban-rural fringe-speech; a war in defence of feral cats *and* against environmental destruction. Against the clearing of land, genetically modified organisms and foods; against pesticides and weedicides and chemical fertilisers; against the abuse of animals. But the poem is a positive action. It does not attain a higher plane, though it might aspire to. Taken as a life project, it is an act of counter-pastoral. In the country house they perform their pastoral masques. Outside, the 'rural poor scrape together a living' – à la Raymond Williams (1973)? The television and video still to be paid off. The harvest fails and brings hardship, and the farmer votes for a racist party. He has no intention of supporting Aboriginal land rights. He says: 'My family have been here for five generations, it's my place.' Another farmer says: 'I know how they must have felt. When I was forced to sell up it was like having a limb wrenched off.' It is how they feel. Poetry from the invader does not bring land rights; poetry of re- or counter-hybridity by indigenous writers might. Destabilising the invading/colonising language. As part of a migrant culture, I write about the paradox of home, about the process of adaptation and change. In cold climates they put tropical plants in hothouses. I am an alien in all places other than the place of language, the place of poetry. I read, the texts become part of me. I write that the texts might infiltrate, mutate, become part of something else. Is this a colonisation? Yes, but a positive hybridity, a sharing of what I am, what has been mediated through my experiences, my circumstances, my set of co-ordinates.

The real and the artificial. A visitant eclogue – the farmer talks with an alien. (Kinsella, 1999b, pp. 60–61). Patriarchal language as a form of address and conversation, the 'external' reply. The same words have different meanings. The range of colour differs. The human eye is a constant – prone to error, to blurring information, to differing interpretations, but it is taken as a given. A semi-precise image. The colour range of a dog's eye is different, we believe. The colour of vowels is different for a dog.

There are no symbolist truths – and there are not simply words. Words are not enough. It is all the reactions that accompany words that matter. The scroll of the computer screen, hypertext, create sequences. Patterns. Systems of decoding. We read through and against them. I hybridise to break the constraints of state control of language, to move away from social and cultural expectation. Liberty, equality. Respect has to remain for spaces into which one is not invited. Appropriation destroys what is positive as much as it highlights the intractability of a particular environment or setting. It cannot be denied, but its implications are challenged and subverted.

My politics and ethics and poetry are inseparable: my vegan anarchist pacifist beliefs inform everything I write. I use language to unsettle a world in which centralisation has denied rights. I believe in decentralised communities creating ethical structures through dialogue and responsibility. Barter as a means of exchange. My new lyricism is one of linguistic disobedience. These are words that open a pathway to what it is I think I write. Poetry is between speech and writing; it is closer to thought than either. When I have written, I defetishise my text, or attempt to. I try to forget about it. It becomes readers'. They reinvest or extract the lyrical intent. They reassign the linearity, imply or decay order accordingly. The page is a field of vision for me, a place of occupation. It is the territorialised environment. I am interested in it only insofar as it implies something outside, something beyond the frame.

Is violent language violence? Is this where context comes into its own? The lyric intent softens the aggression. The song of celebration, the lament, the prayer – the prayer as exchange. What I offer is the organisation of words. Organisation does not have to be oppression. Control can bring freedom. It is a combination of regulation and surprise, disjunction. The four-line stanza, the sonnet, the sestina, the rondeau – the rules govern through tradition and context; to utilise the form is to open a conversation with inheritance, with the gallery of culture. Through form we can undo. An action is taken to improve a situation. Or to resolve it. In the aesthetic, a beauty is entire and yet the process continues; one might say illogically. Lesbia Harford in 'Pruning Flowering Gums' deploys the following:

> One summer day, along the street,
> Men pruned the gums
> To make them neat.

> The tender branches, white with flowers,
> Lay in the sun
> For hours and hours,
> And every hour they grew more sweet,
> More honey-like
> Until the street
> Smelt like a hive, withouten bees,
> But still the gardeners
> Lopped the trees.
>
> (poem LXVII) (1941)

Rhyme is a deft ironiser. It is the illusion of closure, of completion. But this verse goes in circles. Rhyme intimates the circle, and yet a circle in which the end and the beginning offset each other. Complete and yet contrapuntal. Heroic couplets work in the same way – linking and yet cumulative. Rhyme is most effective used incidentally, to short-circuit the process, to make the circle wobble. An elliptical twist. As we are left on the precipice, the line dropping off ... or left wandering aimlessly.

I am interested in surfaces, but there are endless surfaces suggested by our one plane. The prospect is all that words imply, all that they might be doing beyond the poets' expectation and comprehension. The fragment writ large. Refuge is the insularity of the poet, the residual lyrical or ego I, the undeniable. Give me a text and I will trace the narcissistic code. The ubiquitous concrete poem Perspective, vanishing from the p to the e, carries the signature of its author. But we as poets and readers should deny its exclusivity; the word exists in a culture of language, will be curated in a variety of cultural spaces. Interpretation changes. Context unreads, rereads, reads for the first time. The house is a body. Sheltering inside our flesh. We inscribe it with our sicknesses and passion and despairs. The poem is a body. The reader might make it a Deleuze and Guattarian body without organs (1977, p. 9). Filling it, giving it functionality. The book is a machine. It processes, digests, and manufactures presentations. A curatorial machine. It is the end-stopping of data. Enjambment dies in the book.

I am no longer interested in writing overviews of national poetics – old, new, emergent or otherwise. I see all such structures as being complicit in the construction of national identities that inevitably destroy liberty and equality. The machine of the state has many guises, and the poetry industry is one of them. Even overtly political poets who allow their poetry to become part of a national 'heritage' or identity are complicit in this. Language should be used to reduce the influence of the state, to fragment, to create lines of communication between non-centralised communities. If poetry captures the highs and lows of human aspiration, it does so all too often through a semblance of freedom – it plays the games of bigoted and oppressive societies. I am not interested in the idea of Australia. I am interested in bringing attention to tension and conflict behind the face of pleasantness – to highlight the injustices to indigenous peoples and the racisms and misogyny that prop up the Australian government, its bureaucracy, and those capitalist enterprises that support it. I wish to highlight the injustices to animals as well as humans, and to work towards halting the destruction of the environment. Rehabilitation, prevention and a linguistic disobedience.

As a vegan living in a world that is a killing, meat-making machine, I have to adjust my dialogue constantly ... and the same applies to talking about nation. An anarchist for twenty years, I remain so. If my statement uses the 'language' of nationalism, it is because I need to use its terminologies to express myself, to work against it. It is impossible to escape the terms of reference. I will work on ways of overcoming this.

Collaboration. Challenging the unified lyrical self, construct, simulacrum. A pair, a group, a chain of simulacra. Basho making strings with his followers, the process very specific, the rules formulaic – 'The Renku is a unique type of poem with multiple authorship. It normally consists of thirty-six, fifty, or one hundred verses (or stanzas) contributed by a "team" of poets' (Ueda, 1982, p. 69). That's the trick – a controlled environment in which the micros can run wild. Do not hide behind chaos theory. It is not that – it is about manners and courtesy. The collaborators will succumb to territoriality, to suspicion, to jealousy. Best lines are often kept for private projects. How much of the self, of the work history, of the closely guarded secrets of perspective, are held back? But collaboration will undo its own binary – words have minds of their own. They fraternise and resist, the text is fluid. 'I object to your use of the word text when you mean poetry.' I've heard this. Text makes it cold, mechanical – apparently. But what I want is a cybernetic body – words and objects, real objects – data and emotion, metaphor and truth. The melding of the error to the perfect body of truth. Here, I offer you my best words, make of them what you will. 'The world is all that is the case' (Wittgenstein, 1999, p. 5). We both believe in animal rights. We all reflect on the geography beyond our windows. It is a question of location and guilt.

Illustration by anecdote: hay-baling in the southwest with an Italian-Australian family. Breaking up the cultural binaries, moving outside familiar territory, creating connections, finding a language. The signifier is the hay bale; the signified is hybridised pastoral of Italian pastoral song and a pastoral tradition through Spenser via the Australian poets Henry Kendall and Charles Harpur. The clichés are there: the Italian work ethic, the closed family, the creation of a little rural Italy. Two males, brothers, with Anglo-Celtic backgrounds and semi-rural backgrounds pitted against two Italian brothers from Sicily, with a displaced sense of belonging. Competition. Hay-baler on overdrive. Having written dozens of poems related to hay – bales, stooks, paddocks, fields – still, fifteen years later, I have no language to encapsulate the cross-cultural experience. A trans-cultural language. The sound of the hay-baler near the family house at York immediately evokes something. The maleness of the farming environment, the anxiety of influence. The Oedipal farm. All broken up around here, sold off to split up between sons and daughters. They say: see the implication of your feminist sympathies. Fragmentation, decentralisation, anarchism. Here is that Anglo-Celt hay-baling in the early morning: neighbours, but not well known:

> Hay-baling in the early morning: late spring
>
> Between the mountain and the house
> tractors drag hay-balers clockwise
> around the paddock, guzzling
> windrows, coils of twine roping
>
> out in the belly, knots tied
> rapidly as hay is ram-packed,
> metropolis movements sound-tracked,
> che-cha che-cha che-cha,
>
> the bricks birthed rigidly, methodically,
> as if nature has come to this:
> but the steel and mechanisms
> disguise the hermaphroditic birth –
>
> its beauty, its contradictions:
> the offspring's placenta, eaten
> in the paddock, dark cycles
> that sprout like fetishes,
>
> feed the profit. The operators
> push in the early morning dry,
> little moisture in the yellow bales,
> small plumes of dust saying

> get it done: persistence
> is fruitful. Watched, they continue
> unawares, staggered on the clock-face,
> winding inwards, to a point
>
> where they almost meet: these blokes
> in hats and singlets – midwives,
> deftly working the circles, with and against
> the machinery's stiff workings.
>
> (Kinsella, 2001b)

No country to call my own? I have British residency. I am working in the States. The power of anti-federation? All in a name? And I am Australian by birth. I hybridise landscapes. I colonise linguistically to highlight invasion and exclusion. The fens fuse with the wheatbelt of Western Australia. The fens: layers of peat. Water. This is history. The topsoil is ripped from the survey around Cunderdin, Meckering, Tammin. The numberplate of my mother's car: CMT. An international regionalist, I respect the integrity of place but open lines of communication, create dialogues. Through understanding comes respect. Those small communities huddling round the campfire of reason. Cosy. Species diminish, the planet turns tepid. Seasons: unpredictable. The poems grow. To draw these fragments into a picture, we search for unification.

> Lyrical Unification in Gambier
> For Marjorie
>
> (i)
> What remains barely the weather
> report: sentencing labours of history
> against all beginnings, the maples
> leafless, the houses barely porous.
>
> (ii)
> I ride roads I am not familiar with,
> a figure of speech, chrome strips
> between windows. To the south,
> burial mounds. Resolution
> deep and simpatico. Northwards:
> the lake effect, the snow plough.
>
> (iii)
> Deer go down to bow and gun,
> roadkill is a 'cull': beauty
> in the eye of rhetoric
> keeps the engine
> ticking over.

(iv)
Cornstalks like rotted Ceres'
thin black teeth. To end with this.
A season of political arrangements,
remnant snow quarried
like that pitiless ocean.

(v)
The driver must resist
all beauty, the smell
of an unfamiliar passenger.
A door rattles, the car
is almost new. It is shut
properly. Speed limit.
Farm machinery. A (solitary)
white field enclosed
by thawed pages.

(vi)
Maples, oak ... all kinds.
A tornado ripped through here
three months ago and didn't
touch the houses either side.
Birds warble in the engine
cavity. A cord of wood
stretches out below
the kitchen window.
He says we listen
differently.

(Kinsella, 2003, pp. 112–113)

Unrealisable. In Gambier, Ohio, the red cardinal bird centres the frame. It is not a native to the place, though arriving as a stranger, you would think it one of the mysteries, one of the raptures of the region. The signature of a place. Fellow poets include the red birds in their poems. The red bird is of Gambier. It becomes a pastoral motif: here it can be good – despite the imperfections an idyll might, in the very least, be ironically staged. The metaphysical red bird. The bird of friendship and bridging. The bird that takes us to the threshold and says: build words here. It aches to be expressed, to be written:

A Cardinal Influences Peripheral Sight
for Ron and Inese

Through insect screens
a patch of tangled
stems and leaves
works as graph paper;
or is this the way

it seems, in its duns
and browns? The snow-fray
an aura breaking up,
static scoriae ...

We see community
and politics in the starlings'
feeding frenzy, hearted
deep by cardinal

working outwards,
its influence equally
peripheral through
the gridwork,

a blurring that bleeds
cross-species.
The failure of this
transcendent interlude
to contain colour
or snow glare
within the black reflector,
bares molten feathers,
blood vessels woven together.

(Kinsella, 2003, p. 111)

As we might have it in the tentative human condition. The red bird migrated, originally, from the zone they now call Florida. Or something more specific. The pastoral signature? Nature in the garden. Through the study window – comfortable – the red bird sits within the lashes of brambles. Always there in the morning, polarised. It can't see the darkness through the window? Broken up by flywire. Gridded, like the graph paper Lyn Hejinian composes on, composed on. I witnessed.

The lyrical bird? People eat pathetic fallacy.

> Infra Red
>   for that you
>
> Companion blue backdrop
> tense as stretched is taut when
> comparisons are made, unlike
> as error, beneath our spectra,
> our readout: a goodness
> sits there, perched,
> scoped
> as tableau,
> from edges, a view
> of wilderness and suffering
> on outskirts: to look below
> the waterline, companion,
> facsimile: as if to watch you
> enlarged like rage,
> sky upheld, scarified
> by rectrix: bird-type
> like a species of parrot,
> though chevroned
> and saturated in long wave-length,
> we register, I that bird,
> spectre of.
>
> (Kinsella, 2001c)

So what is left but the theory? Overlay the lyrical impulse with analysis. The page as couch. Solipsistic. That signature beneath the deferrals. Without the voice of the unified self, the poem speaks more or less for more than one of us. For the group, the subculture, community, nation?

Consider again Marcus Clarke writing on the Grotesque and the weird in Australian landscape (Clarke, 1893, p. 4) [see Appendix]. Allusion, reference, comparison. The Grotesque given beauty: an apparently new aesthetic. A poetic prose text of assimilation. Even the indigenous dreaming gnawing away in the background. The alienation of the unfamiliar confronted and poeticised. Poetry can make for the most controlling, oppressive systems. Poetry is a machine. Little desiring machines (Deleuze and Guattari, 1977, p. 1), as Empson might have a condom labelled on the stage of the academic pastoral. Poetry draws it all together, focuses language. It apparently creates an order, even where it is not recognised. The Dadaists did not destabilise language after the horrors of the First World War; they gave it an escape route, they gave it an alternative modus operandi. They consolidated art when art had no right to be.

'Poetry after' (Adorno, 1967, p. 34)? Poetry after anything. Poetry joins the fragments. The more fragmented it is itself, the more it fills the spaces. The number sequences are breaking down – the planet cannot hold – and poetry is used like liquid sealant. If we do not recognise this, we have fetishised our souls. Nature scribbles itself, to itself, to us. This is God's signature rewriting, on autopilot. Like the bank teller with a range of signatures for comparison as he or she gets more and more tired. After three hours of signing, this is the authentic mark. The signature. Poets' residencies in banks? Banknotes constructed to prevent forgery, appropriation? The monetary economy? Barter. The signature of God: OMO DEI. So written, in this Latinate language. 'Omo' is a brand of soap powder.

A landscape poet? I came, I saw, I wrote the poem. I lived here long and legitimate my observations through association and experience. He feels the colours of landscape. Through the skin, into the circulatory system. It is all reds and blues: enriched with oxygen, depleted. This poem dwells through colonisation, exclusion, genocide. It ironises and even attacks its own terms of production. And yet it is read. Never written, just read or heard. Someone else does the speaking. I have no rights of belonging textually anywhere. But poetry is the third party, the alternative body. Inscribed, tattooed. It is a venue, a controlled environment that always threatens to explode, to come apart at the seams. The potential keeps us waiting, hanging about. We keep writing and reading. If the potential is not there, where else is it? Below the poem the subtext of self lurks. The author meditates behind persona, the distance of identity loss. Vikram Seth (in conversation at the Adelaide Festival, 2000) said: 'Are you suggesting that she put her name to my work, that I put mine to yours, and so on ...?' Yes, yes I am. And we only gain by it.

Olson: 'Form is never more than an extension of content' (cited in Perloff, 2001a, p. 4). Content forced into form has more to say: that is where the challenges lie. Form is not about line, it is about shape. The relationship between shapes is the key to opening subtextual dialogues. I use the villanelle. I force my words into alexandrines, syllabics. This has cultural implications. 'English doesn't work as verse effectively in syllabics.' Propaganda. Our ears are forced against it. In Australian English, iambic pentameter is often not that. The tonal variations, the dialect, make something else of it. We all write dialect poetries to a point. Otherwise it is simulacrum. I write hybrid synecdoches. A bit of what I am, a lot of what I seemingly am not. Other than in language. The self is mediated.

In the end, it is movement. A journey. But never a direct route –

there cannot be one. Too many ethical hazards. This going somewhere has implications about choice on every level. Nothing is entirely spontaneous; intent is there. The idea comes before the poem. Or something is seen or heard and the words shape themselves around it. The shapes are then pressured, pushed into alternatives. Disparate things sit awkwardly in the same spaces, force each other out, lead us to look for alternative routes.

As a poet I travel from community to community. I do not share in everything these communities offer – many offerings are not for me. But I register them and write them and transport their codes to other communities. I convey. I transfer. My transformations are encoded, recoded, remade. The word 'gets around'. Its growth is limitless. It makes new space to accommodate its potential. Spaces of interiors and surfaces. I represent part of the possibility of this. Each poem, each community, works its own dynamic equivalence. Translation loss is linguistic gain. Genre crossover is poetically exponential – a vibrant source of movement. Water makes up most of our body. Rhythm is flow. Prosody is hydraulics, the schematics of water's movement.

So poetry, for me, is about resistance. It is where my pacifist revolution takes place. It can and does change through communication. It is positive, in the end. To challenge syntax, to challenge common sense, is to challenge the status quo. It is to recognise the language of animals, to recognise the vulnerability of our own conditions. It is about error and uncertainty, about the quirks that appear in the predictable.

First Essay on Linguistic Disobedience

The sing song of the bird
is generic. We follow
its chit chit chit verbally
awkward, passive in its small communities.
Red as always. This lyrical certainty, a linearity as 'comforting' as
Leaves of Grass.
The same sport of democracy
offsetting the house,
the open garden,
the field others wander through.
They designed it themselves.
Joggers surround the house
and ice drops sharp.
There are no curtains
and the joggers look inwards –

machines, made on government treadmills.
The less of, the more: better, kinder
that way. Better
words wanted in better orders:
note the syntax? Note: the tribes driven inwards
as if Ohio might be a name-home, or preconnecting
burial mounds, death-nodes, enclosures.
Crypted over, the house plans
fill room on room, the electrical wirings,
the colour-coded circuits.

In the valley the fraternity
has left refuse and a dead turtle: cans and black stockings – nylons –
adorn the targeted tree. Deer move swiftly by, white high-tailing it
out of there. Security assure us
it's not black magic, and that there
are no shell casings.
In the early morning skunks are shot
by skunk hunters: skunks root the ground over,
searching for grubs. A repellent chemical
is sprayed on golf courses,
where it doesn't reach, the skunks
de-green the surfaces.

These anxieties strut about the houses,
species outside a bird book.
What wrong out of this talk,
these whispers behind closed doors?
Justly, this is our prison.
I entreat gardener and itinerant labourer,
the seed-drill and combine harvester,
or the snake brought in with firewood,
deeply sleep as just as governing
instinct. Protect the snake. Trusts us?
The strength is in its poison
and the power of its jaws to deliver.
The body-spring.

I give this language nothing
the birds' sing song translates as a forest
denuded of trees: these wooden houses
working for nothing.
As if the progress of seasons
doesn't add up –
alienated by smog and effluent,
blue tarpaulins flapping in the wood,

rights of initiation.
The grandfather – mine – was of some
Masonic order and I knew nothing
of it. Parrots are red birds
where I come from, home-
shifting, testing density
of surfaces. That beneath, communities.
The pipes rising up, copper-clouded water
pooling where the parrots' taxes
run out.
        (Kinsella, early draft of poem published 2003, pp. 126–128)

Part 2
Sleep – linguistic disobedience

1.
People seem to know me best by my sleeping habits. Those who have talked or worked with me throughout nights, or have spent days awake travelling with me, know something most of my companions will never know. During my childhood I forced myself to stay awake because I liked the effect. It brought unusual ways of seeing things, and ideas would come that were not simply the borrowed ideas of books. Or so, in my altered state, I convinced myself. Sleep had a spiritual significance for me. It was a communion with the unknown, the unseen. Good and bad things could happen during sleep, with little defence. I learnt to control my dreams, or at least to remember on waking that I had controlled my dreams. I was determined to gain control over sleep because of one dream in particular. I dreamt of a polar bear on a slab of ice. Everything was white, even in my dream the black nose of the polar bear. I could not see it at all. Its eyes were white. But I knew it to be there and thought of it as a kind of spell or maybe prayer. This absolute whiteness was total fear. I wanted it to vanish but it would not. If sleep had to be, I would fight it. And I did. I would read through most of the night, sometimes with a torch under the bedcovers if my mother was particularly concerned about the state of my eyesight and sanity.

I learnt that staying awake was also a spiritual experience, a kind of high of the soul. It was the stuff of prayer, the empirical data of transference and reception of faith. As weird as it sounds, this is what I told myself. I worked in my laboratory, exploring chemical reactions or constructing radio equipment, I created analogues of wakefulness – the reaction, electricity. I played with ideas of perpetual motion machines.

I did not like things that stopped. To stop was to lose control, to have the darkness close over you where only small deaths were possible. I learnt to hate sleep. High on endorphins, I buried myself in work of the eyes; my eyesight suffered. I discovered poetry at a very young age. My mother wrote poetry. She won a tool chest for my father and he cocked an eye, though distrusted it more than ever. They divorced. My brother and I saw aliens in the back yard. My brother also resisted sleep. He went outside at night; at first I stayed in my room. The four walls were my sleep. Poetry was anti-sleep. But it had the comforting cycles of sleep. A hypnotic patterning of breath, of being part of the words and lost between them. A set of certainties but certainties full of errors. Metaphor came with tiredness, with forcing wakefulness when sleep was closing in. But then I ventured out, into the 'landscape' ... the paddocks, the bush, later the beach.

In Sumatra, heading north from Lake Toba in my early twenties, I was awake for the fifth day in a row. I was semi-mad, my head banging the steel bar of the seat in front of me every time the bus hit a bump. Which was often. I had been indulging in a world where sleep was relief – a mystical orgy of skewed signatures and referentiality. Landscapes merged with people. I had been in a place of animism. Places and objects spoke. What I appropriated and took from these I destroyed when sleep took over and left me stranded in darkness for days. I lost something. Years of drinking could not bring sleep back. I started to get afraid. Finally, I stopped drinking, and enjoyed my wakefulness again. Not deprivation but extension. Time up my sleeve. More projects. More conversation, more dialogue.

Prayer is exchange. Poems are prayers. An ongoing exchange with sceptics and believers. I in the liminal zone of self and unself. Consciousness blurring with what lies beneath. And then came email. Open twenty-four hours a day. Just find a different timezone. Three o'clock in the morning in the UK and people are up and happening in Australia. Perfect. Sleep, or rather the tendency of others to pursue sleep at all costs, had been thwarted. From my childhood's four walls, I ventured out to find things to fill my wakefulness, as my brother did. Nature did. No, nature is the wrong word. Too mediated by humans. I do not eat animals or use things taken from animals because they are of me. It is a respect. At night in the bush the tawny frogmouth looks rigidly down from a tree, the owl. Numbats and echidnas nuzzle termite mounds. The forest is silent and loud, sleeping and alive. I discovered something there. A calm that is sleep without the darkness, the emptiness.

2.
Rolling text. Cross-genre. Visions. Speaking in invented languages. Blurring of boundaries. That is what comes from a lack of sleep. My grandmother had trouble sleeping. She said it was old age, but I suspect it was a lifelong problem. When I left the country for the city to start university, I stayed at my grandparents' house in Victoria Park, Perth. It was a short train journey from the city. I would read most of the night, often crossing the path of my grandmother as I went to get a drink, or use the bathroom. She would be up reading – huge books. Anything over 800 pages would do for her. Or writing letters. She corresponded with dozens and dozens of people, diligently, through the night. In summer we would water the garden together in early morning. At five a.m., listening to the magpies. Sometimes I would just be getting home, and she would be watering. That was a strange year. Then I moved out and found empty spaces or zones full of non-sleepers. Or read of sleep in Greek myth. Metamorphosis fascinated me. Sleep was transition but also loss.

Rolling text. Cross-genre. Visions. Speaking in invented languages. Blurring of boundaries. I tend to work on numerous projects at the same time. If the one I'm working on is not firing, I switch to one that is. I work in intense bursts and work through until I am almost burnt out. It is obsessive, that's true. I shut off from everything else. People can be talking, music blaring. When I am not firing, the slightest noise can be irritating. When I am like this I do not even register the need for sleep. I do not drink coffee or take any stimulants. I jiggle my legs, I type or write in pen, compulsively. If it is a critical piece or a cross-genre piece, I might be surrounded by a mountain of books. It might also happen at an airport, and has happened under a floodlight at three in the morning on my uncle's property, Wheatlands.

Out there under the Needlings Hills with the fox barking, and the cold biting hard. The disc plough almost tangled in the corner of the paddock, climbing the fence. A figure-eight to close out the space gone wrong. And then something, out of the bodily tiredness: a poem, a story. A book. Years later in another sleepless binge, it will take shape. The poems of *The Silo* will come together (Kinsella, 1995c). People tell me sleeplessness is an addiction, but for me sleep is the addiction, an addiction I don't want. Rolling text. Cross-genre. Visions. Speaking in invented languages. Blurring of boundaries.

My partner says *you must sleep*, but she is used to it now. As I shift time zones between Australia and Asia and Europe and America I know those liminal zones where time is intensely of the body. The circadian rhythms so disturbed that jetlag eats at the waking hours, over-invests sleep. That is where I live and write.

Part 3
Linguistic disobedience
I write on the level of the word, but in strings or sequences of words. These sequences are not necessarily linear. The intent is lyrical, or unlyrical, or sub-lyrical. The sequences are informed by a sense of compactness, extrusion, and removal of the 'unnecessary'. The pared-back line is made longer by combining short takes. A narrative thread is interrupted by caesuras, breath breaks in the line. The rhythm staccatos, flows; metrics change within sections of the line, from line to line. Free verse combines with 'traditional' verse forms. New verse forms are created. It is the subjective I start from, but the agency is interrupted. There is intervention. The lyrical impulse, the desire to recognise qualities of self, is corrupted. The word has all possible meanings – reinvented and redeployed by the reader, a table becomes a father strapping 'you' as a child. The metonymy is distantly separated. The route from table to strap is seemingly problematic, but it is there. All words are metonymically connected, but also distant. The chalk and the teacher are as far apart as soil and cosmonaut. The space between characters, between words, is loud and quiet. The fuzz on the blank TV screen – the alien messages read by the savant.

The list is adornment. Lists are claims on property: their nature one of verbal possession. Lists decompose when I try to compile them. Lists are the fuel of history, the data banks that flow down the timeline. Control and ownership. The repetition of nouns, of their quality and quantum control – adjectives – builds certainty. The subject links to object/s. Memory takes away possession in action and recalls it when the circumstances are conducive. When certainty and abstraction are required simultaneously. Poetry as analogue.

Adornment, decoration. The unnecessary surfaces create their own dialogues. Palimpsested layers discourse. The trivial, the vague, the vain, the unnecessary, the mood enhancer (artificial paradise), the snow storm over Sydney Harbour in its plastic bubble, the cornice work on the ceiling, the gaudy blobs of gold paint on the portrait of the saint. Rhyme and metre used decoratively. Of the surface. Compiling a list of special effects, a historicity develops. Illuminated manuscripts, the earring, belly ring, nose ring, genital piercing. The radioactive chemical glowing as it charts the circulatory system. The micro-slices of brain tissue with their walnut insignia, thought-maps. Strung up as art. Comment. Discarded in the out-of-date files wastebasket, utilitarian.

Pulled out of the basket and used to give the room character, decoration? Subjectively, this decoration has meaning. The angel figure on the top of the Christmas tree was sexual for me. I eroticised it. Maybe this was the manufacturer's intention. It was not mine when I got to place it there, but standing back it looked, well, exciting. Invested, is it still decoration – an unnecessary bauble? The flourish of the Spenserian stanza or the transliteral innovations of Wyatt. A blending of the two. The decoration and the artistry. Casuistry? Spenser's dedicatory stanzas (1987, pp. 25–33) have to be expanded. A powerful figure at court excluded, a powerful enemy. The utility, the politics of subjectivity. The story is not about Spenser or his friends, at least on the surface. Alternate surfaces – the angle of viewing matters. Unjustified, the poem wanders.

I dedicate my poems; though only some carry names, all are dedicated. Another mediation of the self. We speak constantly, though we meet rarely. The dedication is a simulation of presence and responsibility. I owe it to your dignity to address you in such a way. A dedication as insult would undercut the poem completely. Irony is flow, but sarcasm is a dead end. The dedication is used sincerely. The list of names grows, the list is a history – we must be wary of trapping the addressees in the list of names. Or is the name an allusion, a point of entry into a discourse nothing to do with identity? I have not met X and yet I dedicate this poem to X. It is part of the text of the poem, not something addressed to an individual. This lyrical-I poem is addressed to a building in Chicago, a locus of postmodernism, and yet I have not visited the building. I feel this about the concept of the building, and yet am indifferent to its reality. The dedication, like meaning, shifts. It is about movement.

As with attributive nouns, each poem works as a modifier on the other. I shape books like this.

Affect. Poetry *affects* the world we live in. Cause and '*affect*'. We live in a world *affected* by poetry. There is expectation here. Many see all poetry as decoration – an entertainment or at best a meditative/reflective device with a time and a place. Poetry is seen as 'not work', and in fact interferes with 'work'. In small communities, identity can become value, poetry can become indicative of uniqueness and character, but fluid enough to exchange, share. Value can undo community here. Create competition. Competition creates hierarchies. This is how states are made, to control difference. The eclogue as song competition plays into the hands of a state indifferent to poetry on all but a civic level. My eclogues are not contests. The voices do not attempt to outdo each other. And of course, like the chess game played against oneself, competition is contrived in any case. But the simulacrum of competition in the authorless text will not always undo itself. The imitation can become a convenient reality. A display model, like the display home. Sold cheaper in the end. Only slightly soiled. Shop-soiled. Commodity-fetishised (Marx, 1867/1977, p. 165), the poem becomes pollution. At that point, the civic is offended and the poem is pushed aside. It is necessary to resist this. Participation might become more desirable when offence is taken by the state?

The poet destroyed all his/her poems on paper – s/he can recite them from memory. S/he destroyed the written record because as objects they became things of 'value'. S/he might eventually forget them and the poems will be lost, other than snippets, which might have caught the imagination of a friend.

Does breaking down the centre create alternative or ulterior centres? Possibly, but the smaller the better. Sublinearity is the language of parts. The place of the word, the regionalism of words, clauses, phrases, space. Parataxis is international regionalism: the dialogue of juxtaposition. In rejecting binary oppositions we opt for the volta, the point of contact and turning in the dialogue of fragments. In this liminal space, truth is no longer purely subjective, nor is truth purely qualifiable data. You see, I am not sure if anything is outside my window, or if that is a tree I imagine I see. Confrontation ebbs and flows across the border. The field of the page loses its containment policy. There are depth, height, width and the oral. We speak with the page in mind but do not inscribe. We have learnt to read the book, the paper, the billboard, the road sign.

Correlative and image? Marjorie Perloff writes:

> Free verse is organized by the power of the image, by a construct of images as concrete and specific as possible, that serve as objective correlative for inner states of the mind. (2001a, p. 9)

The image exists within the word. Sections of the line, the stanza, the poem as a whole, focus images. We might cannon image into image, creating a cinematic effect. To give the image dimension, creating points in space, a shape for it, is to control the poetic impulse. The image is of the lyric; the lyrical hybridiser will explore the liminal zone between images. The poem is the Venn diagram. In the following 'House Eclogue' (Kinsella, 2003, pp. 120–122), each 'voice' is composited from an accumulation of words, phrases, clauses, images, prosodic devices. But neither voice is complete in itself. Each relies on the other to enhance the dialogue, to create the subimagery, the hermeneutics behind the text. A paranoid reading (Hodge and Mishra, 1991) will yield the rings of the echo, the harmonics countering and cancelling each other. It is what we are not reading that is illuminating. The radical pastoral, new pastoral, anti-pastoral, the *counter-pastoral*, is the fringe area between rural and urban, between speech/writing and thought. The house is the containment policy that simply magnifies language, inscription. The guest–host relationship in Greek tradition and mythology is sacred. And yet there are always mutterings behind closed doors, conversations kept from the public or private exchange of the guest and host. The host has an obligation to provide sanctuary and nurturing, the guest to demonstrate appreciation and to respect the sanctity of the host's home. Each has an obligation to respect the beliefs of the other. It is a symbiotic relationship. The unsaid is built in – the relationship can cope with the mutterings. Sickness has its own language; it blurs the boundaries.

>House Eclogue

>Host
>This wooden frame might be your own
>pinned with steel at the joints, riven
>to foundations set in friable earth;
>seat of the gentry in the country
>where masques are performed
>like DNA, perfectly cloned
>in this rural setting, seeded
>just after sunrise, deep
>in the woods. Don't let it
>alarm you, the blood-bird's
>black face, the heart-pickings
>as stale as its migratory flight.
>Welcome, eat and drink
>as you see fit. What is ours
>is yours – the household gods
>are gregarious and hungry,
>and glow with confidence.

>Guest
>Typically kind of you, a reputation
>confirmed in the city. I apologise
>for bringing sickness between these walls,
>violating this taboo. Censor
>skies swing low and yet light
>fills every space, language is crisp
>and alive and values lost outside

thrive. These photos of your family,
the soiled shoes by the doorway,
polished floorboards and mandala rugs,
reproductions of Vermeer and Homer,
speak of quiddity and agency.
The potatoes turn green quickly I hear?

Host
We have a kitchen full of refreshing herbs,
of oils and brews to drive your sickness out:
we'll restore you with supplements.
Our grandfather built this house,
and called it ecumenical. Blessed
by every guest who has set foot in it.
It is like an organism living in symbiosis
with its occupants – guest-hosts
all of us, in this place where
flora and fauna grow against
adversity, illuminate the cavities.

Guest
Sealed in against the cold the sick air
will circulate, warmed to blood-heat,
pumped and piped. Plasterwork
inscribes the wallflesh, basement
and attics role-play extremities.
In that room she prays,
in there they're having sex.
Good or bad karma, a history.
In the century-old baby photograph
old men look grim on three month-old bodies.
There is cable and a decent stereo.

Host
The piano harmonises perfectly
with the stereo. In the basement
they dressed the kill. Bone, skin,
fur – wool carpet. Extractions
and sealants. Chairs for carving.
A kitchen vegetable garden
The lawns neatly cut: gathering,
focussing. The porch seat.
The lost toy in the sandiest place.
Please sign the guest book.

> Guest
> Colours embalm in the darkened room
> as if love is loud and hate desperate;
> critical of mountainous blankets,
> rivers in the sheets. Dead skin
> and the signature of fluids
> are loud on the floor. Light doesn't
> always show dialogues. I narrate
> like a spy indoors, to undo reputations,
> immaculate as a character reference.
> (Kinsella, 2003, pp. 120–122)

'Objective correlative for inner states of mind' (Perloff, 2001a, p. 9; after Eliot, 1922, p. 7). The sequence of occasions or encounters in this piece correlate with suspicion and engagement. The inner states of the mind are often contradictory. In 'When Lilacs Last in the Dooryard Bloom'd', Whitman writes:

> And the singer so shy to the rest receiv'd me,
> The gray-brown bird I know receiv'd us comrades three,
> And he sang the carol of death, and a verse for him I love.
> (1865/1968, p. 154)

In the 'Visitant Eclogue' (Kinsella, 1999b, p. 60), I had tried to challenge an objective correlative 'in common' between reader and writer. The reader is expected to think. In experiencing the poem the emotions might only be partly stirred. But to think is an emotional experience, at least for me. On Pioneer 10, now beyond Pluto and heading out of the solar system, Carl Sagan prepared a metallic disk with music, images, and other information intended to inform extra-terrestrials about human civilisation *and* about the planet they occupy. Have conquered. There is a stylus and instructions on how to use it. The means of decoding the information is provided. The aliens will be given points of reference, the input information to create a state of mind receptive to the defamiliarised information. The birds sing death and are used as a symbol of metempsychosis. Death and travel, death and spiritual movement are synonymous. Liberation. The objective correlatives are movements from liminal zone to liminal zone, rather than from object to object. From the de-signified within the image, to the de-signified within the image. The poem is a panopticon. A prison and a liberated way of seeing and saying.

I write love poems and elegies. Someone said this to me about his or her own work. Most of my recent love poems are about the threat to DNA. That love could change in application, in orientation. Genetic modification tends not to appear in my elegies.

Graphology (Kinsella, 1997b and ongoing) is a project – on handwriting, on drafting in pen, on the typewriter and word-processor. On reading and transcribing; the history of the illuminated manuscript, printing press, the notebook. Signatures, marks, imprint, traces of where I have been. To defamiliarise this is to invalidate the signature in my passport, on my bank card. And this is what I have been attempting to do – it is an ongoing project, developing out of the original published volume (1997b). The stains of my hand are a complex of variables. Pressure on the page, mood, angle. Mapping the self, we subscribe to the rules of presentation, publication, performance.

Part 4
Poetics: beginnings are where closure is …: notes from which speeches and essays will be drawn …

Pre-
Beginnings are where closure is, or do beginnings reject closure no matter how neatly turned the end of the poem is? The fragment relies on the whole, but so does the unified poem: all part of an ongoing external dialogue. So the fragment can be as complete as the unified poem, or not. The opening lines of a poem are connections with a previous or external experientiality. They trigger the patterns and processes of interpretation. The reader's expectation of the poem is a-priori – the title, dedication, first lines. Poems work in threads, strings, and sequences of referentiality. They suit canons. We should reject ends for beginnings.

Preface
These remarks are prefatory. Not in a way, I would hope, that dictates the possible ensuing text, or, indeed, to indicate that any text might in fact follow. From the Hegelian refutation of the preface for a philosophical work, to the observation of Derrida that 'Prefaces, along with forewords, introductions, preludes, preliminaries, preambles, prologues, and prolegomena, have always been written, it seems, in view of their own self-effacement' through to his question via routes, marks, and erasure: 'But does a preface exist?' (Derrida, trans. 1981, p. 9), we might be rightfully suspicious of the integrity of the prefatory comment, its allusion to a whole, its 'residue' that will inform and tyrannise our reading of the 'main' data, inscription. Surface suggests there is a confusion of positions here, but the words signal a number of alternative routes through a beginning that allows for a

specific orientation, though offers none. All my writing is prefatory, and what I write is prefaces. For the writer or reader looking for a confirmation or rejection of closure at the end of the text, or towards the end of the observable textual route, the compass will have already been confused. This, of course, can be rewarding in itself, and whether in the poem or the narrative, it is the impetus to drive us to complete the text, to bother informing it with a linearity, to maintain expectation, status quo, and historicity. But this is to close off other routes, dead ends and openings that are equally or more dangerous, enticing, and enriching as that offered by the tying up of an end, or by the precipice of the unfinished, the incomplete. The first line, the first word, is where closure is embraced or rejected. And in the way that fragments and components of the sequence are part of the whole, *and* unique in themselves, in the way that dialogues outside the text create narratives outside the integrity of the markings, so too do beginnings connect with previous openings and ends. This might be cyclical, but rarely is. *Finnegans Wake* opens: 'riverrun, past Eve and Adam's, from swerve of shore to bend of bay' (Joyce, 1939/1975, p. 3), and – though creating a spatiality from the first word – avoids the logic of English syntax and sentence structure, challenges the prefatory notions of order and logic. As a preface, this line defines an argument, though it erases it in the same breath. We follow its residue into the greater body of the text. The skin peels off but grows back; the body keeps functioning. It is surface, it is beginning; we search out more information. Connecting this beginning with the epistemology and etymology of 'river', of 'run', we might pre-connect, or work epilogically. If we compare this opening line with the first line/s of Yeats's 'The Song of Wandering Aengus', the possibilities become obvious. The movement between genres is desirable and not inclusive. And *Finnegans Wake* is a sub-narrative poem as much as a 'novel'. 'I went out to the hazel wood,/Because a fire was in my head ...' (Yeats, 1899/1962, p. 27). Syntax as expected, the digression of allusion and metaphor open up in the second line: metaphor allows alternative resolutions and precipice – it is a passive rejection of closure. Metonym, on the other hand, is an accounting of connection – a defining of a critically expected closure through the word itself – which might or might not exist within the narrative. But to closure in the first line, the opening word/s: the unified self defines spatiality and the certainty of progress. There is a prospect of resolution already. We will digress through metaphor, and alternative paths will be offered by way of allusion, but satisfaction will come. We expect it. We will make it if it is not there or grow frustrated with 'incompletion'. The mark will be alienated if resolution does not come, and its residue will haunt us, will manifest as negation.

A small email conversation with Louis Armand from 2001, without his prompting remarks:

> jk: of course, i am unplanning the town, though the community has functionality and spatiality.
> jk: yes, but i am more interested in erasing the marks and working with residues – per derrida. the next part of the poetics is on prefaces. all manifestoes as this ... as derrida says, 'not just a moment in the hegelian preface ...'. if the form is undone in the overview, then what's to come ...? the argument of course, the illustrations and substantiations. i only write prefaces. i only live in towns thought about. it's all non-municipal.

Hermetics ... the private markings erased and erased ... what (I) write 'unders' text – is there, regardless, though forgotten without reference, those anecdotes told out of hearing.

What is the correlation between the body, landscape, and the poem? All are simulacra. In mapping the body by exposing it to geographies, to environments physical and imagined, we record human interaction with space. The twig that scratches the skin, the prickle that punctures the sole of the foot, the sand that bothers the eye. The poem is the body; it is a zone of marking. The language of landscape is the landscape of prosody, of expressing the inexpressible. If prospect is the text as we receive it, with all possible social and cultural readings opened through it, refuge is the hermetics, the language of the private self that reserves the right for isolation, separation, indulgence. It is imprisoned by its safety. The poem is a mixture of the vulnerable and the open, the private and the public. Language is prospect and refuge, and where these two planes meet, the liminal space of inwardness and exposure, potential resides. Our body is a map of where we have been, as is the poem. The knowledge, the experientiality they encapsulate, work as models for further progress through landscape. This is, in part, the questing motif, so exploded by the materialists, by capitalism. The journey of gain is measured in physical comfort. It is the renewable five-year consumer plan. It is said people tend to read poetry to experience a spiritual comfort, to pleasure themselves through rejecting aloneness. It is said the private space is opened to dialogue, and the reception, the personal reading, is reinvented through each exposure.

As the sequence progresses through landscape, a slight variation on set form challenges its terms of reference, like the animal in death becoming the absent referent when people sit down to their meal of meat: dead flesh, corpse-matter, necrotic ingestion (Adams, 2001). Conceptualisations as much as exploration, the rendering of 'nature' to landscape, negate the possibility of the non-human. We cannot imagine an existence separate from ourselves. All is anthropomorphic. Language must be set aside to break free of this. Language is not mere communication, it is decoration: embellishment, it is the trappings of occupation and ownership. Singularly or collectively, the word owns.

Seventh essay on linguistic disobedience: rejection of landscape through body-map

> This, then, is what I want to address. First, how are the angels present in nature, and second, what does the act of imitating the action of angels entail? – Sardello

> Punctured sole-skin, game of twister
> farmers said would end up with blacks
> winning out, poor white kid a tangled mess,
> landless, language all hit-n-miss, as if...
> decorative, script succoured soft cliffs,
> eroded, wind swept down and out,
> red cross passports and nationless
> creativity ex nihilo, void like self
> on thresholds of disconcerting tortured animals
> joke equinox, utterance, like lists,
> like forsythia and four snows ensuing,
> like Ensign Dale transporting Yagan's head to Britain;
> see this edge, as we hate and conceal
> and scarify, tch tch, as counter-compromised,
> hawks not there for you, this walk, these steps
> highlighting sycamores and conifers, let's delete
> the contrast: Amish buggy, black as global networking vans,
> as vistas are unlayered, we collect plastic containers,
> effete, winged, farmtools at public auctions,
> see THIS threshold, this clysmic recondition,
> blackening rendition as another matter
> drives and eats us out – you see we,
> stringing angels in genetic trees,
> as Arabic in fifteenth-century Africa
> transliterates speech,

> written as, undoing body text
> and words in the canopy, ringing
> changes, connecting families,
> valuing no two cultures, no truth or beauty
> binaries, etymologies regardless,
> synched as packaged, for that's Kulture!
> Give us multi, from standing room only
> to rarefied spaces, servitude and swan heads
> under white cloths: there's your proof,
> you are what you question mark,
> like a signature, gentleman scholar.
> In four days green consumed and scaped,
> seed-proof, evidence; unbodied,
> scatter erotics and wrath,
> prime matter close to the heart:
> cardinals and parrots
> totem-shifting datelines
> speech remnants,
> revelation's backburners,
> a murder of crows.
>
> (Kinsella, 2003, pp. 141–142)

Olivetti Lettera 32

I am typing this on my old portable Olivetti Lettera 32 typewriter. I am in the Western Australian wheatbelt town of York, or more precisely, just outside York at the base of Mount Bakewell. It is early morning and a thick grey mist is rolling over the variegated faces of the mountain. At just one thousand feet above sea level, I guess it just qualifies to be called a mountain, but as it is the highest peak for many, many miles, and a focus of the Avon Valley, it probably warrants the name anyway. I guess; probably ... there is a lot of uncertainty in discussing this place. It is a place of temporal belonging, of incursion. The indigenous Nyungar people call it Walwalinj, the hill that cries, and on a morning like this, pathetic fallacy from a western point of view makes such a description resonant and troubling.

But you cannot think like that uncritically in such a place as York, the first inland settlement in Western Australia. This is a place where great cruelty was inflicted on the Nyungars by early European invaders or 'settlers', by explorers and by the police. There are stories of Nyungars' ears being strung up in kitchens to frighten off Nyungar people; of summary executions. If you talk to local Nyungars about the families of settlers who came in around the time the town and district were founded, they can still name those who were known to be cruel and those who 'helped and respected' the Aboriginal people. As I have noted, Walwalinj is the hill that is crying for its people, calling them back.

The dreamtime legend concerning the mountain revolves around what an outsider might appropriatively compare to a Romeo and Juliet story, or something from Greek mythology. The mountain holds the 'Kunya' of a young man transformed as punishment for going against his family's and people's wishes regarding whom he should marry. The girl he eloped with was not acceptable, and the eventual consequence of their action was that his 'Kunya' was confined to Walwalinj and hers to what the Europeans came to call Mount Brown (Wongborel). (See, for example, the story as retold by Emily Winmar, 1999.)

Mount Bakewell and Mount Brown cradle the town of York. Mount Brown is much smaller, but nonetheless imposing in terms of the low undulations of the surrounding district, the result of age and weathering, of exfoliation of the granite caprock. The legend goes that the young warrior and his chosen partner cannot meet again until the mountains come together (Winmar, 1999). It is a particularly potent story in a more general sense when one considers that this is faultline and earthquake territory, that the epicentre of the major Meckering earthquake of 1967 was not far from here. Furthermore, Mount Bakewell, named after an English farmer who experimented with the selective breeding of cattle – ironically appropriate given that York has become a prime area for GM crop trials – is actually the remnants of an extinct volcano.

So: I am sitting in a shed, in a drought-stricken south-western Australian winter, after a bitterly cold night, typing methodically away at my old portable. Why? I have been using a wordprocessor since the mid-1980s, an electric typewriter since the early 1980s, and before that, electric Adlers and IBM golfballs of the old variety. I have written a poem about the Australian poet John Tranter's first electric typewriter, a Smith-Corona Elect from the 1950s. I have been computer-literate since the late 1970s, when the first punch-card computers were introduced into Western Australian schools. In fact, I used the very first school computer, a Wang PDP 9, and helped set it up one Sunday afternoon. I have composed poems in notebooks and transferred them direct to a computer.

In my wanderings I did, however, find much use for a portable manual typewriter, and much of the content of my first few books was composed this way when I lacked a permanent home. I travelled around the world; I lived on communes, in shacks on the edges of forests, and in shared houses. Quite often there was no electricity. And I enjoyed the physicality of the manual typewriter, its just being enough technology. To type a piece in this way is to have a tactile relationship with what is being written – you 'get in there' with the words themselves. It creates a rhythm, and one I find more natural for poetry – physical, but also meditative. I work so rapidly on a computer that thought and composition entangle and race on together. You find yourself typing almost faster than you are thinking. Not so with the manual typewriter: it has its own metrics, and you bend to its will. And this is why, after many years, I have returned to the typewriter, certainly for poetry, but also for many prose projects.

It was not a conscious choice – I happened on my old typewriter while searching through boxes of books in the shed. The shed is not an easy place to negotiate – it is jam-packed with my brother's shearing things, his grinder for cleaning up combs and cutters, with old bicycle frames, tools, chairs, books, filing cabinets, papers, half-filled wool bales from the eleven black sheep just across from the shed window, gardening equipment, machinery, and so on. Regardless, I cleared a space on a bench, set up the typewriter, found some paper, sat down, and tentatively pushed the keys. The touch was bizarre – I had to work to make the words appear on the page, and watching the carriage travel as the words appeared added to the vicarious interaction with the words themselves. This seemed far more virtual than cyberspace. The poem as it began appearing was a performance. The '28' parrots in the jam trees outside infiltrated the poem, the brother's grinder, the plumes of sparks that fill the night when he gets home from work, burning into the page. And the page itself, burnt with text, the keys and ribbon pyrographic. I thought of John's Ashbery's poem, 'Pyrography' (1985, pp. 212–214). I felt liberated.

Since moving into the workspace of the shed and developing a renewed relationship with the typewriter, I have begun re-immersing myself in metrics and form. Stanzas rather than the word itself, or the word alone, have become the measure of the poem. I am not entirely sure why this is the case, but it is something to do with timing. And it has started to affect the way I draft poems in pen, in my notebooks. I hear the typewriter as I compose. That is another thing: the noise. I place cotton wool in my ears to muffle the sharp, attacking sound. It is meditative, on the level of allowing or giving a sense of more time, of not being able to push the body so hard, though my mother at between 90 to 100 words per minute on a manual puts this theory to the test. Especially since she cannot do that on a wordprocessor, whereas I can – probably a generational thing and a matter of familiarity as well – but it is also aggressive. My ears were damaged when I was a teenager, and extremely acute sounds bother me. This was one of the reasons I initially embraced the computer and wordprocessor with such enthusiasm. But: no pain no gain, as they say, and I am back at it, working the paddock with the machine, ploughing and seeding and harrowing, exploring the implications of what I am doing: the gender and class readings, the sociological and psychological implications.

I mentioned that there is a drought here. Things are grim. Crops that sprouted after early rains are being ploughed back in and reseeded in the hopes that rains will still come in time. The harrows are once again breaking up the soil and covering the drills with their seed grain. The ground so much drier than it should or could be. I composed a poem two days ago, 'The Second Harrowing', on this, here in the shed, with the rain struggling to dampen the ground. It is a poem that could not have been written on the computer within the comfort of the warm house. It would have been an insult to those struggling with the drought.

>
> The Second Harrowing
>
> Sprouted seeds dried and depleted as charcoal
> or serifs, sans in the clot-brown soil, pulse
> lost on watershed, rain too late in coming,
> initial harrowing breaking up and covering
> over as if to damn – arrested or false
> germination, no growth of vision or call
>
> to heaven, just half-formed souls
> lopped off, shrivelled in pockets and wombs
> and envelopes, until new rains kick life
> into the tractor again, and fresh seed makes strife
> for the doomsayers and antichrists, tombs
> opened up and transformed into nurseries, holes
>
> brimming with life. Then the second harrowing,
> the breaking up and covering over, deft
> contradiction, in a breath the prophets
> and patriarchs sticking out their necks, sets
> of divinations raining over the property, cleft
> chins and forked beards of grain growth, straining

> toward clouds and sun, angry and afraid
> of being caught short, should the dry
> return with a vengeance, dragging divinations
> back into earth, *female* and *enveloping*, permutations
> of their self-made hells, their fruits, mystery,
> drive toward harvest, to be betrayed.
>
> (Kinsella, unpublished)

My partner told me a few years back that she had to show some young people how to load and use a manual typewriter, at work one day. They had never used one: no one there was 'old' enough to remember these machines. They were shocked by how much 'work' it entailed. It is work, and that is what gives poetry substance. For my mother, her first typewriter back in the early 1960s was liberation – it gave her freedom to earn money through writing. Her marriage was not conducive to independent means, and with the typewriter and her secretarial skills she circumvented the patriarchal structure of her home environment. It frustrated my father, but she continued. It is why I am a writer today. It is like a body that has been places, seen and experienced and translated those things into words. It has been a process of rediscovering who I am, and what poetry can mean.

I am told that you can hear the typewriter down in the gulley, across the fence, and a short way on the climb up to Mount Bakewell. Then it is lost to the crows and galahs, to the '28' parrots and occasional tractor. Wandoo and marri trees – flowering redgums – increase as the climb gets steeper, rockier. The pasture diminishes and then stops. There are rare alpine plants up there, and rare animals cloistered in the tiny reserves that mark the summit. There is also the communications equipment – aerials and masts – the clash between nature and technology that makes the manual typewriter seem all the less intrusive despite its noise. Walwalinj, the hill of tears, is the source of all weather around here.

Distortions – on questioning the primacy of the accented syllable: notes on alternative spatialities for poetic rhythm

Rhythm is not unique to poetry – and a piece of writing with rhythm is not necessarily poetry or even poetic – but the consistent and regulated control and deployment of rhythm is accepted as one of the foundation blocks of the 'poem'. From the outset, I would like to contest this belief, while accepting that within the standardised and state-culture-centred version of language – that which identifies a particular nation and/or its colonial offshoots – one can systematically identify metrical patterns in the line, in other words can scan with mathematical precision. Syllables can, of course, operate with a shifting or ambiguous stress within the line, but metrics caters for structural variation. However, as we move outside the various canons that inform contemporary poetries, outside the familiar versions of written language, the specifics of literary prosody become more fragmented. The suprasegmental aspects subvert the strictly metrical. David Crystal writes:

> Pitch, loudness, and tempo together enter into a language's expression of *rhythm*. Languages vary greatly in the way in which rhythmical contrasts are made. English makes use of stressed syllables produced at roughly regular intervals of time (in fluent speech) and separated by unstressed syllables – a 'stress-timed' (or isochronous) rhythm. (1995, p. 169)

In Platt, Weber and Ho (1984), *The New Englishes*, we find:

> In some languages, the difference between stressed and unstressed syllables is not very great. In others, such as some varieties of English as spoken in England, it is considerable. Many unstressed vowels occur as the short centralized *e* ... or disappear altogether. A word like *company*, which in some varieties of English, such as American and Australian, has three syllables, may appear to have only two in Southeastern British English: *comp'ny*. (p. 135)

Anyone familiar with an Australian strine, or the infinite variety of Englishes that work in Australian society, will know that locating the accented syllable is not always a predictable process. And this, of course, is what makes it an exciting English to work with from a poet's point of view. Which is not to say that exactly the same flexibility does not apply within England itself, because it does and always has. However, the consciousness through canonical literature of what the benchmark is, is all-pervasive. The following quotes are pertinent here:

A.G. Mitchell, in 'The Australian Accent', says:

> In trying to see the pattern of Australian speech and its likeness to and difference from other kinds of English speech, we must not start with a non-existent datum called 'the English language' and then see any particular sort of English speech as a declension from or a distortion of this. We must start at the opposite end of particularity and see what larger groupings or layers may appear ... (1970, p. 4)

As a subtext to this, Braj B. Kachru mentions that Turner (1966) first called Australian/New Zealand English 'English transported', and that Ransom (1970) used it as a title. Kachru actually calls it a 'transplanted' English:

> One might then say that a transplanted language is cut off from its traditional roots and begins to function in new surroundings, in new roles and new contexts. This newness initiates changes in language ... We might say that there is a bond which connects all the transplanted varieties of English ... There are many reasons for it, one being that the processes which the speakers of these languages had to go through to establish their language identities have been more or less the same. The process of establishing an identity for a language can be as painful and as arduous as the struggle for political emancipation ... The kinship among the transplanted varieties is historical, cultural, and linguistic. (1986, pp. 130–132)

In a bizarre little self-help book, *Speech Training*, C.V. Burgess (1967) argues that a standard, recognised form of the language is necessary for communication outside one's immediate locale or cultural subgroup. In a chapter entitled 'Dialect and Accepted Speech' he divides English into three categories: 'dialects, distortions, and accepted English'. He also goes on to define 'accent' as another branch of the speech family. While recognising the significance of dialect – 'Dialect lends vigour and colour to the language of a country. Without it we should be the poorer' – he warns us off regarding 'distortion':

> Well-spoken dialect is as free from distortions as the best accepted English, and it is pleasant to hear, even though, due to idiomatic peculiarities, it may not be fully comprehensible to the outsider. (p. 15)

The plot thickens ...

As an Australian with an English, Scots and Irish heritage, I grow increasingly incredulous as I self-help my way through Burgess to a version of English that all prospective audiences and converses might comprehend. Where I 'come a cropper', to use an expression that has the rhythms of a rural place I come from whose language is more distortion than dialect, is when I read:

> Speech distortions often occur in big cities in industrial areas. It would seem that the environment of industry, including, no doubt, the smoke laden atmosphere, is the breeding ground for mis-shapen vowels, and sometimes omitted consonants too.
> The flat, almost toneless Liverpool accent – not a dialect – is the result

of a failure to open the teeth sufficiently. The Dublin twang comes from an abnormally high incidence of nose and throat ailments in the poorer quarters of that city.

Certainly it is difficult to recollect a single distinct accent that is pleasant to hear. The hard fact is that distortions are, by their nature, unpleasant. Consequently they are not acceptable. (p. 15)

A Marxist critique of the above is not required to see its prejudices and failings. In terms of English, Australia is a nation of accents and distortions. If poetry is to work against the state rather than be its lackey, it should concern itself with distortion and not accepted language. Herein lies the answer to a question I am often asked: why are certain poets who are not thought of as being particularly linguistically unique within Australia, seen as being innovative and inventive outside Australia, especially in Britain? The answer is self-evident: poems that are perceived as accentual within the culture, are 'mis-read' as distortions without. They comment more on the language/s of the place they are being read in, than they do about the place they originated from.

During my years teaching Australian poetry in Cambridge, I have watched bemused as brilliant students have tried to scan, for example, a Les Murray poem in standard English metrics – which the poems often do – only to lose the suprasegmental reading, the subtleties of tone and intonation. This, in itself, is an obvious enough mistake for the student coming to a new poetry for the first time, but what is interesting about it is that such assumptions are not so readily made in the context of English-language poetry from Africa, the Caribbean, or even from indigenous Australian poets such as Lionel Fogarty and Lisa Bellear. There is an expectation of difference, though most students recognise the subversions of the 'other' in such perceptions and readily critique their own ways of seeing.

As one might expect, this tendency varies greatly according to the students' background and education, with students from countries experienced in British Imperialism tending to be more circumspect when engaging with a non-English English-language text. I am referring not only to, for instance, African, Indian, Caribbean and American students, but also to – often the most vociferous – Scots, Welsh and Irish students. However, there is still a strong expectation among all students that they will be dealing with an homogenous English-language poetry, often failing to recognise significant tensions within the Anglo-Celtic 'heritage', apart from the diverse cultural backgrounds that make up Australian society.

Non-indigenous English-language poetry from Canada and New Zealand, and much English-language poetry from India, is read in a similar way to Australian poetry. It seems the students are assuming that an awareness and a reverential appreciation of the standard-English canon is required, and that all readings should be confirmed by its criteria. Many students have some sense of the insensitivity and inadequacy of their reading, but with a lack of other models, they ask where else they should start. Providing cultural, social, political and historical background is an obvious need, but something more fundamental needs to be conveyed to the student when teaching any poetry. To return to Crystal: 'In French, the syllables are produced in a steady flow, resulting in a 'machine-gun' effect – a 'syllable-timed' rhythm' (1995, p. 169).

In French, true, but also in English and I am sure numerous other languages, at least when it comes to dialect and poetry, often giving an impression of distortion. Syllabic verse is used to both confirm and deny the status quo of English-language poetry. It goes against the grain of 'accepted speech', but confirms with the exactitude of metrics. Allowing for slippage from sound to semantics, a desired liminality in my view, its metrics are of the count, of the metronome, with rhythms coming via intonation and tone variation within the potential meanings of each syllable, each word, each line. I find myself astonished when I read suppositions such as the one by Donald Davie, referred to in the following extract from Fraser (1970). This is a reading I have often heard applied to Australian speech, seen as one long vowel-less continuum from the west to the eastern seaboard, by some outsiders (and a few insiders!):

> The poet Donald Davie, who has recently emigrated to California, has noted in an article in *The Listener* the lack of tone or tonality in American speech. We convey, or used to convey, in English English, much about our attitudes, our social position, our feelings towards those we are talking to by what we loosely call 'tone of voice'. We send signals out by the noises we make. The pattern of American speech, with its tendency to iron out regional and class differences, makes for what one could call a freedom and equality between syllabic units; and it is perhaps no accident that the pioneers of pure syllabic metrics in this century, like Marianne Moore, have been Americans. (p. 52)

In a televised discussion (*Words*, 1999), the poet Peter Porter defended syntax and the autonomy of the line as the basis of poetry, while I claimed the poem was defined by the word alone. I would go further than this – it is the syllable, the letter, the space, the pause a space implies, that defines the poem. This is reading outside either syllabic or accentual impositions. This is allowing for tensions within the syllable itself, between the letters (duration and pitch), alternative pronunciation, even mis-spellings. Distortion happens most effectively on the micro level.

Crystal finishes his paragraph thus:

> Loudness is the basis of rhythmical effects in English (as shown by the way it is possible to tap out a sentence in a 'te-*tum*, te-*tum*' way). By contrast, the length of a syllable (whether long or short) was the crucial feature of rhythm in Latin; and pitch height (high vs low) is a central feature of rhythm of many oriental languages. (1995, p. 169)

This is exciting, but the problem is that Crystal is differentiating between rhythmic characteristic of specific languages. Poetry, I plead, should allow for all possibilities within the language – or languages – of its expression. In recent times I have written poems using words and rhythmic devices from four or five languages, just to undo this metric/rhythmic binary. I am not making an appeal for an Esperanto of rhythm, but for a polymorphous ear. This is not a 'machine' of cultural appropriation, or an aural knee-jerk reaction to globalism, but a desire for the recognition of the organic nature of language, and that poetry's dialectical function is to challenge 'accepted' language.

In Paul Mariani's biography of Hart Crane, *The Broken Tower* (1998), the writer tracks Crane's tensions between a desire to respect and learn from old esteemed models – 'the masters' – and a desire to express the contradictions of the new. Crane's respect for Eliot was slightly dimmed with the release of *The Waste Land* – a poem he found too cold. Crane's 'The Bridge' was to be a poem of similar scope but one of affirmation. It is not difficult to detect 'anxieties of influence' (Bloom, 1973) here. (And Crane's *Collected Poems* was the first book of poetry owned by Harold Bloom, a gift from his sister for his twelfth birthday.) Crane's great achievement was to foreground each individual word so that it seemed almost to have a rhythm of its own. A Crane line may well be a specific unit of, for example, pentameter, but is so heavily substituted that the attention is drawn to the word rather than the line, and produces a unique intensity throughout the poem. He seamlessly distorts language through creating different possible registers of sound within the word. Words often have alternate readings, but Crane offers different sound units – there is no consistent way to read a Crane poem because of this. He undoes his influences remorselessly.

One may ask how this distortion theory might apply equally to different poets like John Tranter and Les Murray. Tranter is the guardian of metrics; in fact, he defines a poem in such terms. He wrote to me:

> Jesus, John – I could go on for twenty pages!!!! I won't bore you with my researches into the Choriambic foot, the Asclepiad (named after Asclepiades of Samos c.290 BC), the Lesser Asclepiad, the Greater Asclepiad, the dreaded Amphibrach (see Martin Johnston's 'European notes') and the fact that in English the word 'amphibrach' is the opposite of an amphibrach; T.S. Eliot and his use of 'Rhopalics', and so forth. Let this do:
>
> Writing in the Manner of Sappho
>
> Writing Sapphics well is a tricky business.
> Lines begin and end with a pair of trochees;
> in between them dozes a dactyl, rhythm
>   rising and falling,
>
> like a drunk asleep at a party. Ancient
> Greek – the language seemed to be made for Sapphics,
> not a worry; anyone used to English
>   finds it a bastard.
>
> Then there's the twenty-two stanzas of strict sapphics in 'Ariadne on Lesbos', in *At The Florida*, and the thirty haibun at the end of that book (most reproduced in *Gasoline Kisses*, Equipage), and – so it goes. (Warning – is the haibun a metrical form? Not really.) (Tranter, personal communication to John Kinsella, 2000)

This seems like a solid argument for metrical consistency, for respecting the rhythms of 'accepted English'. It is not. In that suprasegmental sense, Tranter plays with metrics and destabilises a canonical reading by doing so. These are meta-metrics. They define the poem, but meaning is constantly playing against form. A poet who sees metrics as the basis of poetry and holds the post-modern views of text of John Tranter must, in the main, be ironic. A quasi-satirist, he operates from within the system.

Tranter's allegiances to an American English, over an English English, have meant stress choices that do not match the model. When he takes the end words of an Auden poem and rewrites the rest, he operates on the double-jeopardy level in terms of meaning, but also of form. Auden changed citizenship. Which Tranter is not about to do – but he is making a point about how we read Australian Englishes.

His rhythms are of Col Joye, jazz and American films, as much as the conversations of various Sydney milieus. We recognise this as urbane and witty and worldly. We see the drinks by the pool as the southerly buster comes in (in 'Backyard', 1998, p. 9) as a brash confidence to subvert the foibles of an environment he glides critically yet smoothly through.

A Tranter poem is always tonally controlled. But one should not be too hasty about aligning Tranter's technique with the evolution of American poetry in the twentieth century. In many ways, Tranter's allegiance to technique comes out of an exploration of traditional European and Japanese verse forms (though he started work on the haibun via Ashbery). He even discovered a French verse form called a trenter. One might more readily look at the verse innovations of Arthur Rimbaud than at the rhythmical variations of much modern American poetry. Paul Fussell is problematic here:

> Many contemporary American poets have been tempted to renounce rhythm on the grounds that, associated as it is with the traditional usages of England and the Continent, it is somehow un-American. And it is probably true that the special tonalities of American idiom do require some adjustments in traditional prosodic usages. Robert Frost is one who has perceived that American idiom calls for special metrical treatment, but in working out that treatment he has adapted the proven expressive resources of English prosody. The poet E. L. Mayo has appraised Frost's achievement in embodying metrically the unique tone of the American language ... (1965, p. 101)

Fussell goes on to quote Mayo:

> I conceive it the duty of the poet who desires authenticity of sound and movement to cultivate his ear, avail himself of these riches that lie so close to hand whenever they serve his purpose. In this way his metrical effects become more than merely personal; they become *native*. He thus clothes his naked uniqueness (no fear – it will be civilized and intensified, not smothered by the clothing) in the real spoken language of the time. (1965, p. 101)

In some ways, it is easier in Britain to teach Tranter's poetry than Murray's – students can accommodate the American factor. What they do not entirely apprehend is the apparently separatist and isolationist and culturally defensive Murray. European references and connections abound, but they are somehow 'alienating' and 'foreign'. This contradicts the expectation of metrical certainty. The irony is that in his Bunyah of the mind, his complex pastoral construct peopled with shepherds, farmhands and unpretentious bards and people with 'opinions', Murray *is* speaking a language seemingly close to certain strands in the English poetic canon/s. But this is deceptive. Murray's poetry subverts metrical structures. The 'errors' in his verse come out of what he retrospectively called 'vernacular', but are as much about discomfort in working with 'accepted English' as about claiming a cultural independence.

These quirks are less to do with nationalism than with the isolation of the poet. They are distortions. The poem 'The Cardiff Commonwealth Arts Festival Poetry Conference 1965, Recalled' (Murray, 1998, p. 135), excerpted below, is an interesting case in point.

> ... Uptown, the Bomb Culture's just opened
> its European run,
> discounting many other things on its counter:
> calm tradition is one;
>
> ... the Pleasure Principle's looking quite haggard,
> belching whiskey, sweating scent,
> the belly dancers rhythmically twitching,
> pallid boughs in a current.

It scans, has a neat abcb rhyming scheme. It is a deftly packaged poem about utility, language, poetry, place, and cultural disjunction, displacement, and intrusion. There is the apparent standard English scan (which we should challenge), and the tonal variation: a subterfuge between what the poem seems to tell us and what it is doing. The rhythms are gentle and acceptable – despite the trauma of 'Bomb Culture' and irony of poetry's 'second place' in the grand scheme of things ('mortified to death/to find themselves kindly dismissed/for talk of Wordsworth'). The rhythms should 'pleasure' us: that is, lull us into going with the flow so we can be 'informed' by the poem, lull us into being informed *about* its tensions.

The 'I' isn't there, but this is classical lyrical 'I' poetry. The authority of the voice seems unchallengeable, the poem is (re)claiming primacy. But there *is* discomfort within the rhythms: 'belching whiskey, sweating scent'. There are rhythms of 'meaning', of empirical data, of 'fact', paralleling the rhythms of text – the meta-poem, the positioning of the poem within the collective identity of the English-language 'poem'. Lyrical confidence is never what it seems. It masks a vulnerability, implicit, in the case of this poem, in the meaning itself. As an aside, a gender reading of this poem would disrupt our neat scan even more abruptly. Which entails a subtext: that standard metrics come out of a verbal hierarchy.

And I have just read this as an Australian – I have compensated for laxities in the standard metrical reading because I know where the voice is coming from. Irony mounts on irony.

A poem that I have heard Murray perform, and have used extensively with students in terms of illustrating possible universals in rhythmic structures – those variables, points of reference – that we should question, is 'Bats' Ultrasound' (1998, p. 368) which begins:

> Sleeping-bagged in a duplex wing
> with fleas, in rock-cleft or building
> radar bats are darkness in miniature ...

and concludes:

> ... ah, eyrie-ire, aero hour, eh?
> O'er our ur-area (our era aye
> ere your raw row) we air our array,
> err, yaw, row wry – aura our orrery,
> our eerie ü our ray, our arrow.
>
> A rare ear, our aery Yahweh.

The centrality and authority of the poetic voice are not questioned, but the versatility and flexibility of language and meaning are. Murray comes close to devolving to the level of the individual letter, certainly the syllable. The word itself, be it one syllable, has its own time, even its own prosody; rhythms within rhythms.

We might imagine this is the sound of a bat hearing. Of that tension between speech and writing with respect to a closeness to the 'poetic'. Authority almost fragments, but not quite – the overall metrical control of the poem provides balance and closure. The last stanza and single line are mirrors of the metrical certainty of the first two stanzas – the bat-talk would not exist without the first 'human-speech' stanzas. We might find ourselves imagining that sound and rhythm are universal. In English a rooster says 'cockadoodledoo' but in, for example, French it says 'coquerico' or 'cocorico'. Rhythmically similar, but not the same. Close enough that the sound might be enjoyed by listeners without the language. They would perceive the idea. On the page, however, it would not work for them. Patterns might be recognised but a syntactically logical pattern of meaning (synthesis) would not be recognisable. New sounds might come, or in the case of a language with a different script, only associative meaning and feeling might be construed. But rhythm exists in the visual as well as the verbal, so this is not a denial of the availability of a poetry. Poetry itself as metonym. Roman, Cyrillic, Arabic script, Chinese characters – visual rhythms which are available to us only on a variety of levels. Analogically, this is what the poem potentially does: distorts the 'real', it offers alternative 'truths'.

It is part of Australian poetry folklore that the editor of a prominent British poetry list, went to Australia to investigate the poetry scene, was given a copy of Kenneth Slessor's 'Five Bells', ran his eye through it and said there was a flaw in the rhythm in line x. I have had similar points made to me by Cambridge students. When I point out that such distortions are essential – both to 'capture' the orality of the place (even if it is a construct) and to work against the colonising influence of the Mother Tongue – they become sceptical.

Now, this is not a defence for supposed lack of skill within a chosen standard English metrical register, but a warning that it is vital to consider a poem at the level of the syllable, the letter, rather than the line. That we need to 'scan' the word itself; that letter counts matter as much as syllabic counts. That distortion is a unit of qualification. As the L=A=N=G=U=A=G=E poets have long claimed, meaning resides at the level of the word. (For a range of views on language vis-à-vis the word, and related issues, see Andrews, 1984.) And if context is everything, we are obliged to consider the terms of production; and if it is not – if context is fetishisation – the meaning is generated in terms of both the word itself and the rhythm itself. I am using 'rhythm' as a liberated form of metrics ...

I am making a claim here that rhythm is not a separate entity from 'pitch, loudness, tempo' and the tones of the vocal, of 'paralanguage' – to paraphrase Crystal. That prosody is not easily divisible, though we can recognise unique workings within its components. Some years ago I tried to develop a tonal/metrical/rhythmical system for verse. Through marking stressed and unstressed syllables with a number of between one and four above the text, a comment would be made by the poet about the reading s/he had in mind during composition. The tension between the tone implied by the annotation and the 'accepted' rhythm would form the basis of exploring the meaning of the text on a variety of levels. A dialogue within the line would be admitted. The polymorphous ear would be activated.

For example, in the following line fragment from 'Syzygytics' (Kinsella, 1995b, p. 87)

      4   1
laissez faire a perennial

a 4 marks 'faire', meaning a heavy/loud stress – drawn out; while a 1 sits above the double 'n' of 'perennial', implying a cross-syllabic stress – light/quiet/short – that suggests an alternative prosody within the word itself. The normal stressed and unstressed scan does not effectively allow for pitch, for intonation, for tonal variations within the syllable itself.

However, to use a system like this might be seen to destroy the potential, the ambiguities, the 'mystery' of the poem. It might be felt that a prescriptive way of reading the text is being imposed; that, as ironic as it might seem, it reinforces the primacy of the lyrical I. Its deployment or scoring in 'Syzygytics' is to critique our expectations as readers of poetry – that it should have rhythm, that metrics define the poem. However, one can read against the 'authority' of the register as much as follow the 'instructions' to interpretation and performance.

So, what is the point of all this? To show that language in a poem might be – should be – ambiguous? Even where the line seems straightforward, we should consider alternative readings. A 'paranoid reading' (Hodge and Mishra, 1991) of rhythm, if you like. The information that informs the construct of the text becomes simultaneously vital – as it is part of a greater discourse – but also 'irrelevant', as it is forming the discourse.

James McAuley used this technique as a mode of interpretation of stress fluctuations, but did not advocate its use as part of the text of actual poems (compare this to Gerard Manley Hopkins, who added accentual marks to the text of his poems and meant them to be included). His appropriate differentiation of separate registers for scansion, and separate registers for stress, should be supplemented with registers for stress and metrics within the word itself, and for distortion within the words and across the line. McAuley accurately notes:

> What we must insist on, therefore, is that the scansion is not an attempt to give a full account of the rhythmic behaviour of the syllables of spoken verse, and in particular it is not meant to be an adequate notation of stress values. It has the much simpler task of referring the line to the metrical code under which it operates, giving each syllable the value it acquires within that code (always allowing for variations permitted by the code).
>
> But what is the role of metre if it is this semi-abstract sort of thing, not a comprehensive formula for the actual movement of spoken verse? Its role is to provide a fixed scheme, across which the endless variety of stress-fluctuations can play as one line succeeds another. Our experience of a line of verse is therefore not a single and simple thing but essentially

dual: comprising a simultaneous recognition on the one hand of the constant metrical pattern (with its occasional variations by substitution of feet), and on the other of the actual stress-profile of the line as natural speech would require. The two experiences are mated, they are coherent; they are not radically distinct since metre is rooted in stress. But they are not identical, and a true feeling depends on appreciating the difference. (1966, p. 23)

I would add, even further gradations sub-syllable, and that these encourage 'paranoid' readings, against sense and coherence. Questions of enjambment and linearity must also be taken into consideration: the offsetting of the 'metrical profile' and 'stress profile' of the line by the destabilising 'extra words', the multiple readings that are engendered by the volta of the turning line.

There is a section in the Crystal *Encyclopaedia* – 'Transcribing intonation' – that is fascinating in the context of this paper:

> The first scientific attempt to transcribe the patterns of English intonation was made by Joshua Steele in *An essay towards establishing the melody and measure of speech* in 1775. It had been prompted by remarks made in an essay by James Burnet the previous year. Burnet had claimed that there was no such thing as intonation in English. The music of our language, he argued, is 'nothing better than the music of a drum, in which we perceive no difference except that of louder or softer.'
>
> Steele rebutted this point of view in an original manner. He pasted a piece of paper to the finger board of a bass viol next to the fourth string, and marked the notes on it that corresponded to the various frets. He then imitated the inflection of the voice by sliding his finger up and down the string, and found that the beginnings and ends of these inflections could usually be located in the intervals between the frets. He then devised a transcription which represented these observations – the first systematic transcription of English intonation. (1995, p. 170)

The question of intonation is particularly relevant in the prose poem, where the line does not work as a unit of measurement in the same definitive way. Lines wrap into each other and there is the suggestion of arbitrariness when a line end is reached, especially if the piece is justified. I would argue that the unit of meaning and rhythm still exists at the level of the syllable, but the continuation sets up an expectation of 'narrative' or descriptive or metonymic progression. Joanne Burns, in her poetics statement in the anthology *Landbridge: Contemporary Australian Poetry*, writes:

> Between the late seventies and the early nineties I mainly wrote prose poems – apart from a few fairly playful list poems of which 'revisionism' is an example. I had rejected what I felt was the restriction of the poetic line, and its knotted effect on my poetry, for the looser, seemingly more casual flow of the prose poem. I considered myself throughout all those years a prose poet 'forever'. However, in the early nineties, feeling a need for more spring, tension, and shape in my writing I began to write line break poetry again – but with what I felt was a new prosy breeziness. (1999, p. 73)

Burns is a poet with a project, but this is not to say there cannot be spring and tension and an intense if often variable metrics at work in the prose poem. What constitutes an 'Australian English' is superbly questioned and undermined in its presumptions and bigotries by the prose poems of Ania Walwicz. A sample speaks for itself:

> Wonderful
>
>   tips waves up big dipper fires wings lift me up roll out entry for prince of shiny press into me furbelows bows on tip toes cartwheels in lovely head lamp glower put on her dots dot in dot dotter dot dottie lain in finer blades naps cherubs
> (1994, p. 416)

and so on for dozens of lines. The poem is justified and enjambment produces accents across lines. Rhythm follows a different poetic structure but is recognisably poetry. We can hear it. The beat and pace are distinct, if varied; there is a short, sharp, rapid-fire progression. We spring through the poem. Apart from vitality on the level of language 'in the poem', this, in a contextual sense, implies much about what constitutes the Australian voice. I have heard it said that this is European English, whatever that is, and that Les Murray's is Australian English. I think both poets would be bemused if not amused by this.

To be said to have written a prose poem is very different from being called a prosaic poet, which is considered an insult. It generally indicates 'randomly' broken lines without a sense of 'metre'. If one is trying to replicate a metrical system and failing to do so, then such a criticism is relevant, but not if one is pushing the boundaries of metrics: creating variable rhythms, moving the accents, distorting the expected.

A poet who, to my mind, is revolutionising the way we might be expected to scan a line of verse is the Irish poet Tom Paulin. Of his book *The Wind Dog* (1999), I wrote in a review in *The Observer* (2000b):

The work is both inviting and troubling in its psychological implications. But above all else, this book is about sound – not just 'music', but the sound of being, of oppression, of liberation, of surprise and humour:

how cauld it is
out on air
for the very first time
but not gross and crass
as the first studio in Belfast
its acoustic deadness
– every wall and bit of furniture muffled
not a shred of echo –
where a cheery good day
or – it's Tyrone Guthrie talking –
a ringing roundelay
fell with a dull thud

The language compels us to listen, to hear it – to absorb its silences, the ubiquitous spaces between these busy notes. The geographies of Northern Ireland come through in fragments – like the 'wind dog' – pieces of a rainbow. The genius of this poetry is that it shatters definitions. Not purely a poetry of late modernism, deploying post-modernist techniques, neither is it a poetry of the lyrical self. It is deeply informed by the essence of the word and of the music of the spoken: poetry of the page and of performance. It is political lyrical poetry that historicises the ego-I, takes the lyrical self into a public arena. It might well be the future of English-language poetry – a hybridising organic entity, responding to change and recollection.

My arguments in favour of metrical distortion are both pro-active and symptomatic. As an Australian poet writing in English and teaching in England, I have realised that how I hear my own lines is not how others hear them. Rather than finding this frustrating, I see it as an awareness awash with possibilities. And on varying levels, through dialect and accent, this happens within the spatiality of any language 'centre', especially in Britain with its multiple languages, its distinct geographical, ethnic and social variations and differences.

So, when developing a poem's specific rhythms, there should be an awareness of possible mis-readings, of variations and distortions in the polymorphous ear. The dialogic nature of the lyric – its being informed by different spatialities and idioms – allows the poet to open areas of suggestion and ambiguity that enrich and enhance possible meanings. To be misheard is to be heard anew.

An Australian poet with a good sense of the irony implicit in tangling with the interstices of language and meaning is Judith Rodriguez, whose small poem following is a meta-text of distortion:

> Nasturtium Scanned
>
> Ropey, lippy, loopy, scribbly
> over a brick's edge, she's a riot,
> straggly as random and tricky as a diet,
> tiddly, wobbly, oddly, nibbly
> and flashy as a landmine on her vine-meandrine
> Alexandrine tangle-scanned line.
>
> (1994, p. 210)

Line breaks and back-draft: not a defence of a poem

For me, the measure of a poem is the word, not the line. This is a re-lineation and slight editing (one line) of a poem of mine published originally (1999) in John Tranter's web journal, *Jacket*:

> And Everyone Gathered In Objection Yet Again
>   for Robert Adamson
>
> And suddenly there was a presence,
> as if it were worth something,
> the pylons sticking up out of the water
> like busted bones out of flesh.
>
> A waterbird landed
> but didn't make much of an impression –
> a damp squib by comparison –
> though a couple of fishermen
>
> couldn't take their eyes off it.
> Bloody voyeurs, somebody muttered,
> and the bird, as if taking offence,
> lifted and vanished
>
> into the confident glow of the poem,
> the crowd encrypting itself
> into the scene's diffident colouration,
> troughed and crested
>
> like the hum of the current.

As written above, it basically subscribes to the one-unit-of-thought-per-line, 'natural' if elided clusters of speech, and hypotactic clause structure. The lines, if not end-stopped, are weighted as points of sub-closure within the greater sentence structure of the poem. If the content is not conventional, the layout certainly is, with minor digressions. In terms of what's being 'said', the poem is expectedly periphrastic – it's a roundabout journey to get to the main point because there are many other possible points of departure in meaning and tone on the way. However, the predictable lineation limits the possibilities of this periphrasis, unless as readers we read against the line breaks – say, taking random points within an ensuing line as an end/beginning to the unit of (de-) lineation.

Within the figurative expectations of the poem, I performed this 'adjustment' in response to a discussion on the poem on a metrics chat site, recently brought to my attention. When I draft a poem with line breaks that go against expected or formulaic (in poetry) speech patterns or, as the commentator on the chat site remarked, 'syntactical or rhetorical boundaries', it often begins in that staccato and stilted fashion of much lineated metrical verse. It's a set of ideas and images measured by line breaks – I gain a sense of balance and perspective in the draft, but rarely get the poem as I've seen it in my mind's eye (I literally see poems written before I 'copy' them).

In a sense, I back-draft. The original drafts are often comparatively closer to the linguistically controlled specimens that a more formalist poet or reader might desire. Sometimes I let them stay that way if it suits my broader purpose. But through a process of drafting de-lineation, often in fact relying on the physical measurement of a line in a particular font (which often changes when the poem is published) by way of 'weighting', using the centre of the line not so much as caesura but as pivot, I distract or displace the expected measurements.

Of course, for me, 'syntactical and rhetorical' boundaries are prisons. My poetry is a direct result of my politics and ethics, and form for me is a box to be pushed against; to be used pragmatically at times, but ultimately to be tested at every opportunity. I do not want my poems to give pleasure, I don't want them to be comfortable, and I don't want them to 'tell'. I want my poems to suggest and to bother – to irritate, and to instigate.

Language for me is a generator, and has an organicism that leads to the myriad creation of meaning (out of context); and so is form. Form is not simply the safe house of aesthetic and artistic control that allows us to know a text is a poem; form is not necessarily the guide to interpretation and instruction many hope for. It's how we are taught, maybe choose, to read, that matters. I don't want to package a poem.

Even in the re-draft, the 'dangling' last line might somehow partially gain this effect – a resistance to the bracketings of the previous four-line stanzas – but equally it might provide a more restrictive packaging through suggesting total closure. I see this draft as more anatomically correct than I find enticing. I don't want my poems to leisure or pleasure, but I do want them to allow for a polymorphously perverse interaction with both myself and the reader. They are fetishes, but hopefully with adjustable appendages. They will change with time and place.

The poem cited is not one of my personal favourites. It was written in response to Robert Adamson's great poem of collation and sublimated dialogue with voices of romantic and modernist urges in poetry, 'The Rumour'. It arose from the occasion of a boat ride on the Hawkesbury with Adamson, remembered a few years later in the context of re-reading 'The Rumour'. It's a poem about displacing displaced and re-represented voices. 'Packaging' it would be inappropriate. Here's what Adamson had to say about 'The Rumour' in an interview I conducted with him in the mid-'90s – what's crucial in terms of discussing the lineation of my response is that 'The Rumour' was always a poem about process, about a broader imaginary conversation on process and inspiration:

> RA: ... And then I said that to Creeley, 'Ah, I understand, I understand,' and he was laughing. He said, 'Okay, okay that's fine to understand it. I'm glad I can help. But now what you've got to do is write your poem in Australian.' I said, 'What are you talking about?' I had versions of poems, and that would have been early versions of 'The Rumour', especially that one I wrote before 'The Rumour'. Because it's a bit like Hart Crane, 'The Rumour'. I started it at the beginning and the end, and then filled in the middle. So one of the first things I wrote was that section called 'Everybody Gathered in Objection'. That was an early version. I showed it to Creeley and he said, 'Okay, what you've got to do now is write like Ted Berrigan, only you're Australian so ...' He looked at a lot of poetry in my house and he couldn't find anything that sounded Australian. I grabbed Bruce Dawe and Bruce Beaver and he said, 'Yeah, they're getting there, they're getting there as far as using the language'. He said, 'I hear this language, I've never known it before but I hear it in the air, I've heard it for three days and I can hear the tune you're all playing.'
>
> That's the way he put it. He actually said to me take the high art and put in the language of your everyday conversation. 'You're talking to me in poems that are much better than the poems you've got down here on the page.' It sounds so simple, it really does, but he taught me how to write down the rhythms of conversation and couple that with – this is just technical but it wasn't just technical – couple that with the language of high literature or high modernism, whatever you like, and play that off against it. So what will happen then in the technical exercises, you'll find

– this is Creeley saying to me – you'll find that steeped in language like that, your subject will arise out of the language. You won't have to worry about where you're taking it, it'll come out, or you know, it's just that when you find the right form you'll have the content. So you know, the thing about that was that, in a strange weird way, Berrigan came into that poem, although there's no traces of it in there.

JK: There's a rumour of it.

RA: Yeah.

JK: A fact, something we know, a scientific fact for example, can be bent, can be altered to a certain end, can be propaganda-ised if you like. A rumour inevitably will be because it can't be reconstructed as fact. How does that notion fit in with the definitive poetics that you're trying to explore?

RA: In the book it's very important, that quote from Wallace Stevens at the beginning 'In the long run the truth does not matter'. Now that's really the first line of the poem. So I write, 'In the long run the truth does not matter', and then go on to investigate that. Because truth will be poetry and poetry is the one thing that cannot be corrupted. (Adamson and Kinsella 1997)

In my poem, the boat is flowing against the current, the swimlines are not those of the received speech patterns of 'old-timers' of the river Adamson has so vividly scored in his own poetry, and that I have heard around the river on visiting him. In some ways, I feel it's harder to write against the line when lines are so clearly announced – that is, when they compile themselves in search of a chronological and event-linear format. I believe this is the case in the above version, with maybe the exception of 'as if taking offence' – and there I have deleted the key 'on their behalf', going for a more conventional ambiguity through tight expression – a lie I've re-admitted to the poem, and maybe in tune with issues of honesty and untruth in 'The Rumour', but antithetical to the drive of the poem).

On the web chat site I have referred to, my poem was cited as unredeemable 'writing' (the title and first stanza – which remain the same across both versions – were not included, though a link to the *Jacket* URL containing the entire poem was), and its line breaks described as 'radical' and sometimes 'silly'. The protest was against a supposed 'modernist' urge towards creating lines of the same physical length, creating seemingly arbitrary line breaks which add nothing to meaning/sound, and so on. The general prosiness of contemporary poetry was deplored, and then the discussion sidetracked into contemporary poets being read solely by contemporary poets because of this. I have paraphrased this from memory, but think I have the basic gist of the arguments.

The idea that 'radical line breaks' (to quote one of my critics) involve the breaking of units of common speech or expression and associative meaning, might be allowed, I guess, in a kind of obvious declarative enjambment, where meaning carries over the line for a specific dramatic effect (and I'm all in favour of enjambment), or as an antidote to the repetitive staidness of the end-stopped line, in the same way that substitution of a foot in metrical verse brings relief to the reader, and good opportunities for the poet to show how elastic set form really is. This is all good, but working within the shape and framework of the deformalised poem, one can, of course, go further. That's what interests me: keeping enough of the form for it to be recognised as coming out of some kind of 'tradition', but radicalising enough to question the heritage and the need for variation itself. It's self-damning as much as 'illuminating'.

If we view the basic reason for line breaks as rhythmic, and rhythm in poetry as directly connected with mood and meaning, then it inevitably brings us to the question of what necessitates a particular rhythm in the first place. Back in the Western Australian wheatbelt, and surrounded by paddocks, I make use of my brother's full drum kit to vent some of my ... er, rhythmic urges. Drumming can drive itself. You start with a basic four-four beat – common time – then maybe slip into doubles, then compound a three-four beat into a six-eight, a waltz to Spanish variations – and build from there and break away (you can frame anything, do it in any denomination you want); or you can listen to (or hear in your head) a piece of music and drum to it with the same principle. My brother drums to words – lineated and non-lineated!

Either way, the ability to keep time is the skill; the art comes in breaking free of that – to my mind at least. And I'm not only talking about jazzlike innovation – divergences that ultimately take you back to a point of reference – but rather the notes of discord or arrhythmia that genuinely contradict the form you are working in or through. It might be that one aspect remains consistent – the accent of the drumming, for instance – a little like the length of the line becoming the measure of rhythm rather than the integrity of speech grouping or associative meaning. In other words, the line forces us to hear what we wouldn't hear by reading for literally expressed meaning (even where it's 'figurative') – it forces to listen against expectation. It doesn't have to sound pleasing at first listening, but a different way of listening and thus hearing is suggested.

On the Microsoft Help and Support site on the web, the imperialism of correct expression finds its most paranoid and authentication hungry expression. It's where the new media self-validate through the philanthropy of assistance and explication. It struck me: what of the line faltering between email packages – a common experience for poets and editors. 'Because I have problems with lineation, I have marked the end of each line with ...' Anyway, here's a little MS internationalism at work:

> OL2002: Posts Do Not Honor Line Breaks in Plain Text Format
> View products that this article applies to.
> Article ID : 287816
> Last Review : June 27, 2001
> Revision : 1.0
> This article was previously published under Q287816

SYMPTOMS

> When you create a new plain text formatted post that contains line breaks, the line breaks are removed when the Auto Remove Line Breaks feature is enabled unless there are two successive line breaks. However, the posts do not display any indication that this has occurred, other than the change in formatting. The information bar message about extra line breaks does not appear, either in the Preview pane or when you read the post. This processing appears to happen when the message is initially posted.   (http://support.microsoft.com/default.aspx?scid=kb;EN-US;q287816)

Experiencing this lapse in day-to-day emailing might mean confusion of meaning for the reader untried in the vagaries of email, but generally we'd be able to nut our way through it. For the poem – especially one that doesn't use capitalisation to begin a line – it offers a real problem: a probable defeat of the original intention behind the poem ...? Or, even worse, a misreading that might lead to an accusation of shoddy craftMANship. I WANT that software. I want my line breaks to falter and differ from recipient to recipient. One error in a book is just irritating, but a generative process that recreates text in an infinitely varied way is deeply appealing. It's probably as prescriptive as 'syntactical and rhetorical boundaries' – the same line break 'errors' for all or most recipients. The third party infiltrates the text, but it's just their word against yours. The reader is left disappointed, maybe, but the error has been built into their expectations, their adjusted sense of rhythm. The irony is, though we can with a skilled ear detect line breaks when verse is written in metrical stanzaic forms, and quite often in free verse, it's an extremely visual way of listening. There's nothing wrong with that, but rather than sight and sound interacting, it's more a demarcation of the two.

Gertrude Stein, in stanza LXI (Part V) of *Stanzas In Meditation* (Sun & Moon, Los Angeles, 1994, p. 201) wrote:

> I wish once more to mention
> That I like what I see.

We can hear that line break and don't really need to see the page. But knowing it's Gertrude Stein we might doubt it a little. Stein had an intense sense of the line (one non-believers called prosaic, despite its musicality), and where the expectation of a line break might be ... broken. Seeing is to gain comfort. Milton's great sonnet of his blindness is a poem about seeing as much as loss of sight. Few poems embrace the blindness of the line, think outside the kind of drumming that simply keeps the beat. I've always admired Keith Richard's wise words about Charlie Watts, sublime drummer of the not-so-sublime Rolling Stones, that went along the line of: 'a lot of drummers have the rock, but Charlie has the roll' ... The roll happens alongside the rhythm, and is part of it, but it's also the slippage between the lines. Something to aspire to, maybe.

So, to cut a long story short, here's the published version of the poem with its much-drafted line breaks:

> And Everyone Gathered In Objection Yet Again
>   for Robert Adamson
>
> And suddenly there was a presence,
> as if it were worth something,
> the pylons sticking up out of the water
> like busted bones out of flesh.
>
> A waterbird landed but didn't make
> much of an impression – a damp squib
> by comparison – though a couple
> of fishermen couldn't take their

> eyes off it. Bloody voyeurs
> somebody muttered, and the bird,
> as if taking offence on their behalf,
>
> lifted and vanished into the confident
> glow of the poem, the crowd
> encrypting itself into the scene's
> diffident colouration, troughed
> and crested like the hum of the current.
> (http://jacketmagazine.com/06/kins.html)

The poem itself occupies an indefensible position in terms of consistency in line breaks, but I stick by them and the means of getting to them – they were certainly more bothering to write than the first version shown above. I believe the poem gains in periphrasis, and though remain fairly conventional in expression (it's not a paratactic poem, as such), the line breaks bring a suggestion of a dislocated clause structure. Readers are encouraged to read against expectation, to ironise their own process of reading through the poem ironising its own production. The observations have a sense of the matter-of-fact about them, even flatness (the 'prosaic'?), a participation in the rumour that displaces the process of witness, telling and insight. A possibly frustrating characteristic of the poem, for anyone reading and expecting a certain kind of lineation, is that the poem is primarily lyrical, though refuses to settle into the rises and fall of lyrical song rhythms. I would hope that the distraction and displacement of lyrical impetus makes the poem more volatile in its register, more evasive, and that as Andrew Zawacki noted in his *ABR* and *Notre Dame Review* piece on *Zoo*, "And Everyone Gathered In Objection Yet Again" plies an eerie natural and aesthetic transfiguration...' (*Australian Book Review*, November 2000, Issue 226). In this case, the upsetting of the givens is as much a result of the 'radical and silly line breaks', as it is about the words used.

What's it about? Maybe it's just about an unidentified (choice or lack?) water-bird – the lack of naming encrypting the rumour of it having been seen. So, the biggest irony for me is that 'everyone gathered in objection yet again'. Maybe that's the other point of the poem. I'm sure Jo Shapcott felt the same when in the early years (late 1990s) of the *Poetryetc* email discussion list, a well-known British avant-gardist denigrated Shapcott's astonishingly technically accomplished poetry as being inadequate because her line breaks were supposedly 'without volition'. Coming from a self-proclaimed innovator, this struck me as being rather imperceptive, or even hypocritical. Women poets often get the line break and form argument thrown at them – I say, thank goodness that some resist expectations of form and convention. If Joanna Russ had been a poet rather than a science fiction writer, she might have had a chapter in *How to Suppress Women's Writing* (1983) on the male policing (or 'masculine' policing) of female line breaks. The gendered reading comes from the outside as much as from inside the poem-text. Lineation can easily become a security, a status quo, that needs, on occasion, to be resisted.

My partner, poet Tracy Ryan, wrote a response to the criticism of Jo Shapcott's line breaks as part of a series of poems entitled *bloc-notes*. I leave the last words to her:

Masterclass

You're nobody without prosody. Let me show you how it's done honey. I told the bitch, I said. I love her instinctive but without prosody, without volition. The definition of lack. I broke her line like a twig for her, like a waist so slender my hero hand could. Like a neck. Snap, a match like a rhyme. Tinder and flame, just begging for it. It wasn't force but you couldn't say consent. What she needs is a good enjambment. This thing is private. Lil ol me. The lines just lay down like that. Lil ol me. I have always relied on the kindness.

Line breaks coda

Adapted from a recent email sent to Marjorie Perloff

I have been thinking a lot about the issue of 'tighter' verse, and have come to the conclusion that I am trying to create a verse (on occasions) that is somewhat akin to Philip Sidney's prose narratives of *Arcadia*, but merged with his metrically tight poem sections as well (configured mainly through the eclogues). How to create a sense of narrative and still retain the integrity of 'individual' poems? This issue has occupied me for some time. When one deploys the overt – and often 'small' – lyrical moment in the poem, it contains itself; but what happens with larger, freer verse units that create a cumulative effect? Why does one choose to break against the 'natural' break (and especially a metrical break) or break in unit meaning? But it's more than that – it's not simply a matter of the prosaic in verse, or, indeed, the prose poem (totally different), but rather of melding speech rhythms and this cumulative way of reading and interpreting the world (how my odd brain works, in some ways).

I've come up with a term for what I am trying to do formally – create an 'articulated' line in poetry. Articulated in the sense of 'connected by joints' (*Oxford English Dictionary*), as in an articulated vehicle – articulated clauses, even articulated morphemes! – plus the 'uttered as articulate sound; distinctly spoken' (*Oxford English Dictionary*) ... for me, in the face of the devastation of the rural and 'natural' environments, there's a reconstitution of language, a filling-out of the lost spaces of language in verse (and as you cleverly point out, Marjorie – the antipastoral's reformulation as pastoral). Now, this is not an 'outing' of the hermetic, but rather a dialogue with the unseen, the disturbed, the lost and damaged pieces of language. This 'articulated poem' or 'articulated verse' or 'articulated' line becomes the partner of parataxis – actually achieving something similar, but in a more directly dialogic, maybe conversational, way. It's where I've found myself in trying to deal with issues of pastoral in Australia.

The search for the new idea, the unique? Against poetics?

I fear when poets feel that poetry needs terminologies, needs gimmicks, needs the new idea. It seems that poetry lives in a narrative cycle that requires plot gestures, actions, possibilities, in order to keep going, to motivate itself towards newness. The poet becomes a fetishist not only of self and language, but of community. S/he annunciates to those around, declaring interstices of experience and the subliminal, empirical and sublime, and other binary combinations. The desire to discuss how one writes, as much as why one writes, seems pandemic at times. Is it a lust for a stage, and for an audience? It forms the basis of the creative writing thesis, and many poets at some stage of their 'career' will make some utterance of independent thought, either by interview, or by declaration. Some of us even have students writing group-poetics. The codes of writing and reading are broken down. Perhaps what I am talking about is my own constant need to comment on process. It is myself I fear.

One of the characteristics of poetics-making is the coining of 'new' approaches to language, to prosody, to the act of writing, that place poetry on the more general stage of community. These interstices are as much part of an anxiety that evolves out of fearing indifference from a broader public, as they are of a desire to inculcate poetry into a broader discourse. It also suggests a possible 'failure' to believe in the poem itself achieving this, or a desire to make poetry into another discourse (especially in terms of literary theory), or the manipulation of the poem to serve a pedantic, dogmatic or propagandist purpose. The propaganda often comes out of the most abstracted poem, the most nonreferential, non-lyrical I, even non-lyrical. The poet refuses to 'explain' in the poem (what good poem does explain anyway?) on the level of line and word, but seeks to rectify this by explaining in a poetics. Having one's cake and eating it too? Possibly, but so what? Why not? The poem and the explication form a symbiotic relationship – or maybe they were always part of each other.

On the more positive side, there is a genuine desire to express the inexpressible (is this not what poetry does anyway?), or to develop terms of reference and discussion that allow bridges/connections to be made between the apparently irreconcilable. These are digressions, but they underpin my concern with issues of originality in my own work. What purpose does originality have, outside feeding a life-narrative driven by the need for change? I would argue that the innovative piece of writing is not necessarily more likely to bridge the gaps, to create new possibilities, than the apparently tired old four-line rhyming lyrical-I poem that works on the overt level of 'meaning', tells us something that might surprise us on the level of content, more than of form or 'language'. Sometimes apparent innovation becomes the most overt form of fetishisation, of art for art's sake: audience is variable, and meaning will change according to who is reading/listening, but in many ways poems attempt to construct a 'kind of audience' as part of the fetishisation of a uniqueness, an innovativeness. The notion that one is unique, and deserves a unique response, goes hand-in-hand with an expectation that the audience will be privileged because it 'understands' what is not readily available to most.

Even within the group-poetics, the individual voice might be heard. The group behaves as a unique individual; then there are the obvious digressions and disparities within the group that will be articulated on the micro-stage of self. After all, our bodily functions primarily work independently of other people. Our bodies are different poems that share a group-poetics, but also declare their own poetics. I have found that a compulsion for collaboration (anarchist) seems to bring a desire to articulate one's variation, one's difference.

So I have felt a need to discuss what I do and why I do it, and to connect myself with what has come before, to allude to what might follow. Or in distancing myself, to over-emphasise what else has happened by refuting it. The claiming of an idea quickly disparaged by evidence that someone has claimed it before. Did they write the same poem, story, essay, anecdote, theory ... word by word, do a Menard (Borges, 1962)? Is what I am writing given relevance by its being different, unique? This is not an issue of good or bad, or of quality control, but of separation and isolation. And that is what I fear, and that is what compels me to collaborate not only with other poets, but artists, composers, even scientists.

With web saturation and search engines, it will be shown that our individual thinking is a mirror of, or 'coincidentally' connected with, many others' 'individual' thinking. There are more crossovers than we might like to accept. Maybe not to the extent of the Borgesian (1962) word for word reproduction, but certainly on the level of content, language-deployment, articulation of what it is we are attempting to do. If it is a case of plagiarism, then that carries its own meanings and discourse, and these shift with motivation and intent (parody, abuse, theft etc.). What about the idea you have that is unique, and then you discover it has been had before? Okay, as the cliché goes, there are no new ideas ... but what if the language you use to express it is exactly the same as the way someone has previously expressed it? What if someone expresses it as you have already expressed it?

The email discussion list, the listserv, is a wonderful short-circuitor, or maybe circuit-breaker, for new ideas in poetry. Ideas are subtly, and almost unconsciously, built up over hours, days, weeks, even years. Theories are formed, poetries change, adapt, 'increase' and diminish in response to the collaborative cut and thrust of exchange. Declarations of dissension cause upset, some are 'thrown off' lists, but the process is absorbed. Lists are subverted, undermined and abused, and the process of assimilating or capitulating or adapting to this becomes part of the lacunae of the poem, the poems floating in over the life of the dissent, debate. Peripheral argument becomes part of the whole. So many words have been absorbed, hijacked, adapted (these lists keep forming), into the general poetics of bourgeois western poetries.

The claim is that the academy eventually absorbs them, but the truth seems more likely that academy-envy produced them in the first place. For example: the idea of fiction theory becoming poetry theory is enticing, and given that life-narrative needs changes to keep it kicking along, given the annotations of *The Rime of the Ancient Mariner*, why not?! A friend once made the (un)original observation that sex was like a Russian novel. Now, he didn't say that as theory, he was just going off with his partner into another room and told me they were going to write a Russian novel. I thought of Lyn Hejinian's *Oxota* (1991), and drew a blank (...) I thought of *War and Peace*, *Dead Souls*, all of Turgenev, and almost settling on the *Brothers Karamazov* for some perverse reason, settled on *Anna Karenina*. Now, there's a poem and poetics rolled into one. There are answers there. Anyway, I scribble to frame the text.

Can I write a rural poetry without referring to a single concrete/inanimate object? Keep people, animals, plants ... get rid of ploughs, tractors, feed troughs, knives, hooks, incubators? You could – but would you want to? It is a semi- (I'm sure) unique idea. Or maybe the uniqueness would be in writing a 108-page book of these poems. Or maybe spending one's entire life writing the same poem over and over. I no longer consider myself, for example, a hybrid of experimental (or 'linguistically innovative' – and that is going to come under scrutiny shortly) and 'traditional'. It does not account for my love of the draft, as physical entity, the piles of rejected pages from the manual typewriter, pre-electronic conversion, transcription, and always transformation, even if not a word is changed. Photocopies, each time the same poem would be different.

No: I have a new word to ponder in a poetics context. I *think* I have coined it, but I am sure someone else has used it in the specific way I intend, probably on a stormy day in the northern hemisphere, and in an *English*-speaking country. I wish we spoke Latin. Anyway, the word is variorum. Not in the retrospective 'variorum edition' sense, but as an active writing process. I consider myself a poet of variation, and those variations build into an oeuvre, a life project. The difference is a sameness. Maybe I am a 'variorum' poet. I haven't plucked this out of thin air; there is a precedent. I wrote an article nine or ten years ago on the validity of the poem draft as poem in itself. I have always rejected closure, and never see a poem as complete – even if it is written in a specific form, with a tight metrical system. I digress again. I have seeded the word 'variorum' into my latest poem draft – I would guess the word will remain throughout all drafts of the poem. But it might not.

The journal forms a pivotal part of the variorum poetics. There is a note in my journal from July/August 2005 that refers to the 'borrowing' of an idea I had by a friend: 'As an anarchist, I feel I must accept this plagiarism graciously – but coming from a friend, it does make it very uncomfortable.' The irony is, I have written an essay on plagiarism in which I say that if the intent is not malicious, then basically I do not mind. And I believe that publicly.

What I have just quoted is from my private 'under-lock-and-key', hand-written journal. It is not a blog! The blog seems antithetical to the unique idea. The unique idea is a fetishisation, so maybe the blog is a decoding of this. Unlikely. There is one persona for the private stage, and a different one for the public. My papers are archived: some have privacy protections, but eventually they go public. Now, nobody might read them, but the point is that they can. So, once outside my life's narrative, do I perceive them as becoming something else? No doubt, someone has written very similar words, somewhere, in some language, with cultural variants possibly, in their own journal. Intentionality, apart from context, becomes the definition of uniqueness. The private, or even quasi-private, space suggests a necessity of uniqueness. The dialogue with self, where truth is a different variable.

I would like to quote a few pages from the last week before writing this:

20th May, 2003

Aggressive storms this evening ... Had a tooth extracted today.

Am thinking about two Mummers' style plays – one a plough play ...

***

23rd May

Replacing Modernism and de-valuing Modernity

Insomnia. Poetics. Heisenberg (the presence of the observer alters the nature of the observed). Schrodinger's cat – vile analogy. Superposition and the poem – the word.

If one thinks what someone (else) has already thought – independently, without knowing – can it be 'second-hand'? Or should we investigate its newness and originality? Its spontaneity? I reject determinism. A new poetics is forming. I do not recognise myself as being part of any modernism. Mine is apocalyptic. [Though not as in the Apocalypse poets ...] What I think is not what I say. Sometimes it approximates, but that's as close as it gets. [I read a poem aloud and think of another poem in my head as I am doing so.] I am alive and dead. This era leaves us no choice – no expectation of life. The poem is alive and dead. Recent correspondence with a linguist friend over an article of mine re metrics has made me consolidate my belief that English is only English because it's not French or Chinese etc. I do not recognise an organic language, empirically intact. I do not write in the simulacrum English. I write in a language of superposition – English, and not English, metaphoric and non-metaphoric, rhetorical and unrhetorical, and all other binaries, which together make 'structured' confusion that resists binary examination. As a vegan, I cannot recognise the validity of Schrodinger and his cat, the cat he wishes he never met (this wish must have been the key to his social life!). The vegan won't even conduct the figurative experiment. Now, the cyanide might be real. And yet the empire has created conditions of terrorism. That's the flaw in the reasoning. We can't measure the particle as movement contradicts expectations. We can only expect it. That's the gap in the poem. The flaw is where the poem might locate itself.

Schrodinger's cat is a scapegoat.

A poetics is unique to the poet because there are the poems! The 'creativity' of the texts gives an axis for the ideas to turn around – to be confirmed and negated accordingly, respectfully. The uttered opinions are secondary to the texts – it is believed ... But they are both of the same poem. There are no separate poems. For a single author, for all authors ... once they are written. Language as art subverts originality. The real poem is outside language, pre-speech/expression (writing).

The qualifier 'for me' is a ruse – 'for me' is a proxy for those who share language. A version [of]. We retreat into 'dumbness' and refuse to answer the doll/marble question. We refuse our cultural informatives, refuse the determinations, refuse the text.

Do I need declare the name, shape, and nature of the god/s I believe in?

Mime.

Slippage – it's not all rhythm. The shed is my retreat.

Eschatological?

These claims we make:

Metaphor is rhythmic – or, rather comes out of the rhythmic disjunction between different word and idea strings as they dislocate from poetry before utterance, and the materials of the utterance, and the expression that is lost, shifted, transformed in this movement. It's the kinetic energy that surrounds the transfer, this change. Concept = a lot of agitation between the pre-cognitive, or even 'thought' poem, and the poem as language. The pre-uttered poem is part pre-thought, part thought – it is restless between states. Part of it is beyond the manipulation of the deaf re marble and doll. The dead refuse the manipulation. The isolation and declaration of the informatives of language are a denial of poetry and a form of abuse: of cultural, social, ethnic, and physical control. The poet and audience are deaf, all deaf. And this is what allows them to hear the poetry. Poetry is why we have a term like 'mystical'.

Now I must sleep. Retreat into the hypnagogic where I forget the words for what I see, and see my mouth with no words 'hearing' out of it. Soon

I change locations. Soon a disruption will create heat and energy.

The insecurity of language.

Bi-lingual, tri-lingual household – destabilising the sign.

My linguist friend pointed out that an idea in my article that I seemed to imply was original had in fact been articulated by a linguist some years ago. However, I have not read that linguist, and still have no idea what he says. I will investigate. She recognised that my context and application were different. I felt quite good – I am not a linguist, but thought of an idea a linguist came up with not so long ago. But maybe it is just a condition of the environment we both work in. Maybe numerous people have had this idea – it becomes 'first in print' to claim it as unique. It becomes absurd. Why it is being said – the intention behind usage – is the point of ethical 'validity', surely?

Another extract from my journal:

31st May, 2003 Kenyon

Read in Cincinnati yesterday. A wrong turn over the bridge took us into Kentucky. The bridge, a liminal zone over the certainty of the Ohio River.

Extending the metaphor. 'Linguistically innovative': I used this expression long before I read that it had been 'coined' (by Gilbert Adair in 1988). I believe I came across it in translation texts. I think Margaret Atwood used the expression in her mid-80s anthology of Canadian poetry. I can check. Maggie O'Sullivan used it as a subtitle of her anthology *out of everywhere* in 1996. I discussed it in my Australian poetry anthology of 1999, *Landbridge*. I used it long before this. Independently. Uniquely. I certainly wasn't conscious of the Atwood then (was this early 90s, late 80s?), and certainly not of Gilbert Adair, though I would have a complete set of *Angel Exhaust* by late 1996. When I write about it, I don't do so in any way I would recognise as belonging to the discourses of these others. It is a fetishised expression – personally, as well as within the so-called discourse. I coined it for myself. To express something I couldn't express otherwise. It's like 'linguistic disobedience'. I wrote seven essay poems on this – a derivation of Thoreau and pacifist-anarchist-vegan politics – before seeing an advert for a Russian poetry reading in New York quoting Joseph Brodsky as saying certain poets were 'linguistically disobedient'. It was an isolated usage, I believe. Maybe not. I'd written essays on the subject before hearing this. Others have probably used this expression as well. Now, here's the rub. For me, in both cases, uniqueness is not lost, but enhanced. The problem is not in the repetition of expression, or even ideas (ideas and usage being clearly different, if overlapping), but in the concern and desire for uniqueness. How can claims be made for ownership? Does coincidence inform as much as circumstance, condition of language and production? This concern is a denial of my public politics – which relishes the undoing of the fetishisation. It becomes the generative flaw, the location of the poem. But this contradiction (Walt Whitman) is another draft, in another context – they are drafts of the same poem. They are no replications, or renditions, or unique entities, they are just variations of translations of the pre-cognitive, the un-uttered. Poetry has never been about ideas – it's about the desire for ideas, and evasion of conclusions.

So, that is the most recent entry in my journal at my current point of writing. The ideas – convoluted, gestational – might inform my poems, if nothing else. In a sense, it becomes a way of removing the feel for the need to express ideas overtly in the poems. It might create something more allusive, more ambiguous in the poems themselves. If so, the poetics plays a role in keeping the poem in that liminal zone over the Ohio River. However, I have grown increasingly convinced that the poem is actually unutterable, and in some senses, becomes a 'poetics' – a how and why we write – the moment it is uttered – articulated, written. No matter how crafted the poem itself, it is a victim of the poetics that created it. Whatever name the utterance goes by.

In the end, the production of the poem becomes a search for a combination of recognition of uniqueness, and a call for dialogue (writer/reader, friend/friend, text/concept, and so on). The fact that uniqueness is always contradictable, or accountable, would seem to belie this desire. But poetry is delusional in so many ways – its indirections allow diversion and distraction, for a façade of uniqueness to be maintained. The irony is, then, when a uniqueness, and an inability to translate a poem, occur, many poets go into pseudo-critical, self-reflexive mode and critique it themselves, just to ensure the reader realises exactly what it is or is not they are saying, and just how unique such an achievement really is. I am going to persist, at least for the time being, with variorum(ism), but only as a term of convenience that has a set of meanings within my personal vocabulary, and a sense of familiarity which allows me to connect with real or imagined audiences, with all the problems that entails. What I feel sure about is that I will continue to write a poem over and over again, regardless of the name I give to the process.

On *Graphology*

A pseudo-science? False science – alchemy – always interested me. I worked in a laboratory during school holidays, I planned on becoming an organic chemist. I did research into chemi-luminescence and read Meister Eckhart and Paracelsus. Exact and figurative sciences blurred. My mother always had handwriting analysis books around the house – she was a whiz. It was like fortune-telling and opening a secret dossier simultaneously. The fiction writer in me might have had a vague interest in the latter, though my politics steered me away from intrusion. But the mystical inexactitude of the former was attractive. I studied history at university, and English, and politics. The timeline of graphological studies, of a person's life read through the development and dissolution of their script, a different kind of history. It all ran together. My own handwriting is almost illegible.

Loop and angle, aggression and passivity, 'handwriting resonates/ like the voice' I wrote in *Graphology*, Canto 1 (2004a, p. 269). In the same canto:

> those amateur graph-
> ologists from Suetonius
> to Poe legal & validated
>
> by time, which fades
> like a secret signature
>
> (2004, p. 269)

So it was always historical, or perhaps undoing the 'big events' – coronations, battles, politics of vanity – by verbal, visual, and musical subtext. As for the exactitude, the precision of the science:

> Degenerating
> the unconnected writing
>
> as theory angles
> & forms against curves
> of food production,
>
> the specialist items
> labelled brightly
> in the specialist shops:
>
> the upstrokes vigorous
> amongst the arrhythmic ...
>
> (2004, p. 270)

Spatial lyricism

Disorder – the error zones in which the 'non-linear' (as Marjorie Perloff [2001a] might have it) poetries form. The practical application of physics led to:

> The mechanical skill
>
> of the Victorian cursive
> as the moon full & deliberate
> flourishes amongst the tide-
>
> riven ripples of the river.
>
> (2004, p. 273)

And the identities of history merged with the language that held them and their attempts to record it, or be recorded. The sign of presence and liberty becomes the signature. It is an inscribing of the world's different bodies: earth, water, air ...

> as formniveau
> is underwritten
> by the rhythm
>
> of variations in
> pronunciation:
> Ludwig Klages'
>
> Handwriting and Character,
> and later Max Pulver
> preoccupied by the world space
>
> of a sheet of gleaming
> white paper ...
>
> (2004, p. 277)

It is spatial, and that is what *Graphology* has always been: a translation of spatial dynamics. *Graphology*, a poem with a tentative beginning, and no possible closure, locates itself from the late 1980s – the earliest material was lost when two tea-chests of drafts and artwork were accidentally destroyed. In its second incarnation, *Graphology* began with a book-length group or sequence of poems, *The Radnoti Poems* (1996) though in some ways it began before that with *Erratum/Frame(d)*(1995a). The *D & G* poems I constructed via fax (in English, German, French, and Latin – handwritten, typed and illustrated) with the Swiss-German avant-gardist, Urs Jaeggi, in 1995/96, are tangentially connected. However, the *Graphology* project 'proper' began with the Equipage (Cambridge) publication of *Graphology* (cantos) in 1997. From that point on, sections have appeared in print and internet journals, and on sites such as the Electronic Poetry Center at Buffalo.

The pieces were occasionally composed in a sequential/chronological format, numbered accordingly, though at other times the numbering leaps and reverses and becomes – seemingly – inconsistent. This is the nature of memory and the instability of memory, text and sign. History changes according to the time and spatial co-ordinates it is viewed from.

I envisage *Graphology* to be a lifework. It is certainly absorbing all of my major concerns and is 'adapting' linguistically as time passes. Time and the unrealisability of permanence are its focal themes, or questionings. The signature, written by hand, is a false fingerprint – it is a construct. And this is the clue to decoding the work as it unravels. It is also a poem concerned with issues of belonging, ownership and recording identity.

III

MANIFESTOES

Anthologising the nation

Since the mid-1990s, I have edited a number of special Australian issues of literary journals from Britain, Canada, and the United States. I have also edited an anthology of contemporary Australian poetry, *Landbridge* (1999a), and am at present completing a two-volume historical anthology. These projects were very different in orientation from the process of including Australian poetry (and prose) in the many 'general' issues of literary journals that I edited over the same period of time, and indeed over the last dozen or so years. Apart from the obvious agenda of representing place and culture – or especially with a continent-country as large and diverse as Australia, places and cultures – there is the constant undercurrent of bypassing or making connections between differences to create a broader context of identity. Shared identity. To open lines of communication between different kinds of poetries coming out of a spatial zone that implies shared language, geography, social and cultural concerns, and political frameworks, can be useful in presenting a picture of how that place works subtextually. But it is also limiting, and tends to help establish a nationalist discourse, a collective identity that places those outside the fabric as Other. This Other varies in degrees of rapprochement and alienation, but all those outside the place denoted by the rubric 'Australia' become the necessary counterpart in a binary that defines collective identity. This can easily become the machinery of oppression, the emotional and potentially propagandist means of oppressing those who are not of the nation.

Australia is often called a young nation, because it was settled by Europeans just over two hundred years ago. But the indigenous peoples' connection with the land has spanned something like 35,000-80,000 years (figures vary). The land is geologically old, *and* old in terms of human habitation and cultures. Furthermore, the idea of modern Australia being a single collective entity collapses under even vague scrutiny. It relies on an image peddled by governments and organisations with a vested interest in maintaining the primarily Anglo-Celtic inclination of Australian culture, especially its close links to Britain (to the point that the British Queen is actually also the Queen of Australia). During my years of anthologising 'Australian' poetry, I have increasingly tried to work outside the expectations of the official culture. This is not always easy, especially in cases where the government has indirectly funded the payments to authors. I am not suggesting that there has ever been any attempt to direct editorial content, but there is certainly an element of expectation in the general culture – expectation of 'quality', the inclusion of those poets who have contributed to the national literature, who are either resident in Australia or have Australian citizenship, and so on. As time moved on, these various projects began to work without funding from Australia, and I have felt a greater freedom to use such potentially nation-asserting projects to undermine the idea of nation. In an issue of *The Literary Review* I wrote:

> So, here's a selection working against the idea of 'one' nation. It's a selection that works in terms of communities and alternative identities – not just in terms of whether people's surnames are from different backgrounds, but in the way they interpret the world around them. Few of the writers here – though I can't speak for individuals, only for the overall impression – would be likely to spout patriotic anthems, though all are intensely aware of the implications of being identified as Australian. This label, to the overseas reader, is most often associated with the geography, topography, and geology of the land, certain clichéd cultural icons, and a few signifiers from television (location for *Survivor*, the Olympic Games, the place where backpackers are murdered), but to the Australian writer it is loaded with contradictions and ambiguity. (2001d, p. 8)

The expression 'one nation' has particular resonance here, since the official political party of Australia's far right is called One Nation. This party is about exclusion of Asians, of refugees (as is the present Federal Government itself), and segregation (through assimilation by removing special rights) and suppression of indigenous peoples and their rights. In many ways, One Nation is just a personification of the Australian bureaucracy, and its inexorable drive towards the universal cliché of exclusiveness – that is, what differentiates Australians from the rest of the world. Instead of being part of a broader humanity, it has its own special label: Made In Australia.

The challenge has been to work outside this exclusivity, not only by aiming at the representative diversity in poetic styles (and, hopefully in the future, languages), but by clarifying how liberty of expression can be packaged to deny a liberty of day-to-day living. The marketing of the Bronzed Aussie, of the sports-mad high-achieving athlete bred in the wide-open spaces of Australia, is part of a campaign to market something different and special. But it begins with language. Australia is a multicultural nation (as opposed to the official 'Multicultural'), that is linguistically rich, despite trying to impose English on all its new citizens. Australian English is unique because of the pressure under which standard English is placed by this diversity. To track these language differences even within the official English of 'Australian Lit' becomes imperative.

In no place will you find such a volatile linguistic space as in poetry. Australians are generally proud of their poetry, or the poetries of their particular cultures within the idea of Australia, and poetry has a great significance spiritually, as well as pragmatically, to the indigenous peoples. It was also the vehicle (specifically through ballads) used by those forced to Australia through convict transportation (freedom songs, especially for Irish people). In the early part of the nineteenth century, 'Frank the Poet' (Francis MacNamara) wrote:

> I was convicted by the laws
> Of England's hostile crown,
> Conveyed across those swelling seas
> In slavery's fetters bound.
> For ever banished from that shore
> Where love and friendship grow
> That loss of freedom to deplore
> And work the labouring hoe.
>
> (1979, p. 39)

Poetry also played a part in building an identity separate from that of the colonising country. What was it that made Australia different? Marcus Clarke wrote in 1876:

> Our April bears no blossoms,
>   No promises of spring;
> Her gifts are rain and storm and stain,

And surges lash and swing.
No budded wreath doth she bequeath,
　　Her tempests toss the trees;
No balmy gales–but shivered sails,
　　And desolated seas.

Yet still we love our April,
　　For it aids us to bequeath
A gift more fair than blossoms rare,
　　More sweet than budded wreath.
Our children's tend'rest memories
　　Round Austral April grow;
'Twas the month we won their freedom, boys,
　　Just twenty years ago.
　　　　　　　　　　　　(1956, pp. 48–50)

So within these imposed categories, different forms of nation become different forms of expression. The problem comes when you attempt to collect them and call it 'Australian Poetry'. As with any other 'nation', the foundations of inclusiveness are shaky. To include is to exclude, to attempt to define is to imprison and usurp context. An agenda comes into play; a value-adding fetishisation of language, to suit a particular end. Originally I started these editing projects to bring to the attention of those in the English-speaking world a poetry (or, more accurately, poetries) that is in a constant state of flux, that is linguistically diverse and interesting, and that, because of the tensions regarding identity, was quite radical and revolutionary in its sometimes laconic or quiet way. This is not always easy to see in the 'official' anthologies of pre-1890s Australian verse, with their preponderance of traditional verse forms and attempts to force Australian English (or other Englishes) into an acceptable colonial-inspired model. But if you look more closely, there have always been poets testing the edges, from 'Frank the Poet' in the early nineteenth century, through the astonishing Lesbia Harford and Zora Cross in the early twentieth century, the hoax-poet Ern Malley, the dense and twisted beauty of Francis Webb in the 1940s and 1950s, on to the great innovators of the late 1960s – Michael Dransfield, John Tranter, Robert Adamson, and so on. All of these poets worked within English – but there are also Greek, German, Chinese and most other languages, with often nearly hidden histories of poetry in Australia.

Most significantly, the indigenous poetries of Australia have effectively undermined the primacy of English. Often under the threat of genocide, the astonishing song-poetry of these people has persisted, and adapted into an English-challenging poetry of connection between many different peoples. Also from my introduction to *The Literary Review*:

> Indigenous artists, sportspeople, activists, and members of the varied indigenous communities in general, live lives connected with notions of Australia, but also parallel and independent cultural existences. They deal with histories – and I mean this in terms of a European construct – of genocide, of having children removed and transplanted by law into white families (The Stolen Generation), of land removal, of 'economic' destruction (traditional food gathering, spatial and temporal associations, etc., devastated or denied), and operating within the framework of 'modernity', at considerable social and financial disadvantage. Kim Scott, Samuel Wagan Watson, and Lisa Bellear, write out of this 'history'. (2001d, p. 7)

Furthermore, the representation of poetries under the cloak of nation often goes hand-in-hand with overlooking spoken and 'sculpted' poetries. The marking of the body, sand-painting, rock-carving and painting, and the corroboree and ceremonial song-cycles are usually written out. Indigenous traditional song-cycle poetry in Australian anthologies has often been used without permission of the custodial peoples, and via transliterations that do not respect original meanings and spiritual significance. Appropriation becomes the key to anthologising in this context. To build 'nation' out of the theft of often-oppressed peoples' cultural identity is deplorable, and easily done. And it is done with every anthology of nation, as earlier times are plundered to validate and define the modern nation and its geography. The English historical anthology that utilises traditional ballads does a similar thing, especially when the material is translated out of medieval languages, and the desolation of Scots or Irish or Welsh (and many other) poetries by the anthology of nation (Britain) is a standard publishing pastime. One does not have to think hard about American anthologies to find the same thing.

What goes out is a packaging of culture that is portable and recognisable for those we wish to influence. And that is the point. With good intention, I might try to bring an awareness of the diversity and organicism of poetry in the landmass known as Australia, but in reality help suppress that diversity. Surely poetry is to challenge the way we receive information, to make us question how and why we perceive language in the way we do. But to collate and market is to control, to remove poetry's energy. Individual pieces might surprise and inform us, but the conversations implied by the anthology also constrain. To challenge this, I have attempted to create alternative conversations, to show the disjunctions and discomfort along some of the seams, to make the conversations vigorous and demanding. I am often asked why I mix 'innovative' and more traditional work, why I bring cross-genre pieces into the poetry environment. The more one can challenge the categories, the more one respects the fact that poetry is part of a resistance, as much as an engagement with what is. It has a political role that should subvert the expectations of the reader ('I want something that tastes of Australia!').

In 2002, in New York, I participated in a programme at the UN for World Poetry Day. A lot of useful dialogue came out of this, but one of the things that disturbed me was a net-project presented by some participants to represent all nations of the world with their own poetry sites, under the umbrella of an international festival site. The notion sounds a good one, but all poetries were to be translated into English, adding fuel to the argument about the imperialism of English (a universalising language). Yet more disturbing for me was that no matter how much I challenged this, no space would be created for those without nation or who reject nation. On requesting that such a space be created (again), I received the following message from one of the organisers:

> Thank you for your suggestion. But we do not think such a special domain will be necessary. We use the division in countries for practical reasons. On the website itself this division will not be as prominent as you might think. For example language will also be an important entrance to poetry and/or information about poetry ... We seek to mix the poets and the information from different countries as much as possible. The concept as it is now, already includes poets in exile, refugees, poets who are against nationalism. They will resort under their native country or country of residence. Their poetry will speak for itself. (Personal communication, 2003)

The problem is that the 'practical reasons' are why the oppressions exist in the first place. We must recognise that poetry packaged in terms of nation contributes to the conflict between nations, becomes a pawn in creating prejudices and separations. The most apparently apolitical poet is immediately made political when used in this way. What about the poet who is without nation, or in exile, and writes about the beauty of a flower, without any overt political message? Is he or she labelled as, say, supporting the country of his or her oppression just because the poem does not say: 'my' Nation did this to me? It does not necessarily announce directly, and only within the context of distancing or rejecting national origins does it take on a different overt meaning.

Two projects with which I was involved – a special 'Culture and

Place' issue of *The Kenyon Review* (2003) (which I co-edited with its editor, David Lynn), and a special contemporary 'pastoral' poetry issue of *TriQuarterly* (2003) (co-edited with Susan Stewart) – both seek to break down the borders, to look at the way nation is frayed by cultural affiliations, divisions, and movements. The poet from the space known as the United States sits next to the poet from the space known as Lithuania, the essayist from Tasmania with the essayist from India. They speak out of and across ideas of nation, through music and geographies, investigating the language of difference without the need purely to validate and confirm a specific identity that sets them apart. Difference, diversity, and undercurrents of change. This communicating between regions through international dialogue is what, in the past (from 1997 onward), I have called 'International Regionalism'.

Notes towards netdeath and the loss of page style: working 'off the page'?

Shortcuts (as per Robert Altman?) (*Short Cuts*, 1993) are no way of making life less complex. If, in the glimpse, destiny can be observed and ascertained, then the time between such cuts is inconclusive. In reality, we are given nothing, just incidents and their implications. The prologues are suggested, traced, and incremented. Poetry works in the same way. The threads that fill the space-limitations of the electronic 'page', the message quota, and archival space, are shortcuts. They slice into each other, run for a while, morph into another argument. They are quick and fragile. When asked, back in the early days of the 'British-poets' email discussion list, whether or not archives should be preserved, I said absolutely not. My reaction is probably archived somewhere. I'll find it. The writing will break here:

> Now, this is a healthy move. De-archival! Electro-dissolution. Yes!
>
> Best,
> JK

The writer Alison Croggon felt the same way; most did not. Here are the list-manager's eventual conclusions:

> By popular demand, Mailbase have agreed to maintain the Britpo Archives indefinitely. Nothing will be deleted. So every halfbaked thought, every correction, every second thought, every badtempered riposte which seems so witty at the time, is there, in its linear glory, for future phds to pore over ... RC (Caddel, 1998)

When I started 'poetryetc' (1998), on the listbot list server, I maintained the archives, keeping them open to the public to create dialogues external to the list, then closing them to non-members because of spammers taking information, and then finally altogether because of agendas of sabotage on the part of undeclared list members. Proof of identity, closing down and restarting – the variations multiplied. Those early archives from 'poetryetc1' and 'poetryetc2' still exist. Sitting there, unused, on listbot. At times I have had plans to salvage them, but just do not go through with it. For the reasons mentioned in my message to 'British-poets'? Or out of a strange respect for 'literature'? I would not destroy a notebook of someone's poems found in an attic. But these archives are in limbo, and the dialogues they contain, having moved on, are in limbo. They have suffered what we might call a netdeath. Interestingly, if you search for 'netdeath' on the web, you'll most often come up with the Hunter S. Thompson fan page and the Net Death Hoax – the rumour of Thompson's premature demise. In the realm of Gonzo, this seems as fitting as anything else.

'Netdeath' is not in any direct way derived from the language of Erich Fromm, but it might seem convenient to create links to an analysis of the mechanisms for escape from freedom that Fromm isolates: authoritarianism, destructiveness, and automaton conformity (1969). In each of these categories, comparative models with regard to net usage might be established. Fromm writes in his introduction,

> Although this book is a diagnosis rather than a prognosis – an analysis rather than a solution – its results have a bearing on our course of action. For, the understanding of the reasons for the totalitarian flight from freedom is a premise for any action which aims at the victory over the totalitarian forces. [p. viii]

The net, under its guise of capitalist individualism, is as much a 'category' of totalitarian escape from freedom as any of the categories Fromm named. Netdeath is a stasis that is an escape, of sorts. It is only partial escape, and exists between escape and freedom. It is a gesture; it is notional. Almost a paradox: a symptomatic response to oppression dressing itself up as freedom. We must be wary: apparent freedoms often turn out to be different versions of control and subjection. Poetry can be a freedom rather than an escape, but the environment in which it operates might push it one way or another. Private or public escapism ...

'Poetryetc' moved from listbot to mailbase, and then moved with other mailbase lists to jiscmail when mailbase closed. The list is thoroughly archived now. The archives are open – many people follow discussions without becoming members, or join when a thread appeals to them, often leaving when the thread is 'finished'. So, archives as participation. Those who have been with the list from its inception know that there is a core of dialogue/s out there that work as pre-text to present discussions. The dynamic might change again – the present archives being electronically dissolved ... What are the implications of such an act? A freedom to be unconstrained by records, proof? Such an act would be met with strong opposition. A desire for restraint, for precedent. For confirmation?

It is assumed because one engages with the net that one admires 'technology', or rather, 'the technology'. This is not always the case. I do not admire the web. I do respect community, and subversions of centralisation through fragmentation and dissemination. I believe 'information' should be available. But the web is as much about the page as the book is – it has just changed the perimeters, the spatiality. The nodal points have increased in number, the possibility for variations on a theme are broader. Genre barriers are easier to cross. From a creative and even political/cultural/social/point of view, these are all positive qualities, but as Cheryl Buckley, in her essay 'Made in Patriarchy: Theories of Women and Design – A Reworking' (1999), notes:

> Using Adrienne Rich's term 'the politics of location' to theorize the specificity of female subjectivities, Rosi Braidotti argues: 'The politics of location means the thinking, the theoretical process, is not abstract, universalized, objective, and detached, but rather it is situated in the contingency of one's experience, and as such it is a necessarily partial exercise. In other words, one's intellectual vision is not disembodied mental activity; rather, it is closely connected to one's place of enunciation, that is, where one is actually speaking from.' (p. 115)

The hyperspatial nature of the linking of quotes and texts says more about the way language is used within its own terms than it does about its medium of presentation. The page should be treated with suspicion – its iconic solidity questioned. The text as written feigning authority. The net presents the same problems. As advertising and commercialism consume it, the irony – of the scroll, of the link, of the coding that hides the true marks of the text as it really is (the symbols that encase, say, a poem, that in reality make it a different poem, or an alternative poem) – has been lost. Questions of authority and – given the ease of circulation – of dissemination, authenticity. Politically, for an anarchist, this might seem enticing. But it is not if people accept it as a truth, if they refuse the irony. That is choice. Or is it?

Consider this from Derrida:

> There is, as everyone knows, a poetics, a tradition and a genre, a thematics of smoking. One day there appeared a sort of journal, Poésie 1, that presented itself as an instrument in the fight to defend poetry. Its first issue proposed an anthology of poetries of tobacco. It bore the subtitle 'Poets and Tobacco' and contained some sixty classical and modern texts; but its principle title marked in an ingenuous way the extent to which the poetics of tobacco does not expend itself at pure loss and above all does not let itself be disseminated in smoke. This title was: 'La Poésie ne part pas en fumée (Poetry does not go up in smoke)'. Indeed, in this case it goes up so little in smoke, it keeps itself and keeps itself so well from going up in smoke that on the back cover there is an ad for Gitanes Internationales and, on the title page, the editors thank Seita (the French national tobacco company) for its support: 'We thank the Seita, whose help, whose dynamism, and whose wealth of archival documentation allowed us to produce this special issue of Poésie 1.' (1992, p. 113)

The rest of the above paragraph is a treasure, which one may track down in the bookshop – or on the net, as the original or in some translation of varying quality. The relationship between poetry and smoking is similar to poetry's relationship to the net. And both cause death. By lung cancer, throat cancer, mouth cancer, heart disease ... or by netdeath.* The poem on the screen becomes text, which is not necessarily undesirable; in fact it is desired by many. Imagined audiences are created, and the poem, regardless of intent, becomes its own signified. There is a new thematics of poetry. What has not changed is the page. The net does not take poetry off the page; it just increases the debt, ironic or otherwise, to Gitanes and their brothers. I do not say sisters, because like the tobacco company and the book, it is made in patriarchy (nonetheless a problematic word in its potential erasure of difference in women's experiences). Safe spaces for women there might tenuously be, but the need for those in the first place says it all. The net is gendered, and no matter how many more women than men might use it, it comes out of a discourse that at its base is oppressive. The poem on the page is not the liberator it might be. The screen is a finite space, as is the paper page. These are the limitations we must avoid if poetry is to break male dominance. The scroll is only an illusion of change.

In an email exchange I had with the artist Ruark Lewis, he noted that

---

* Extending the analogy, our bodies die but out genetic material might be preserved, with or without our knowledge. In a similar way, our net movements and textualities leave vestiges, shadows, and trails (exhaust).

he would prefer me to be working across the landscape, instead of the vertical. This makes sense to me. It means spreading across pages, across pages on the screen – lateral rather than vertical scrolling. Foldout books? Screens next to screens? Of course, it means more than this. Poetry should be taken off the page literally, it should become (or be becoming) part of the 'environments' it works through. Through the streets, floating in the pool, spread out in the sand. Moving away from the literal, there is a conceptual space worth recognising here. It has nothing to do with 'technologies'. The moment a medium becomes prescriptive, the moment it becomes a repository for achievement and replication, it loses integrity. This does not mean the poets/writers/artists/conversationalists and so on have lost integrity, but the space is compromised. That is what social interaction is, a process of compromise and adjustment.

'Poetryetc' has been through many phases – at the time of writing this, it has a four-person editorial team, apart from myself. We collaborate on ideas to 'stimulate' discussion, to make it more than a conversation, or space for simultaneous alternative conversations whose crossovers create 'cyberspatial' text, hybrids that might or might not prove fertile. The deterministic language here *is* ironic. The list, in reality, is linear, and no matter how many forms of indexing or multi-directional movement are created in the process of archiving, it remains linear. The language itself might reject linearity, but the package is linear. Technology strives to overcome this linearity – virtual, three-dimensional, depth of field – but it is still confined to the sensory limitations of human perception. But poetry never was – it has always been about containing and breaking out of these confinements. It is a paradoxical use of language that has never been confined to the page, and neither will it be to the screen.

The page is decoration rather than a field, the screen is style. These definitions are reversible. Plenty of other catchwords work as well. And maybe style and decoration are 'necessary'. But confinement is death, and the page wizard is solid, even with glitches, and the computer virus is solid, and the flawed software is solid as well as the patch that repairs it. The nicotine patch, the pseudo-solid, the placebo field. Netdeath is the rejection by text of the materialism that makes it. The archives hang there, mimicking stasis. As vulnerable as the book is to fire.[*] Lost in the attic, it burns undiscovered, but there.

---

[*] Vulnerable indeed: since the time of writing, Listbot discontinued their free service and with short notice deleted the entire Poetryetc archives based on their server. Unless they exist in vestigial form, these messages are now gone.

Thinking landscape rather than portrait here ... of ash and flow. Let's undo it all: linguistic disobedience.

Consensus

I have talked about the nature of prefatory remarks (page 70). Extending this, we can see that it could also be a warning: for a preface prefigures a conclusion. And if we are looking for conclusions, for closure, we are sadly misguided. A conclusion would be absolutism: the consequences would be narrowness and inclusivity. Our responsibility is to question, to open our discussion to a wider audience, to create a space for poetic dialogue. We must accept that we will create nothing more than a preface, that the main text is unreachable, that it will always elude us. And this is desirable.

I would like to suggest an expression pertinent here, one I have referred to earlier: international regionalism. If globalism is about ironing out the differences on the level of the international marketplace structures and bureaucracy – an -ism driven by a lust for markets and profits – international regionalism is the opposite. It is the process of opening international lines of communication while respecting regional integrity. Difference is good, desirable, and not the individual's to negate outside his or her own self and community. The world wide web has been friendly to international regionalists – one can retain a sense of place physically, and enter the international source of the net. But how international is it? Most people log on to sites in one language, and though all or most national languages have a presence, many dialects and hybridised tongues do not. And languages change and evolve; the movement is significant. How does the net cope with this? Of course, in itself, it does not. It is without ethics. Protocol, and the laws of individual countries and international law, might restrict certain contexts of availability, but ultimately it is the individuals, communities, groups, governments, religions, and so on, that constitute and direct it. The boundaries between different spaces are highly fluid – filters and firewalls are nominal infrastructural control. English is it at the core of the web – the colonising language to beat all colonising languages has found another power vehicle. Should we be wary of this? It goes hand in hand with decisions made on a global level within the United Nations and its affiliate organisations. Specific languages carry specific proto-cultural agendas. The international regionalist is aware of this, and moves through language barriers. I am not suggesting a hyperspatial Esperanto, but I am suggesting a non-monolingual approach to the issues of cooperation, sharing, and understanding.

International consensus* is a variable in its effects. It can be oppressive, as in the case of the sanctions against Iraq, which worked only in part in placing pressure on the cruel regime of Saddam Hussein, but worked in entirety in oppressing the people, when it served the interests of the majority to isolate and destroy a minority. It can be selective, when the environment is contaminated by greed and profit, such as the selective whaling ban that sees whales taken for research ending up on commercial production lines. It is also exclusive – recognised nation states having the only say, or cultural minorities having their say diluted through the process of departments, representatives, and collective voices. More optimistically, consensus can be used to insist a wrong is put to rights, or that the hypocrisy of one of the above examples might be put right. In Lyotard we read:

> the principle of consensus as a criterion of validation seems to be inadequate. It has two formulations. In the first, consensus is an agreement between men, defined as knowing intellects and free wills, and is obtained through dialogue. This is the form elaborated by Habermas, but his conception is based on the validity of emancipation. In the second, consensus is a component of the system, which manipulates it in order to maintain and improve its performance. It is the object of administrative procedures, in Luhmann's sense. In this case, its only validity is as an instrument to be used toward achieving the real goal, which is what legitimates the system – power. (1984, p. 60)

Accepting that we should be suspicious of any declaration of a specific number of possible outcomes – two in this case – and also of any text that qualifies with 'men' instead of 'men/women' or 'people'; it is worth considering this statement carefully. If we are to accept the expression 'dialogue between cultures', which originally came out of the marginal-

---

* I differentiate between grassroots consensus (say, within an anarchist collective) and sovereign states' tendencies to majority and 'rough consensus' in international forums where not all parties necessarily agree, and where some parties might well 'vote' out of political expediency that in fact goes against their own interests and beliefs. In making such decisions, representatives of these states push towards decisions that might influence other 'outcomes' in other contexts more suited to their interests; they may also, of course, be coerced into voting against their own interests without return. All hierarchical power structures make participants complacent and more willing to agree with / concede something they might not morally or pragmatically value. Of course, such dilutions of consensus also take place at grassroots levels. Anyone who has been part of a collective will know that one often makes decisions that go against one's interests, and even what we might believe the group's interest to be. Hierarchical power structures in collectivist environments rear their heads in numerous ways.

ising and culturally insensitive 'dialogue between civilisations', then we share territory with the point Lyotard makes about dialogue between individuals, or their representatives, and free will and knowing intellects. We are aware of the conditions of language and the social and cultural environments in which we operate. The dialogue is framed by variables that are recognisable. And our aim in coming together from various parts of the globe is to discuss issues relevant to language, to poetry, to the validity of 'presenting' poetry to an international or internationalised audience. We will attempt to find points in common and reach consensus, to mark the page, to mark space with our shared goals. I am sure we would all agree that the outcome of such a course of discussion and epilogics is desirable.

However, we must be wary that the second possibility is not in fact the outcome. In some ways it is the more likely. We talk about co-ordination, advocacy, missions, marketing, fund-raising, implementation plans, and reports to the Secretary-General of the United Nations; we talk about an internationalism using the net that relies on the sponsorship by countries operating within the selective consensus of self-interest, of profit, and the corporate colonisation that is globalisation. If not, we are at least skirting these territories. We run the risk of becoming that instrument that legitimises, which reinforces power structures we might wish to challenge as editors, as poets and writers.

A poet is not necessarily going to challenge a power structure, but I feel strongly that to evolve an ethical consciousness, we must place pressure on language, encourage its growth. It is clear that I feel the poet is obliged to challenge the centrality of the state, to challenge controls over free will and intellect. But these expressions themselves are the product of 'Western Civilisation' – of a culturally appropriative machine, a religion absorber, a product substituter, and above all else, a systemiser of patriarchy.[†] Most poetry canons are the extension of patriarchy. The poem is the body inscribed with codes of conduct. The four-line rhyming stanza, the Petrarchan sonnet, all control the corporeal shifts of information. We are obliged to test these forms – not to reject them, which would lose control of context, but to challenge and reinvent them, recognise them for the controlling forces they are. Han-shan, poet of 'The Cold Mountain', knew this twelve or thirteen hundred years ago, despising 'regulated verse'. The poems of this Buddhist monk recluse (1990) were collated from the page that is the tree, the wall.

[†] The word patriarchy here is used only to mean 'the rule of the fathers', and not as part of an arasure of difference among experiences of women worldwide, mentioned earlier as a difficulty associated with the term.

Language is a most effective colonising force when used aggressively, but it is also a most liberating force. To articulate is to define self and community. As poets we should place pressure on language, to undermine it at the points where it has become a control factor. This is 'linguistic disobedience'. My call: rehabilitation, prevention, and a linguistic disobedience.

If we are aiming to utilise poetry as a means of cultural dialogue, we must consider its liminality – where it genre-shifts into prose, into other forms of expression. To isolate this dialogue to 'pure' poetry, if such a thing exists, is to close off any number of possibilities. It is also culturally disrespectful: the poetic unit differs not only between languages and cultures, but also within languages and cultures themselves. We should also consider the place of visual art and music in this exploration. If we start prioritising art, it becomes just another commodity fetish.

To develop an international web portal for poetry, as discussed at the World Poetry Day held at the UN, is to open the possibility of religious and cultural offence. The words that liberate for one people may oppress another. The possibility of reply, of dialogue on the site, should be created. Nothing should be closed off. Copyright, for example, might be the writer's only defence against a loss of income and exploitation for a morally offensive purpose, but it is also the straitjacket that helps maintain and legitimise the system Lyotard notes above. To control language is to empower oneself, the group, the nation, and increments of that. But to share and give language, to exchange language, is to create something far more respectful and liberating.

Apart from issues of respecting regional and personal integrity, the issue of how publications and ventures are funded is significant. As someone who deeply objects to the monetary market economy, I would ideally like these processes to be driven by good will, exchange, and community. Of course, this is just not going to happen. It is not the world we live in – yet, at least. My vegan anarchist pacifist small-community barter-based hope is certainly not immediately at hand, though when one thinks about it, it is surprising how many communities within oppressive state structures still manage to operate in such ways in actuality, disguised by a veneer of participation within the nation. Anyway, given that money is going to be a factor, we must consider what kind of funding we can attract, and what kind of funding we want to attract.

The present Australian federal government's treatment of indigenous peoples in Australia is reprehensible – I certainly would not fund a dialogue using their money. Neither would I personally knowingly take money from companies exploiting animals. Some of my readers might. Is this a consensus question, with its obvious exclusivity, or is it a recognition that internationalisation is only achievable through an ongoing dialogue, a community of links? There are major net spaces that bring together different literary journals, political and ethical groups, religious groups and so on. Maybe the word comparative could be used here. Do we want a controlling centre, or do we want many smaller centres, or better still, a series of fragments that are greater than the whole, that never really add up but are constantly discussing, disagreeing, exploring possibilities, accumulating small outcomes as an ongoing process?

The group, linguistic innovation, and international regionalism: prelude to the preparation of a group manifesto

A community of hybridity is evolving at Kenyon College, Ohio, USA. Both internationalist and regional, the group maintains concerns for cultural respect and independence, without censorship, while appreciating that context informs the relevance and nature of this 'free' expression. To create links, but to respect the integrity of the individual, and other groups that individual might 'represent' in the moment of collaboration.

Theory classes, prosody classes, and so-called creative-writing classes are inseparable, becoming increasingly blurred. Who can separate music and musicology, art and architecture from the experience of poetry? We no longer trust our 'selves' to control our lines of expression, and have allowed language to assert itself. The implications we codify are not lost, but re-emphasised. Our intent is displaced by the intent of the reader. There is nothing new in this, but the concerted effort of the group to speak through and among each other is generating interconnecting projects, interconnecting projections of the individual voice.

We attempt to identify and consolidate our own 'voice', but also to bring this into question. Collaborative exercises and compositions, performance and presentation, cross-genre writing, editing, and the fetishisation of the manuscript are ongoing nodal points of our investigation. It is all part of an evolving, organic 'poetics'. Individual compositions are secondary to the formation of a group poetics, through which individual voices might be clarified. What we take into group is text, not a set of separate masterpieces.

Two points in particular are rejected from Olson's projective verse manifesto:

(2) is the *principle*, the law which presides conspicuously over such composition, and, when obeyed, is the reason why a projective poem can come into being. It is this: FORM IS NEVER MORE THAN AN EXTENSION OF CONTENT. (Or so it got phrased by one, R. Creeley, and it makes absolute sense to me, with this possible corollary, that right form, in any given poem, is the only and exclusively possible extension of content under hand.) There it is, brothers, sitting there, for USE. (1997, p. 240)

Form is of the unconscious and generates its own meaning. This may not be desirable, but seems inevitable. Shape is an integral component of form. Even spontaneous or automatic writing will have shape, no matter how randomly it seems to manifest itself. The shape of the page, the topography of the surface of writing will restrict content – form will manipulate or inform the processes behind the presentation of content. The use of language is indicative of experience and experience is encoded with encryptions of form. We spend our lives accepting, challenging, or adapting systems of forms. Form can create content. The second point we reject:

> Now (3) the *process* of the thing, how the principle can be made so to shape the energies that the form is accomplished. And I think it can be boiled down to one statement (first pounded into my head by Edward Dahlberg): ONE PERCEPTION MUST IMMEDIATELY AND DIRECTLY LEAD TO A FURTHER PERCEPTION. (1997, p. 240)

The interconnectability of things is undeniable, but the nature of perception is changeable, within the moment. The self is the self's unreliable narrator. Explication lies outside perception as much as within its field of content, or activity. Marginalia, lacunae, the liminal. The potential of language is predictable, but never quantifiable. Its decay is its resurrection.

The poem is 'defined' by a combination of rules and slippage. The rules are:

1 A poem is a translation of the unutterable, exists between speech and writing, and is potentially close to thought. It has anchor points – references that will work outside the authorial perceptions, speak across boundaries: cultures, class, prejudice. A proper noun, a noun ... an idea that has through cliché become concrete. A verb that denotes activity beyond the meaning of the word. It sounds, it echoes out of the activity of the body. And error zones – those ambiguous points where referentiality collapses or is displaced, or

just uncertain. Where meanings can be rebuilt and certainties replaced. We are never sure what we see is true, and our position re this seeing is fluid. The voice is of the group, of the other, the voice of self is constantly in denial. This paradox drives the poem. Linearity suggests the trimming of excess, the programming of translation. But this is a deception: the line is not the measure of the poem; not even the word is. The moment before articulation, the suggestion is the measure of the poem. It is biological, it is chemical.

2   Slippage from linearity/end-stopping into persistent enjambment, the hybridisation of shape, is the accompanying action. We see the poem as a shape, as shapes conversing. The poem turns within the word, within the line, within the form as a whole. Point, counterpoint.

We are conscious of the potential political, social, and cultural effects arising out of the production of the poem text. We read the poetry as readers, not as manufacturers. Slippage will take meaning away from intent, but possible interpretations will be considered, and the code made more complex to cope with this. The point of 'disinterest' will be furthered as much as possible. This is not the paternalism of the author, but the concern and investigation of textual implications of the reader. Accepting always that language is greater than the sum of our selves, of the group, of all those participating in the conversation. Awareness and control are different factors.

A number of points have arisen out the investigative process; more will be added:

1   To record observations as data: names of plants, spatial observations (a fence, a house across the highway and river, an Amish buggy heading into town behind a postal van where the highway split the forest, and so on), the individual's relationship to this data ('being a city person it was the red roof of the house that interested me', say, more than the deer tracks), and then a consideration of what the recorded words mean on the level of language. From something as trivial as a pun on 'red' through to more complex considerations on etymology and the politics of representation.

2   What does English mean in the mid-West, or in Bangalore, or in the wheatbelt of Western Australia? Among which family, which community, between which families, which communities? The prevalence of certain expressions and 'ways of saying' things in the mainstream press, on television, the radio? We are extending the

idea here, but that's what comes of the collaborative process – we pick up registers of concerns and critiques and play them out further. Gender of observation and presentation become an imperative dynamic – the words hybridising, even trans-sexualising across the group until the certainty of persona, voice, and authorial integrity become blurred. Who reads it, how it is presented, make differences.

3 During an incursion into the forest we ask the group to be conscious of the two fundamentals of landscape theory – 'prospect' and 'refuge': that is, what can be seen and why, and what is hidden and why? We use nature as a refuge, but we might destroy it out of fear, to ensure our lines of sight. A simple principle that works its way into the texts within the materiality of the poems, these are places to be seen or places to hide. The landscape becomes the text, and vice versa. We use the word 'text' consciously here – maybe what we are creating is poetry as a separate field of engagement between the said and the unsaid, bringing the empirical and the spiritual into question?

4 To see poetry as a translation process. Looking for varieties of dynamic equivalence and placing them under pressure. Through journals and note-taking we are constantly engaged in this process of 'collecting' material to bring to composition. To produce a piece of 'lyrical-I' poetry, where some real or imagined unified-'self'/unified subject centres the voice of the poem, directing the reader with certainty. To challenge this, to deconstruct it, to write against these certainties. Of course, the 'I' is such a highly nuanced concept that this opens transitional space for activity. The relationship between subject and object being constantly questioned.

5 An exercise: produce conventional poems of observation and experientiality. 'Feeling' poems, or 'ironic' takes on 'feeling'. Then go on to remove the self from the poem entirely. Quite literally. No consistent *I* or *we* or *you*.

6 Make intense use of enjambment, parataxis, and disassociation, using the same base material. Expect more than a set of variations on the original – create sets of independent poems that share many of the same words. The words have different meanings, as the song goes. The micro versus the macro. Experience isn't going out travelling the world, getting smashed, having disastrous affairs, but travelling through the potentials of language. Words make their own meanings. The references can be internal to the poem.

7 Develop a lyrical narrative poem. A sequence of events told from a 'confident' narratorial position. A non-'lyrical I' piece using annota-

tion to create narrative – Bakhtinian dialogics with text and tale (1984). The annotations to discuss process within the poem. That is, a conversation between the marginalia and the poem itself. Of course, in truth, it's all part of the same poem, the same organic process. Deleuze and Guattari's 'body without organs' (1977), reterritorialising the poem itself.

8   Consider Coleridge's 'Rime of the Ancient Mariner' (1798/1996, p. 744). Think outside the frame of the text. The idea that most things happen beyond what is actually 'said' in the literal poem and any accompanying commentary. Group members might annotate each other's pieces – these annotations might or might not be then worked into the original. With the production of each new text, the participants write a hybrid poem text.

9   Group collaboration – a 'movement', as a group evolves an identity that is both compatible and contradictory. Interact at readings, absorb bits of each other. A volatile sense of community evolves. The group fragments, implodes. It feeds the group that collects the remnants.

10   Fragments and sequences are important in the process of collaboration, and in learning to shed expectations of solely personal achievement within poetry and poetics. The sequence allows for multiple voices with ease; it allows counterpoint and play within forms, and is convenient for collaboration in the sense of students compiling or adding to previous intact contributions. This can then be developed through fragmentation of the integral component parts and the interpolation of rogue or stray texts.

11   Questions of violation, intrusion, compatibility, fusion come obviously into play. From a gender perspective this can create tension and challenge the desirability of creating text itself. It is the same process that the text undergoes when someone of another gender, or another set of world views, engages with it anyway. It is just a matter of making the possibilities active rather than passive.

12   Consider Marjorie Perloff's essays (both 2001) on 'After Free Verse: the New Non-Linear Poetries' and 'Language Poetry and the Lyric Subject'.

13   The I speaks: object–subject relation. The tree is in the window, through the window the tree – the unified self says it with certainty. Parataxis, enjambment. The window tree limbs loosely I see wood glassily. Line length, metrics, and breath. Neat definitions. The line rolls on and on, written in sand. It blows away shortly after implying completion. It can neither begin nor end, being perfect in conception but decaying as it is written, inscribed. Plato would have a field

day. We do not want poets in this organisation.

14 To believe work moves through the many nuanced layers of the 'lyrical I/non-lyrical I' construct. To use sequences a lot: within the sequence a textual dialogue is created. Even the narrative destabilises itself through alternative relationships being set up between different sections, chapter, occasions, events. Numbered, asterisks, roman numerals: different languages. Annotations work in a similar way: dialogues within texts, within the frame of the page, across frames, between different surfaces. All poems are part of a larger project. A greater sequence of language usage. Nothing exists as a thing-in-itself. Efforts to disconnect create new connections.

15 Another way of approaching writing poems in a way that brings 'self' into question is to fragment the whole. Differentiate between fragmented poem in parts and the sequence. Sequence may be composed of fragments but doesn't have to be. Three general sequential types: (1) narrative, where sections work like chapters in a book; (2) lyrical/cumulative, where an overall picture is built by adding parts that share linguistic qualities and may offer different angles on the same subject matter, but don't tell a story (amplify, augment); (3) the conversational sequence, in which the disparate parts speak to each other 'dialogically'. One might also add another possibility – (4) the sequence of fragmentation in which the parts may seem to operate totally independently from each other, and may be broken down not only on the level of the line but on the level of the word itself. Narrative and lyrical/cumulative types can comfortably fit within the lyrical-I tradition though you could have non-lyrical variations on this. Third and fourth types lend themselves very much to the non-lyrical-I approach. Fragmentary sequence undoes narrative as much as creates a sense of movement. Parts of the whole don't necessarily add up.

16 Sequence can be hybridised in the same way as what was done with lyrical/non-lyrical I poems. A poem might be in six parts, some of which might be straightforward lyrical, some not, some hybrid. If these are put in a sequence, the reader will create the links.
Another characteristic of this nodal, branching pedagogy is digression. In the process of writing a poetics and fostering the growth of both individual poetics among group members and a group ethos, we find ourselves wandering outside the guidelines. It's all connected, but the outcomes are never entirely predictable. Discussing this issue of the 'lyrical I' via email, Marjorie Perloff notes: 'When people talk about unified lyric I, they don't really mean are you a coherent person, so to speak, but when you present

the "I" in a poem do you consciously try to distance yourself from your selves, so to speak? It's complicated. The best thing I've read about it is an essay by Antoine Cazé on the "fourth person singular"' (personal communication).

Cazé writes:

> The lyrical subject is not located fully in the empirical dimension, nor can it be reduced to the fictional (be it autobiographical). Rather, it is pierced through by multiple voices, thus clearly debunking the myth of Voice as expression and disseminating it as traces of presence (close to Derrida's analysis of writing, then). The lyrical 'voice', if it can still be called so, is an *alteration* (making other) of the subject which becomes what Maulpoix shrewdly proposes to call 'The Fourth Person Singular': 'It is finally reduced to a mere inflection of voice. Not quite the same and yet not quite another, it occupies the empty place, the place to which each of us aspires, that is to say the very place of voice itself as it constitutes an invisible link with the other, a coming out of oneself, as it signs and signals the most singular but remains however impossible to pin down, evanescent as long as it is not put down in writing.' (*Ibid.*, 160) The rhetorical construction of the subject is the foundational gesture of lyrical utterance. (no date, no page number).

18 This nodal feeding of the discussion will play into the formation of the 'next' group, into the creation of isolated texts by group members. It will form part of their own ongoing dialogues with their previous poems, their poems to be, and will feed the developing poetics of new participants. It will become part of the ongoing process of poetic collectivity – the group will continue in absence, the lyrical voice of the whole will accumulate fragments in which the inflection of voice will in turn be placed under pressure, testing the lyrical-I questionings of the previous incarnation of the group. The subject becomes the Group which is an utterance of its component parts. It is one possible Self, it is one possible empty place. Waiting to be filled, or for the emptiness to outflow?

19 Where possible, conversation with participants might be ongoing through email, letter, exchange of texts, of text, visual, and musical materials. Hybridising the movements from one zone to another, engaging with the problems of appropriation and infiltration. Poetry is always political.

20 Landscapes of Ohio rhizomically connect with the landscapes of the wheatbelt of the Avon Valley, the Fens of Cambridgeshire, the

jungles of Indonesia. A circumvention of quarantine? Of restriction? Challenging purity and sterility while protecting the regional. International regionalism. Mutual respect. A sharing of links. A hypertext between participants. The pedagogy becomes process, the voices are no longer influences but conversations. The lyrical I is sublime enough to shift on the vibrancy of utterance and the 'body language' of the words and poetic forms themselves.

21 The page is not a field isolated from the spoken. Performance and visual presentation create new languages – group and public readings, a developing awareness of how voice and persona work in the public space, and on the stage. Dramatic monologue, dramatic irony, persona as mask, and so on. A verse play is the distillation of this journey. The stage as decoration?

22 The appreciation of texture and layering in surface and adornment. To forget about surfaces is to forget the delicacy of environment – both textual and natural. To innovate, an understanding of 'tradition' is necessary. Explored in a critical light, set form becomes liberating. The appreciation of accent, intonation, context, and chaos in the reading and presentation of the poem will bring a new dynamism to metrics. The conscious deployment of substitution, the displacement of expected rhythms. We do not simply count, we fuse and mingle stress and unstressed syllables. Between syllables, stress levels fluctuate, and there 'meaning' generates. Thomas Wyatt, adapting the Petrarchan sonnet to English, was the greatest of innovators (1988, p. 344 onward). Skelton's doggerel is a rich zone of textual destabilisation and innovation – fresh and revealing (1983). Free verse has given way to tonal versification, and the vigour of noise in the line.

23 This said, subtle variation can often lead to the greatest change. The addition of a spondee in an anapestic line in one line out of five will jar the sensibilities as much as in every line. It will, of course, have different implications, and if we read across the stress differentiations within the feet, such declarations become dubious. However, on the surface level, variations will be read in this light. A declaration of duality, of the 'dual-coding' referred to by Jencks (cited in Portoghesi, 1983, p. 10) and many others in the context of postmodern architecture, is a good starting point.

24 The deployment of form for a love poem, an ode, an elegy, the capturing of a 'single' moment will contextualise that presentation in the same way that regional or national address might. We should be conscious of and work against and through this. Nation is totalising and might diminish the group and the self. Poems of national

celebration and praise, even poems of national loss, seek to be representative, even when critical – for they will be read in this way. The desirability of this will vary within the group, but an awareness that nation forms the primary discourse for presentation should be realised. 'Free' societies are only ever so free. We create fugitive meanings that will shadow the text, make even the surface seem one way to one reader, another way to the 'censor'.

25   Paolo Portoghesi writes:

> On the other hand, the end of prohibition in architecture is a conquest that brings the discipline into an area of linguistic freedom that all other artistic disciplines had either conquered without causing scandals, or had never lost so completely. Who would ever dream, for instance, of taking away the patrimony of spoken languages from modern literature, and abolishing traditional codes. Who ever berated Saba or Eluard for writing sonnets ... (1983, p. 10)

We might wonder if Portoghesi had ever heard of Ern Malley, and further question whether he places the reader in the same zone as the occupier of a building? The reader, assaulted by propaganda, reads contextually – gleaning furtive meanings if those meanings are against taste or desirability. Maybe this fugitive reading engenders revolutionary tendencies. There *are* restrictions in the articulation of difference. A love poem can incite change, and as such reading habits will be monitored and changed through the classroom, the media, within the municipality, the culture at large. The dominating cultural identity (the umbrella culture) of nation. The use of the word 'conquest' brings to mind John Crowe Ransom's discussion of R. P. Blackmur as a representative 'new critic' (1941, p. vii), and analysis of words in an Emily Dickinson poem. Blackmur (quoted in Ransom) notes the word 'renunciation' in the poem 'belongs to a special department of experience or contains in itself the focus of a particular attitude, a department and an attitude we condition ourselves to keep in abeyance'. He then notes that 'Only one word, *piercing*, is directly physical' in the poem fragment (an abstraction of context here), continuing 'something that if it happens cannot be ignored but always shocks us into reaction' (1941, pp. viii–ix). In this light, 'conquest' works as a cross between the two: the spiritual triumph of the ineffable (art/architecture) and the physicality of the victory (stone and metal ARE dangerous). The group is against 'conquests', and only interested in recognition and departures. The quote within the quote, the atmosphere of New

Criticism, is relevant but only as a source of reference and as a dialogic nodal point. As the genetically modified corn crops, pollution from cars, and the brilliant red cardinal on the maple bough outside the window that might only persist metonymically. This is praxis.

26 Metaphor is not juxtaposition but an attempt to reconcile differences. A resolution is not desirable.
27 To read against narratological 'devices' of order, duration and frequency. (Genette, 1980). Metaphor is the compaction, distortion, and irruption of 'time'.
28 Closure is registered in the opening lines of the poem – composition is ongoing and all poems are drafts. They read against beginnings as much as towards ends. The poem is intact despite extraction, fragmentation, distortion.

Intensivism

To examine something not once, but over and over from as many different 'angles' as possible.

To accept that such examination will be likely to create agendas outside the actuality of the object, scenario, place or identity being examined. The subject will invest the object with conditional, circumstantial, and contextual meaning.

That context is variable.

That 'politics' is the effect language has when experienced: language changes and provides momentum, even when repetitious. This is the political effect of poetry.

To accept the irony of constraint: systems introduced to convey meaning, intention, or effect (atmosphere) are an extension of social forms of control. The stanza, metre, the line are units of imprisonment. Form is to be used with an awareness of this implication. Language might work against form. The poem should undo itself in negotiating this contradiction.

The ultimate aim of the poem is liberation. It is the place of religion undoing religion: heaven and hell are modes of social control. Heaven and hell exist in all poems.

Poems can attempt to be machines of de-gendering.

Poems *are* generators. They are cybernetic and have a life of their own when being written, when read. However, they die without a host. Poetry is parasitic; at best, symbiotic.

To concentrate on as small a place as possible as an anchor point for a continuously expanding argument. That is, to see a world in a grain of sand, but also worlds beyond the grain of sand. To work locally, to be regional. To maintain or allow the possibility of 'international' lines of communication. To be international regionalists.

Language is only part of it, and the poem does not exist alone.

Pastoral Intensivism takes into account traditions of song and idyll, of rural celebration in the eyes of the invoked, and the political propaganda this is used as. In describing a very specific geography, even one that is devoid of 'nature', an awareness of the songs of place, the laws of the rural, or of the human in nature, will form an echo of the powers of description, of observation. Spirituality comes out of this; so does science.

The object is not merely a thing-in-itself. It is intricately connected as are all things in the observation of the apparently – on the surface – finite place.

Intensivist poetry has a tension, a dialogue between the writer and the poem, the poem and the reader, but most relevantly, between the poem and the subject material.

Not deep ecology, though the impact in this small place will be elsewhere as well. The impact is mediated by the poem, but not necessarily changed. Though without being didactic, the desire of the poem is to prevent negative impact. This is in degrees, and even textual interference is never desirable, but to observe without realisation of the consequences of being present, of remaining physically aloof though textually intrusive, is creating art for art's sake. Intensivism is everything that art for art's sake is not, though recognises that the process is always going to be caught up in this.

Intensivist poetry can have a symbolist effect, though not necessarily. Intentions coming out of the observed are the signature of each individual poet.

The design of the poem is always going to reflect, or reflect against, the observed. A structure that seemingly has no connection, no synthesis, that seems mere decoration, is going to create a dialogue between words and form that will generate focus. Apparent ambiguities and errors are generators of readings, of potential meanings.

The writing of the poem *in situ*, with memories adding layers to the text. All external noises and sensations – birdcall, a plane in the distance – becoming the text, or challenging the text, becoming synthetic with the poem, or at odds and creating points of juxtaposition. Such points might be metaphoric, but also create associations – metonymic stand-ins. The bird reminding one of a moment elsewhere, and with it an object of that moment. A hybrid of metaphor and metonym might form. The metonymic metaphor is the metaphor that stands for a metaphor prior to it, even following it. Order is to be disrupted – the poem is an entry into a range of times, though always with the realisation that consequences are felt in the pragmatic real-time.

Hybridisation is a tool, not an end result. It suggests that only through taking on a variety of linguistic values and registers will a desirable reassertion of identity be achieved. But with the small space observed repeatedly, humans are only one part of the equation, and hybridity will always be an occupation. It is not a solution, consequently.

The 'ego I' is a distraction. The lyrical-I, the lyrical self can only ever go through degrees of separation. It is always there – as soon as language is used, manipulated, thought. The lyrical self in the poem will always be contingent on its relationship to the observed: it is a manifestation of the observer, the observing, but its presence is defined by what is being observed. The 'how to' takes precedent over the 'who'. The so-called unified self is about how we deploy our observations, about a point of relativity. The more intensively we observe and rewrite the same place – altering and atrophying is what it was, is, and will be – the more the unified self seems an absurdity. The moment of stability exists in a time that is immeasurable – eternity is in the grain of sand, but only symbolically. As a working tool, the unified self is desirably unstable!

Saturation. Total immersion. The displaced method-acting of poetry. To document ...

Excursions and field trips. Other locations, small spaces interlinked, a network of comparisons, differences and similarities to highlight the specific space.

Words speak louder than action. Poetry is a statement.

Publishing volumes of poetry makes resources of the world's natural environment. How we publish poetry is relevant. The poem is an extension of our life choices; our life choices cannot be hidden by the poem.

Language does not exist itself alone, but can be manipulated to appear as such.

Poems are landscapes. Landscapes are the linguistic restraints of the natural. The intensivist seeks to undo landscape to liberate nature. The intensivist seeks to undo the landscape of poems.

To challenge hierarchies between poets, within poems. To be linguistically disobedient.

Hyperpoetics and the curvature of subsets

An approach
Poems by accumulation
The theme stated in the beginning of the poem existing as residue towards the end. No direct restatement of theme – and if so, as counterpoint (often ironic). For example, discussing light in buildings at the beginning becomes the luminosity of canola, the shock of a white wandoo, a haunting at the end of the poem. This is not (or no longer) a rejection of closure, but an embracing of distracted, digressive, or partial closure. The curve is part of the circle and not the plane, but in the set theory of the poetic curve, the plane is bent into the circle, and the circle broken and opened out such that it can include the plane (tangents) within itself.

Poetry is not about the words themselves. Words as a shell, a husk. It's what's inside the words – textually and figuratively – that's relevant to poetry. Words are always aleatory. Connections – articulations – come from within.

I saw a circle on the horizon – a close horizon yesterday. I think it will persist for a while. It is upright – vertical. Like the mouth of a cylinder lying on its side, but just a circle, a disc even. It has another side, but it might be reflection of this side, as we can't see it. I have become fixated on it. It is the poem.

The circle might be the lens of the eye. What is on this side might be projected upside down against its back surface, but the same happening within us, we see it 'the right way up'. It is real but what it casts or takes in, interprets, is not necessarily. Or not the reality we perceive. This is the poem.

Donald Hall differentiates between the poem and poetry when talking of Dylan Thomas in a memoir piece in his book, *Their Ancient Glittering Eyes: Remembering Poets and More Poets* (1992). He says that the poem is intact and complete but that Thomas most often accumulated poetry rather than poems. He cites stanzas that could be left out or substituted for another. The examples he cites are some of the best lines of Thomas's. We need all the lines. Digression and repetition increase the ways of viewing. They are endless. Poems are poetry and they and it are endless and cumulative.

The study at the back of the house is small and looks onto Walwalinj. The distance between the room and the mountain is vital: it curves downwards and lips up like an unbalanced bowl, and twists into indentation and heavy tree-growth and caves like a dented metal pannikin. At sunset, the high silhouettes and the lines curve and straighten. The room is a room within a room. There's a storage room – longer and narrow, then another door, and a cubicle which is soundproofed. It has an L-shaped desk in front of a large sliding window that starts a short way above the deskline, then breaks right at right angles. An L! There are shelves above the wall side of the L. Beyond the wall, a bedroom. The room has a variety of books and a few CDs and maps of the district on the wall. Close-up, detailed survey maps. One is missing – lost somewhere in America. It's of the place where the room sits. The view from the small room is immense, overwhelming – though the mountain curtails the view, smothers it. You can't see far but it's immense, though at around 1200 feet it's not a large mountain, only just one, but certainly the largest peak in the flat eroded wheatbelt. It is the summit of the Dyott Range. The lines from the room, its spatial architecture outside the earthquake-proofed steel frame and brick and gyprock structure with iron roof hit by lightning last year, are the key to poetry written within it.

The imagined, precognitive poem: poem as $\emptyset$. No set is a member of $\emptyset$. If an empty set exists, an empty poem exists: $\{\}$.

The poem is not empty but the set of the poem is empty until it has found its visual or verbal parameters.

The poem begins in the imagination as the empty set containing all boundary and interior points, making it both closed and open.

We might talk of the 'arity' of a poem. The number of parameters in the imagined poem is 0, therefore the arity of the operator (imagined poem) is 0: the 'preservation of nullary unions'.

The poem is closed once it finds expression on the page. It re-opens with each draft or configuration, but becomes closed once the words are read over, even if the reader returns to them or reconfigures through slippage or a text generator what s/he reads. The printed or visualised poem is closed because it is equal to its closure.

The possible parameters are n-ary: unlimited.

If the axiom of extensionality applies:

$\forall A, \forall B: A = B \quad (\forall C: C \varepsilon A \quad C \varepsilon B)$

then we might challenge it through the ur-elemental nature of the precognitive poetic word. Words are empty shells, and as imagined are gestures moving towards expressive meaning. Chemical, electrical, cognitive stored information, interact/react to make the empty set that will form as sets of words, of information to elicit reaction outside the composer. To equate or make equality between the ur elements and empty set a variation of the axiomatic extension might be desirable for the sake of logic, but is the 'flaw' through which metaphor forms within the empty set.

Axiomatics and articulation of the poem

Axioms of pre-poems break down with and within the axiom of regularity, or foundation axiom. Excluding its necessity, we can interpolate the likelihood of non-well-founded sets pre-cognitively arising. That is, hyper-sets that evolve out of experientiality, chemistry, spirituality, imagination (in their confluence). Given:

If $A \in A$, then $A = $ a non-well-founded hyperset.

Which leads to a positive set theory for the pre-cognitive poem, a theory allowing for the opening of sets which are classes whose topology is compact, that the 'closed and bounded' (finite experience, finite functionality of the machine of the brain) – that is, if its covers are held within a finite subcover. This allows for empirical limitation, but the infinite branching of the figurative that is eventually limited in language (though language suggests the opening of these nodal points in branching all over again – maybe the same, maybe different).

The articulated line is the eroded letter-morpheme-word-line that emerges from the precognitive merged with more eroded letter-morpheme-word-lines. Articulation is readily recognised across the long line, but is also present between syllables, even within syllables. A diphthong relies on the articulated. A caesura within a line is another form of articulation. The set of the line contains the fragments (or elements) of the precognitive as translated into the possible contents of a visualised set. This would seem to insist on the consistency of the axiom of regularity.

Poetically, there is not a contradiction in juxtaposing or making necessary the axiom of regularity and positive set theory. The slippage between precognitive and manifest (visualised, spoken) poetry demands concurrent and overlapping theories. There is curvature. The attraction and repulsion of 'ideas' or 'illuminations' or mental stimuli cause the pathways to the manifest to bend, to curve toward and away from each other. So much mental illness with the resultant inability to clear expression is poetic because of this.

The articulated line is the concurrent and juxtaposed presentation of alternative sets which share elements in common, are the same, but unique.

There is no necessary correlation to situation theory, of importing a situation to words per other words (properties/relations). Information is paramount to the formation of fragments to be articulated, but not the 'meaning' of poetry. Pre-cognitive poetry adapts meaning, but is not meaning. Meaning is translation and communicative. Poetry does not have to be communicative, even in its manifest form.

More curvatures
Roman Jakobson wrote:

> 'The poetic function projects the principle of equivalence from the axis of selection into the axis of combination. Equivalence is promoted to the constitutive device of the sequence. In poetry one syllable is equalised with any other syllable of the same sequence; word stress is assumed to equal word stress, as unstress equals unstress; prosodic long is matched with long, and short with short; word boundary equals word boundary, no boundary equals no boundary; syntactic pause equals syntactic pause, no pause equals no pause. Syllables are converted into units of measure, and so are morae or stresses ...
> Measure of sequences is a device which, outside of poetic function, finds no application in language'. (2004, p. 356)

This is patently untrue – unless it's for an imagined traditional reading of western poetry. It undoes with oral poetries that vary from speaker to speaker, as much as it undoes with interpreting the signs on the page. Syllables can be (and are most often) converted to units of measure, but this is obvious. In the formation of a poem, sounds and syllables do not necessarily match, and syllables don't form or are deformed. The poet imagines s/he selects the appropriate words and arranges them in the combination – the arrangement of communication. Measure of sequence is a manifest device, in which the curves have been forced into parallel lines of conformity. Hearers (or readers and writers) think they hear a poem because conformity suggests form and its artistry. We might listen across line breaks, we might fall from line breaks or get caught off or hang over their precipice; so can we within the syllable. In the syllabic poem we count syllables and count lines, but what are we counting with such certainty? The poet plays the manifest game by being conscious of his or her own limitations – but maybe the poem exists between the syllables, or by removing the spaces between words and reading against their combination. The articulated line does the job but might also be an unholy alliance. The effort required to haul the trailer focuses on the linkage – the coupling, the articulation. But there are numerous other linkages within the line, and they are equally relevant. Don't always look to the caesura, or even the word.

I once met someone who claimed to be an ex-lover of Jakobson's on a train going from Copenhagen to Paris. She was in her eighties, I'd guess. I was twenty and it was 1983. In a compartment full of teenagers drinking beer, I gravitated towards her. I drank beer as well. She took a few sips when it was offered. She was immaculately dressed and groomed. What do you do? she asked. I write poems. Might I see some. Yes, I have just had this booklet published: *The Frozen Sea*. You have talent, she said, and I wanted to believe her. I placed my head in her lap, and she stroked it, telling me of Jakobson and his love of poetry. Of his belief in poetry and poets. You will be a poet, she said. I wanted to believe her, I want to believe her now. I know that poetry isn't what we think it is, and we don't know how to read what it is we have translated from the curvatures of precognitive poetic space. She would be long dead now.

Treatise on rooms and windows

South...?

I have eyes in the back of my head. That's okay; at school I was called 'four eyes'. I can see out of the 'north window' of the house at the same time that I can see through the 'south window'. This is a large house that stretches east to west, a house of many windows. Facing north there are large feature windows and glass sliding doors, but the 'northern window' I focus through is that of a small room behind a store room. The 'south window' is actually the window of the library. There are a variety of rooms between these north and south windows, and they are not opposite each other in any way. Still, I maintain, I can see out of both simultaneously. Within both I am motionless, I am enclosed within their surface, though what is outside is also timeless, motionless, and includes all other points. I am of a set that contains itself, and this is the poetry I write. It is wheatbelt Western Australia. The farms that surround me – us – are primarily 'wheat and sheep', though some canola and cattle have come into the district over the last decade. The town is the oldest inland town in Western Australia. It is a nexus of dispossession, though that's not how most of the non-indigenous locals see it, of course. I wrote a book a few years ago in collaboration with the American fiction writer and editor David Lynn on 'The House'. The houses I utilised for that book were this one and the one in which I was living with my family in Gambier, Ohio. David wrote very short fictions, I wrote a series of poems. The book remains unpublished; we never really pushed for a publisher. I was interested in houses in Australian poetry, and I see I am far from alone in that. From a 'personal poetics' point of view, I am interested in the specific spaces of two rooms, looking out. In vistas and their contractions. I write on an old manual typewriter in the north room, and on a word processor in the south room. I write in pen in both. The house – this house near

York – was designed quite mathematically. I am becoming more convinced that, like music, poems are really maths, and that words can be dispensed with. I am looking for a different kind of nomenclature. But it all overlays, and that was always and will always be the case itself.

Over recent months I have been compiling a new poetics. A protopoetics that will never be anything but a prototype. That's part of this manifesto too (see previous section on 'Hyperpoetics and the curvature of subsets'), as with the poem 'Windows', referring to the north and south windows, and the spatialogue poem dedicated to Graham Nerlich (both poems are included as appendices, along with a letter by Nerlich engaging with some of the ideas posited in this book), and a few diary entries. There are no boundaries or borders outside the page to the diary entries.

West of the north window, about forty metres away … Sitting on a chunk of granite enclosed by 'missed' long stalks of wild oats rustling hyper-dry around me. Against my ear, like electrified cellophane, combustible but with a static so low it won't ignite from the friction. As emptied signs of a painting I'm in. Wind is picking up from the south-west. Warm. Unsettled. On the edge and brooding. A short-cycle cicada vibrating in the hydra-headed York gum behind me. The mountain – Walwalinj – Mount Bakewell – 'the hill that cries' – releasing its storm energy – pent up. No birds – no, there are a few songbirds. Disturbed singing. Broken, deleted. Odd willy wagtail – jiddy jiddy – on fence wire, pirouetting around the rusted barbs imposed by earlier 'owners', let fall by us to red earth, dust. Glare intense, my glasses and sight polarised.

Epiphany (extreme delusion of motion)
Fiercest storm here I *remember*. I am outside the south – library – window. Wongborel (across the valley, town 'cradled' between, the companion hill to Walwalinj – distraught and separated lover – named Mount Brown by colonisers) is being clawed and ripped up by fork lightning. The thunder is deafening – eardrum crushing. Hail and violent rain are stunning the corrugated iron roof, spray is whipped up off the gravel – I am as electric and wired as any moment since childhood when I was struck twice by lightning. I cannot delete language of tense and memory – I write *in situ*. Space expands, contracts. I pulsate. The verge of still birth. The epiphany. The showing. A double crack of thunder and an incendiary odour. I am on the veranda on the other side of the window, the looking-out-at as might be imagined. On this side, I could be destroyed. That's the (in)security of glass. The registers here are dull and manic. The sheep have few places to shelter. The wasps by

the window ledges have literally sealed shut their mud-earth chambers. York gums are buckling and branches separating. A ring-necked parrot is vaporised in the haze. Tumbleweeds rolling from no origins (I have searched for them outside high winds). Picked up before the storm, they are ploughed into earth and their fine machinery made capillaries, hair-roots. The setting sun peers through as a sick fog-like eye, to its close. Beige stubble won't resprout green afterwards – only still and false breathings there. Though new growth will come even on the damaged trees. It was the hottest day today in ten months. I am writing by the florescence of lightning – sky and ground elided. Wongborel has vanished. This is the southern view. I will struggle around the house – leeward, and view the north, Walwalinj, from the eastern wall.

Comparatively sheltered here. Walwalinj is just an outline, a one-dimensional drawing that's not even a silhouette. Ochre water is flooding the lower ground. Bees are latched to the rough surface of brickwork. The greens of the jam tree, York gum, and flooded gums, are caught between bandwidths. Windrows of uncollected hay are turning inwards, away from the show, the bloody viscerality of the pre-, the false, the still birth. The dog is terrified. The damage inflicted on the mountain by paraglider pilots and their crony farmer-mates is lost in the blur – only the high-up alpine wandoo scintillates. My mother has an escape plan in case of lightning strike. It can burn here even in torrential rain – I have seen it *before*. It haunts me. I look east, and distance is a grey blank calm, the aftermath of the storm approaching its beginning and never getting started. Over there. Setting itself up until lightning's hooks and jags say otherwise. All electrical equipment inside the house is shut down and unplugged, even the telephone – the interiority of the house outed to the acreage, the hectares, the 'block'. This is the country. There is a scale to it. It tempers sublimity. People *remember*. Other people – those close or distant throughout the district. This house is earthquake-proofed and storm-resistant and senses our lurid imaginations. It makes myths of us. Brings security to epiphany. Now – honestly – all light is golden.

Note: I have had constricted lungs, and now, after the storm, I can breathe freely. The house's Bachelardian 'intimacy' is a falsity – the intimacy is outside, beyond the windows, out in the risk zone where I was struck by lightning.

> All great, simple images reveal a psychic state. The house, even more than the landscape, is a 'psychic state', and even when reproduced as it appears from the outside, it bespeaks intimacy. (Bachelard, 1994, p. 72)

No: the intimacy is without, in the paddocks, in the bush, and we hide from it within the house. Hiding is not 'nesting'. Space is light and darkness; in the storm our darkness is fractured and altered by the branches and nodes of light. It is a living death. It is the house fully opened out. Thus the myth or belief or hype of 'God's House' ... God is shape. Curvature from and against which lightning cracks the bowl.

The hole
The storm has almost passed – a yellow and tungsten light, almost bright as burning magnesium at times, despite night. I am in the north room looking through the increasingly occluded 'hole' (almond trees in the foreground growing rapidly to cover the disc, the hole). Running sweat. It is beyond 'close'. I flood over book, seat, floor – I touch many points at once. My DNA touches many points I don't make contact with in terms of my corporeal self. The delineations of 'body'. Do I touch with 'being'? The storm has reconstituted and quickly contracts, disconnects, touches and withdraws in its many local spaces. Duration is measure, not time.

In *The Shape of Space*, Graham Nerlich writes,

> Now if we do think that space is problematic, but it is also clear that we must have spatial elements in our privileged language, then a great deal recommends topology as the geometrical part of the privileged language. The relation of one thing's touching another, of the material points of an object forming a neighbourhood of which each is a member, of the surface of an object enclosing these points and constituting the boundary of a contractible space which encloses them, are all very tangible, immediate and familiar to us from all sorts of experience with simple manipulation of objects (see Piaget and Inhelder 1956). (1994, p. 156)

I am sweating so much that multiple surfaces of this object – the pages of this book I hold, Nerlich's book – are stained. I lean back to prevent more run-off – it changes, blurs, my perception/s of outside, beyond the vertical blinds that cover the window of the southern room. Outside is dull/bright/dark light. The blinds are angled seventy degrees.

The hole is exit and entry point. It is formed by branches of York gums and the funnels of jam trees. It is a perfect circle, drawn with a compass of darkness. A thick outline. A disc. A mirror. Centrifugal. Tracy has also seen it – sees it daily. It is always there, if covered over a little. She verifies it. It is a few hundred metres away, across the stubble, the clumps of dead wood, low granite cairns. It is adjacent to the thirty-degree gradient of the hill as we look across it. A funnel, the barrel of a telescope. Through it, the light falls away into precipice.

There is gentle rain on the roof now. The remnant light is that shed by lightning in darkness. Purple, mauve, visceral though finished. Blue shifts under the west and the aftermath is there now rather than the east where it earlier suggested itself, where the storm is now blown and where I sheltered. Shelter. Will shelter.

I have drawn the blinds against what I can no longer see. I have drawn pictures of window frames and blinds and curtains for over twenty-five years. I have drawn – sketched – pictures – coloured them. I drew them for months in the Royal National Hotel, Bloomsbury, London. Pissing in the sink. Loss and return. I measured their frames imperially, converted to metric for here is where I measure them also before drawing. And all the hundreds of hotel rooms I have been in. I look through them to see here out of here, closed. I gradate. The northern view from the back-room study is the narrow small room at the end of the storeroom concentrated behind a door whose opening is half its width, vertical blinds there too opening out to segment the highest peak in the eroded, ancient Dyott Range. Angst and trauma at always seeing its abuse. I have even contacted the environmental protection agency, resorted to pragmatics within my umbrella anarchism. Anything to stop the damage. The rough drafts I type in there always focus the experience of looking out through the planted trees, through the old-growth trees of the uncleared laneway, gazetted to reserve and never opened, through hay and horse paddocks and the grazed liminal zone of jam trees and wandoo gathering at the impenetrable cleft, the dark fold that cannot be traversed that remains as intact as possible – sanctuary for bats, roos, small marsupials despite cats and foxes, birds inhabiting all heights of vegetation ... place of shapes overlaying shapes: polygons; quadrilaterals: triangles (isosceles, right ...), squares, circles, oblongs, rectangles, trapezoids ...

Mr. Dale's Journal of an expedition whilst exploring the country eastward of the Darling Range, 1830.

August 10th. Finding it impossible to make any further progress with our horses which were completely exhausted by their unusual exertions, and having secured them we left our tent pitched, considering them as a sufficient protection against the natives, none of whom we had as yet met with, and proceeded with two days' provisions to explore the left bank of the river towards its source, not deeming it prudent to be longer absent from our encampment than that time.

Recommencing our journey the medium course of which was South South-East we, in six miles, arrived at a remarkable range of hills (which I propose naming the Dyott Range in compliment to General Dyott the colonel of the 63rd) rising abruptly and almost perpendicular from their southern base and presenting a wall-like barrier to the river, they had a rich and verdant appearance and were clothed with grass to their summit, and moderately wooded with gum trees. At this spot we heard the natives whose traces we had been following this morning hailing each other at no great distance. We were fortunate this night in finding shelter from the rain which was pouring down in torrents, under a shelving rock, it was of considerable size, having the shape and appearance of the thatched roof of a cottage. In the neighbourhood of our Bivouac and for some distance around were large masses of granite; in one of these we discovered a cavern, the interior being arched and resembling somewhat in appearance the inside of an ancient ruin; on one side was rudely carved what was evidently intended to represent an image of the sun, it being a circular figure about eighteen inches in diameter, emitting rays from its left side and having within the circle lines meeting each other at nearly right angles. Close to this representation of the sun, were the impressions of an arm and several hands. This spot appeared to us to be used by the natives as a place of worship. (p. 7 of Battye Library transcription, provided to author in 2004)

I need not decode this and template against the hole, the imperialisms, the making a house and city of the land and distancing of the indigenous. Othering, primitivising, and ethnocentrism are common to most explorer-narratives of the period (or any period, it could be argued). Imagine it written ironically, which it wasn't, and it translates itself, translates the disaster that is the north window looking out, imagined and seen through the south window looking away from the Dyott Range.

The empirical view of centre that is the focus of 'my' window/s – the northern room actually part of a house extension going at a right angle, so going north–south in contrariness or in intersection, as point of the compass complete and complemented; the room added on to increase functionality and privacy: workspace and inspiration, a form of inseparation, with the walls (even) sound-proofed. The walls covered in maps. Between the north room and the south room, we live. South, we look into the wormhole loosening time space in its precise blankness; north, we look to the extinct volcano, core of the Dyott Range. Dale is yet to reach there. The sacred is visible to the north, tangible, tactile. You barely need imagine it. It is visibly tracked, parodied and mocked by paragliders swinging 'freely' in the thermals.

Open the vertical blinds again. Stray lightning flashes over Wongborel. Leaden. But dogs are starting to bark again, sound easily carrying the five ks from town. Cars are doing massive burnouts from gravel to bitumen – you can taste the rubber. Local police are saying such behaviour will result in temporary loss of vehicles and the cost of de-graffiti-ing the road will have to be covered by the perpetrators. No one is ever caught. I cross those fishtailings regularly, driving in and out of them, enclosures in which points are inside and outside, Euclidean broken down by distortion. Inside out.

The positives and negatives of seeing opposites reflected ...
The portal (south) and mountain (north) are mirrors. The specificity of direction regarding my windows is a false paradigm – in the north we peripherally find the east (making the window actually north-north-east and not precise to the compass, thus the rest of the house); in the south we find glimpses of the west. I see out of each the true direction, and the 'off course' ... and even these factors (members of the set) are interchangeable, or are one and the same in the abridgement of description. I look out one window and see around the curvature back into the other. Straightening the lines out, we look back to ourselves. Inside out of 'place'. The axis is/axes are crossed over by the fracturing of fork lightning, smothered or wrapped by sheet lightning. In *A Treatise on Time and Space*, J. R. Lucas notes,

> The symmetric and alternating groups provided two different, though linked, sorts of geometrical sameness. The association of the positive sign with transformations of the alternating group, and of the negative sign with those transformations of the symmetric group that are not also members of the alternating group, accommodates our urge to say 'equal, *but opposite*'. The most typical case of two things equal but opposite is that of a reflection in a mirror. And we can see that this does, in our three-dimensional world, correspond to a single interchange – transposition – of axes, if we consider a mirror standing vertically and facing northeast. North then will be reflected into east, and east into north (and south into west and vice versa). Thus it seems reasonable to identify reflections with odd permutations of axes. (1973, p. 173)

So far so good. Do I have another account outside my own experience of the same view in different directions, one allowing for disrupted axes of compass, the error of estimation and abbreviation? Or is this searching too hard for a proof we don't require anyway? The hole is a mirror, as is the mountain. When the sign on high is super-bright, the glare of the mountain induces imaginings of reflection. Of the south in the north. And the hole – the wormhole – is either pure mirror or pure emptiness. Or wormhole.

Lucas thwarts us/me, a little:

There are, however, objections to explaining reflections in terms of interchange of axes. We naturally think of a reflection not as interchanging two axes, but as reversing the sense of only one axis, leaving all others unaffected. It was an artificial example to have the mirror facing northeast. We should naturally think of a mirror facing, say, north, and reflecting north into south, but leaving the east–west axis unaffected. More generally, in mathematics we should take as the standard reflection the transformation of the point $(x_1, x_2, x_3 \ldots x_n)$ into $(-x, x_2, x_3 \ldots x_n)$, not the transformation of it into $(x_2, x_1, x_3 \ldots x_n)$. We picture the mirror as being in the hyperplane of all other axes, $Ox_2, Ox_3 \ldots Ox_n$, rather than in some diagonal one.' (1973, p. 173)

But this gets closer to the 'truth'. All peripherals are absorbed in the reflection. In the contained space of mountain and 'hole', we have vista and panorama, or their potential. Their lack suggests the possibility. Removing it from the one dimension though, the sign reversal is unnecessary. In the same way, the sign denotes the poem – a one-dimensional textual space for expressing the multi-dimensional. The poem imagined, or the poem thought before expression is the actuality of the poem: converted to signs, it becomes a formula. Lucas: 'Moreover in one dimension, it does not make sense to talk of interchanging axes, whereas it does make sense to talk of reversing the sign, and we regard doing this as a degenerate case of reflection.' (p. 174). The 'make sense' will be of less interest to the poet, and maybe this should be the case also for the philosopher who quotes Herrick at the front of his treatise: 'Then while time serves, and we are but decaying / Come, my Corinna, come, let's go-a-Maying.' Have your cake and eat it too. Know the poem exists without being written or spoken, that it loses in the translation, but do it anyway . . .

I had a dental x-ray the other day – a full rotation shot: as I clenched a mouthpiece with my front teeth, head locked in place, the x-ray camera circumnavigated my jaw. I became machine. My teeth in diorama. Panorama. Vista. And so the x-ray of light here – swinging from window to window, partial evidence accumulating. I suspect a simultaneity. At the south window there will be activity, and also at the north, and vice versa. Mirrored. And east–west and all other diagonals. Under the darkness, it is still liminal blue-gold in the west, but that's the rim of the planet and a long way off. Being struck by lightning at nine is my axis: struck on the axes in constant mirror reflection. That was twenty ks from here. It is my mantra, my rotation. The same day, the farm and surrounding farms burnt.

Internal coda
Mum's partner John A. actually went out in the height of the storm to collect figs, lest they be knocked down and damaged by high winds. This mirrors three years ago when, during a similar storm, he went out to clean the rainwater tank so it would fill cleanly with the expected liquid bounty. It was terrifying, yet he didn't care about the lightning all round. I wrote a poem, 'Cleaning the New Rainwater Tank During the Onset of an Electrical Storm ...' about that occasion. It seems to be a poem about time but is actually about narrative. And for me, narrative is not time, despite Genette's categorisations (and the poem's): 'Scene', 'Summary', 'Ellipsis', 'Descriptive Pause'. They are all of the moment, and motionless. They are before, now, and after.

North ...?
Stuck in the mud ...
Whenever our toddler, Timmy, doesn't want to do something, or doesn't want someone to do something he doesn't like, he says they are 'Stuck in the mud'. It comes from witnessing John A.'s car buried to the axles down the back – had to dig and tow him out. He had been scraping firebreaks, and down he went. For Timmy, 'stuck in the mud' denotes non-action, but also a general cessation of time. All is folded in the moment. From the north window I can see through the trees the firebreak along the fence line where John A. got stuck in the mud.

The day after Epiphany unloaded the strongest storm seen and felt here in years. In fact, the town flooded. That's a week ago today. In the *meantime*, Cyclone X crossed the north-west coastline and made its way inland, quickly degrading to a rain-bearing depression. It dumped 82.5 millimetres on our place near Walwalinj. Today it is said the Avon will flood. It is mid-summer. This weather is not usual. I am writing looking out of the north window. The mountain is visible; yesterday it was almost entirely swallowed by cloud/mist. It is called the 'hill of tears' or the 'hill that cries' by the Ballardong people, and indeed it looked as if it was weeping. The debate about climate change rages around it. Yesterday morning a guy from the EPA visited to discuss my concerns over the clearing of native vegetation on the summit. He will examine aerial photos taken in 2001, 2003, and more recently, to map the changes. I am making myself increasingly unpopular in the district for my stand on this and other issues. It's been in my poetry for decades, but they can tolerate it there. Not, though, when it comes to issues of money, recreation, ownership, control, power, and authority. Poetry, apparently, doesn't fit any of those categories, even when it resists them. A local farmer left a phone message for me to call him back 'for a chat', I would guess, to do with my opposition to aerial (and other) spraying. He is reputed to be one of the strongest advocates of herbicide, pesticide, and fungicide-spraying around. My mother fears we'll be driven out because of my stand.

It is overcast with a slight breeze coming from the north-west, which is unusual. The crows are speaking in semitones and the songbirds are intermittent. It is humid again. I can see the rain gauge clearly from here – it's just been emptied. The ground is so sodden (bizarre) that trees are toppling over and are having to be staked and tied. A few months ago we had a series of intense fogs. I heard that the paraglider vandals (agents of 'freedom'), were actually jumping off the mountain in fog – flying above it, then landing (on the neighbouring property) in the fog. Dickheads. I would sit here in the north room during the fog and write poems – 'fog' poems – about perceptions of space/distance – of imagining how things were behaving – imagining them to be as I had last seen them, but not really knowing.

The closest fence-line is a constant. I know its angles. In Ohio, USA, we lived without fences, as did most of the community. The deer crossed zones, infuriating locals who called them 'giant rats' and plotted their demise, even outside hunting season. Still, they felt not having fences was a statement of freedom, but then were obsessed with private-property ownership and armed themselves to keep intruders OUT.

Each fence here, looking from both windows in all mirrored diagonals, is topped by a single strand of barbed wire – legacy of a past we don't employ. All are staked with star pickets. Thinking over Wallace Stevens's early *Harvard Advocate* editorials on 'the Fence Question', as I often do (and encourage others to do so), I resist the fence in all senses. Having said that, it partially eases the aggression of neighbours here, though they perversely exploit the 'line' – making the precise liminal when it suits; for example, by spraying herbicides on both sides to keep weeds that grow on 'your side' from growing into theirs.

You can see Stevens's poetics in those early editorials:

> 'Putting a fence around the Yard strikes us as being the easiest way of achieving order out of chaos. One reason we have spread out through Cambridge in such a loose fashion is that we have had no point of concentration, the Yard, as it now stands, extending wherever you choose to have it extend. For instance, it is still a question whether the unknown land back of Sever is part of our geography. But a fence would settle all this; it would bring about a definite spot and turn it into a point around which new buildings could cluster. In addition to this, a fence would unquestionably bring back to the Yard some of the prestige which it has lost. To be within the walls would soon come to be an envious posi-

tion; and thus the yard would regain the hold on our imaginations which it is gradually losing. For these reasons, we think that a fence would be about the best thing that could be built by those whose aim it is to improve our present conditions. (March 24, 1900. (1997, pp. 757–758))

The confines of the room focus the poem, the text. I like it being a room of corners with little in between. Bachelard, second-hand spatial philosopher that he is, gets close with this:

> Consciousness of being at peace in one's corner produces a sense of immobility, and this, in turn, radiates immobility. An imaginary room rises up around our bodies, which think that they are well hidden when we take refuge in a corner. Already, the shadows are walls, a piece of furniture constitutes a barrier, hangings are a roof. But all of these images are over-imagined. So we have to designate the space of our immobility by making it the space of our being. (1994, p. 137)

No. We don't have to. This is *stuck in the mud*. Looking out from my compact eight corners, I synthesise my being as external, as the still moment without. Looking out, I am out. When I was a child my aunt wrote an ode (narrative, metrical, and with at least occasional rhyme), for the Avon Valley Arts Society poetry prize (I think she won), called 'A Mountain in Time'. The title and the traditional form are all I can really recall of the poem. But it has stuck in my mind. Walwalinj (she wouldn't then have known the indigenous name), is said to be an extinct volcano. It pre-dates the organic 'time' so often utilised as a yardstick of mortality. Looking out, time seems no more than that title. I am of these corners that hold no being, no tenses. No past, present, future – or all of them at once. I am as culpable of dispossession as my ancestors. The crimes of Ensign Dale are my crimes. In *The Existence of Space and Time*, Ian Hinckfuss sums up a number of arguments relating to issues of tense in 'The Debate of Tense Elimination':

> Considerable debate in recent years has centred on the attempt by philosophers including Smart, Quine, Reichenbach and Russell to de-tense language, and rid our language of reference to the past, present, and future. On the other hand, C. D. Broad, Richard Gale, Arthur Prior, and others have thought it enormously important to resist such attempts. What is interesting is that most of the philosophers on both sides of the debate have thought that something would be lost in the de-tensing process. Those in favour looked upon the loss as a loss of confusion – confusion which leads to mythological beliefs if not downright paradox. Those against regarded the loss as a loss of important conceptual abilities needed for a complete description of the world. (1975, p. 88)

Within eight corners, or held in the photograph of my being in this small room, the north window (as opposed to the larger south window of the library, with its shelves of books, that absorb, create barriers, deflect, the contractions and expressions of the hole framed by the rectangle of that window – the metaphor within the stanza), the presence of the moment (the 'picture'), doesn't mean the absence of another. The moment is the set that contains itself. The moment is metaphor folded into the finite subcover of the poem.

The maps on the wall I have in here are survey maps of the district. Incredibly detailed. Pink, as opposed to its use elsewhere for empire, represents intact or reserved bushland. The room of inversions. I can touch these maps from where I am sitting, swivelling on the chair. I can touch desk, paper, books, typewriter, walls ... open the window. And I can touch the trees and dead grass outside, the paddocks, the barbs on the fences, the vegetation on the mountains, the granite, the aerials that mount it – a visitor a few weeks ago thought it'd be nice to have a restaurant up there (horror of horrors). I mentioned this to the EPA guy and he wryly quipped, 'Yeah, a revolving one ...'.

Walwalinj 'blocks' the vista from this window, the view of the paddocks, the sheep, the wheat, the smaller hills and undulations of the valley. And yet, through its ancient granite, I can touch them all, and more.

First inland town, nexus of dispossession. Ensign Dale wrote of the 'discovery' and naming of Walwalinj – Bakewell:

> 1830. August 11th. Having only brought two days' provisions with us, we regretted being now obliged to retrace our steps to where we had left our horses, and proceeding North by West we, in seven miles, arrived at the base of that part of the Dyott hills which rises so abruptly from the river. In twenty minutes we reached the summit after a fatiguing ascent, and were amply rewarded by commanding from it a greater expanse of country than could be observed from Mount Mackie; to the Eastward it presented a view of lightly timbered Forest land, rising in alternate undulation and expanding itself from nearly North to S.S.E. till it finally disappeared in the distance from 25 to 30 miles off, seemingly partaking as far as we could discern of the same character as the adjacent country. This being the most conspicuous Hill of the Range I propose to name it Mount Bakewell in compliment to a friend. I had also an imperfect view of an elevated peaked hill which I had ascended while on an expedition into the interior in December last, bearing nearly S.W.
>
> Quitting these hills we, at the termination of seven miles reached our old encampment which we found had not been visited by the natives during our absence.' (p. 9)

Neville Green, often challenged as too liberal in his views and history, has written of York in its early days. I feel Green is often accurate, and his quoting of settler documents accurate. Of the violence at York his subjectivity is, to my mind, appropriate. It is clear it was a place of great brutality in the processes of dispossession, as he writes in *Broken Spears: Aborigines and Europeans in the Southwest of Australia*:

> In July 1836 Lieutenant Bunbury and a detachment of troops were transferred from the newly-established depot at Williams to the York trouble spot, where he nonchalantly recorded in his diary: 'shot a few of them one night'. (1994, p. 122)

And:

> Settlers in the York district responded to Stirling's instructions and refused to permit Aborigines to approach their farms; Mr Heal set his dogs on a group of Aborigines forcing the women into a deep pool of water. In revenge, several men crept up on Heal and his partner, Burns, as they worked in a paddock. A well directed spear pierced Heal's cheek and lodged in his throat and only the timely action of Burns' wife rushing out with a gun saved the two men. Angered at the attack the York settlers contributed sheaves of wheat as a bounty for the capture of the attackers. The reward was never claimed for 'the natives afterwards held a friendly corrobery (sic) with Mr Heal and adjusted all matters to the satisfaction of both parties, and the two men who threw their spears at him assisted this industrious settler for months in his farming and grazing operations'. (1994, pp. 122–123)

What is being configured and reconfigured is touch – surveillance from up close, distantly … from exploration, 'settlement', ship, London … The 'bringing back' of samples of flora and fauna – flesh and bones of the indigenous inhabitants. Touch. To hold, to ease, to relieve. Guilt, security, aspirations. To discharge static.

In his 'classic' (and to me disturbing) work, *Space, Time and Life*, C. H. De Goeje, 'Extraordinary professor of languages and ethnology of the West Indies in the Leyden University (retired)', writes:

> In Space we meet with many objects, having in common the peculiarity that when I touch them their surface resists or breaks up (f.i. a soap-bubble). Touching is a kind of mechanical process and when I touch the objects separately I can count them. Touch strongly links my psyche to my body and my body to the material world.
>
> The psyche lives in a wider sphere when it is not interested in the individuals separately, but more in the characteristic properties of the species (the expressive, S #5). This reality announces itself in my mind

as a *concept*. To primitive people (and also more or less to Plato and Goethe) it announced itself in a vision or a dream. And this might be so vivid that they took it to be a manifestation of the essence (Father- or Mother-spirit) of the species, from which spirit the properties of the individuals emanate). With modern man the relationship is inversed; according to his opinion the things one can touch and see are real, and the concepts are abstractions. Primitive man was an introvert, modern man is an extrovert. (1951, pp. 28–29)

In my modern primitivity (to reject his offensive simplification), I catalogue *and* holisticise. I count my concepts, and what I touch are abstractions or dreams I don't need to believe are real. Is this because I can touch from within to without this room, from the south room (and through it) as well?

From the enclosures of my rooms I look into the enclosures that are the paddocks, to the enclosure of the hills and the preciseness of their 'place' of the geometrical properties of these, outside the distortions of my text, outside the distortions of fractal organics. In 'Some topological ideas: enclosures' in *The Shape of Space*, Nerlich says:

> First, what is topology? It is the study of a certain class of properties which are invariant under the transformations of the topological group. The group is easily enough defined: it is simply all 1–1 continuous transformations of a space into itself but without including transformation of improper elements such as the line at infinity. The transformations are called homeomorphisms. More vividly, if less exactly, plane *differential* topology looks into whatever properties of figures would be unchanged if they were drawn on a rubber sheet which was then *smoothly* (diffeomorphically) distorted in arbitrary ways without cutting the sheet or joining parts of it. We could mould a clay sphere into a cube without tearing the surface or shearing the stuff internally (though since it creates corners, it is not smooth). Nor would we need to join new points of it up to other points – provided we were careful. If cube and sphere can be deformed into each other in this way, then their differences in shape do not concern topology: they are topologically equivalent. But neither of these shapes can be transformed into a toroid, or into arbitrarily looped and joined pretzel shapes. These shapes are topologically distinct. Differential topology is clearly more general than projective geometry, though it does not (usually) transform improper elements. (1994, pp. 126–127)

So, add to those mountain shapes the doughnut shape of the toroid plus pretzel shapes. Place consists of the topologically equivalent, and the topologically distinct. We can touch both. In the poem, we work and rework the equivalents to make the common forms of poetry. The acceptable. We create the distinct by breaking with syntax, by upending rhyme and metre, creating arbitrary and toroid-like shapes. As the place of the mountain, as the view through and against the hole of the south window, are essential as one view, so the poem mixes these topologies. The poem becomes enclosure (which, to my mind, is to be resisted). Out of curvature of sight – the roundings of the corners of the room to create a smooth and absorbable shape, a curving of the paddocks, deleting corners to prevent refuge, to open it out entirely into the what-we-see, the outwards – or to make the inwards outwards – we forget or ignore corners, and round off. Here is the paddock the rooms are in. And here are the rooms threaded through the same poetics:

1 North Window 1

2 North Window 2

3 North Window 3

4 South Window

For me, these topologies are never stable. In fact, I challenge them with distortions. Also, I want all points enclosed in my closed curves.

I suggest the poem is a world without motion that needs to be distorted (a motion, of sorts; the poem forced into motion through distortion). In this/that there's the still point of the north room–south room reflections, enclosure within enclosures. Take the great paradoxist, Zeno of Elea, whose teacher in roughly 500 BC was Parmenides. Wesley C. Salmon notes:

> ... Parmenides ... held that reality consisted of one undifferentiated, unchanging motionless whole which was devoid of any parts. Motion, change, and plurality were, according to him, mere illusions. (1975, p. 31)

Zeno's best known paradox was The Achilles (and the Tortoise) paradox. Without restating it, I favour the regressive form of the Dichotomy in which Achilles remains motionless – a sequence without an initial member is established thus creating a regression – that is, Achilles cannot even get started on his race with the tortoise (who starts ahead of him):

$$\ldots 1/16, 1/8, 1/4, 1/2,$$

To quote Salmon again:

> The recent literature on Zeno's paradoxes has contained a good deal of discussion of so-called 'infinity machines'. These are idealised devices that purportedly perform an infinite sequence of tasks; they have been introduced into the discussion because of difficulties they seem to encounter in completing the infinite sequence of tasks (a 'supertask'). The resolution of the problems surrounding the infinity machines is strongly analogous to the resolution of the progressive form of Zeno's dichotomy paradox. The motion of the Trojan fly up to and including the moment Achilles overtakes the tortoise involves exactly the same considerations. So far, I am not aware that anyone has explicitly introduced the kind of infinity machine that would be analogous to the regressive form of Zeno's dichotomy paradox – a machine whose difficulty lies in getting started with its series of tasks, in contrast with the usual infinity machine whose difficulty lies in finishing its series of tasks. (1975, p. 50)

The old innovator's adage of resisting closure was a bum steer, a falsity. Closure is an unrealisable (and undesirable, admittedly) absolute. Infinity machines that are poems are claimed to be unable to reach the end of their sequence of tasks, or rather, are told they can and that it is ineffectual, and offering poor return in figurative, metonymic, or anaphoric possibility. I argue that the infinity machine of the poem is regressive, and never gets empirically started because its beginning and end are in the imagined, the precognitive non-expression.

The poem is a motionless enclosure in its written and spoken form (as opposed to its infinite imagined and unimagined or not-yet-imagined form). It is looking outward (inwardly) from the north and south windows, and being at the axes of the backwash of reflection, the fracture of lightning. The written poem is a topology, and most often simply an equivalent topology. I wish to introduce distortion into the topology of the poem – a semblance of motion, a guise of motion. The emergence of a new set theory of poetry. A post-enclosure poetics.

IV

AGEING, LOSS, RECIDIVISM ...

Domine, refugium ...

> I look into my glass,
> And view my wasting skin,
> And say, 'Would God it came to pass
> My heart had shrunk as thin!'
>
> Thomas Hardy (1898)

The crumbling foundations were solid in my childhood. Is this ageing, or something that happens outside time? Temporal? Reincarnated, I can expect another exposure in a different body. Ageing fuels visionary dreariness, but the spots in time are empty. The child is long in the tooth, the curtains are drawn. Marginalise, contain. The Home. The piano. Dancing with hip replacements. A nomenclature of ridicule. And that smell, so emphasised from early memory, yet not noticed until it is too late. Too late? In God, in wisdom and respect, the elders are spiritual leaders, guardians. The codes we have to work with. The planet is so old, the solar system older, the galaxy older still, and beyond that, red shift; or maybe moving back towards the beginning of the ageing, blue shift. Can light be beyond? Twisted nomenclature, misuse of specific terminologies ... Navigation is calibration and measurement. Growing old has nothing to do with it. We can begin at zero degrees and disappear below the horizon, moving into the negative until we meet our beginning. Do circles negate ageing? At eighteen, he got to vote and drink – the birthday before, he could drive a car. He did all of these things – well, not vote for government, avoided the draft –

before that. And other things out of keeping with his 'age', or in keeping with the age? Epitaph. Birth notice. Wedding banns . . .

I was born old, or so I was told. As a child, I certainly wanted to grow old, to free myself from what I perceived to be the prison of childhood. Yes, there was imagination, but it had to operate within physical constraints which I found compromising. It is not surprising that I 'cut loose' in my mid-teens and tested the limits of society's capacity to cope with a fairly libertarian view of personal freedom, if one constrained by a sense of responsibility and guilt that edged into paranoia as I moved further and further away from what was expected and hoped of me.

Children are a great way of measuring one's concept of ageing. I noted recently that my own childhood and school memories were being semi-deleted as my daughter grows older. School Year 5 for me changes and disappears – or rather, is overlaid, palimpsested by her Year 5. What replaces it is an adult interpretation, a need to be adult in the context of her being in Year 5. In similar ways, all memories/experiences are reprogrammed by experiences, especially of the need for responsibility as one grows older. I have never cared much about my grey hair – white or silver or whatever – it came when I was still in my twenties; nor about the other physical declines that mark the ageing of the body. Neither have I placed much store on accumulated wisdom, as every new wisdom seems to replace something else. For me, ageing has been a twofold question of rights and loss of freedoms. Confronting different types of social bigotries.

I am fascinated by the way ageing is treated in poetry anthologies. At school. The picture of the wizened old man, old woman. 'That is what you'll become so you had better be nice to "them", understand them.' The 1970s in Australia were not a great time in most schools for the reinforcement of respect and value for one's elders. I cannot answer for the Catholic schools, where 'we' imagined old nuns made you older. There was growing old enough to gain independence, which was what I wanted, and the growing old that took away your rights – that placed you in a home, that had you in hospital on morphine dying of cancer. I remember the smell of an uncle's gangrenous leg. We all remember phobias of being kissed by the elderly, the combination of soft and aged skins. It is the realm of opposition and fetish, as much as affection and security. That is it – the security of a long life to come, that one might grow older – look, there is the proof, the evidence – but also the loss of faculties. Age becomes polarised.

A poet of ageing, of the loss of the ability to love in 'those' ways, Thomas Hardy was my favourite poet at sixteen and seventeen. I never believed in 'ageing'. I intended to have burnt out by twenty-four, but if

I lived I would keep doing things until I dropped. I would live outside the ageing of my body. My grandfather's gradual decline into Alzheimer's served as a stark reminder of the gap between the mind and body. He knew; he always knew. He would tell you what was happening to him and then forget. My mother was deeply offended one evening, watching a news programme on which she unexpectedly saw her father, confused and out of control in hospital – a programme about the disease. They had intrusively ignored his rights; he had lost his freedom.

The child of three who cannot yet articulate his or her needs shows them in ways unacceptable to older children. The older brother or sister has accumulated experience, the social skills – partial or full – that enhance freedoms by bending to the needs and expectations of others. In gaining these freedoms, spontaneity is subverted or even lost. Loss of innocence, the growth towards corruption. The riddle of the Sphinx, Plato's dissection of our loss of knowledge with birth (and later recollection of it) as demonstrated in the conversation between Socrates, Simmias, and Cebes; there is a language of progress and decline, of decline to decline. Decline and loss *are* in there. A loss of virginity. The soldier shooting his first victim. An awareness that people do not do unto you as you do unto them. It is loss on loss. Or is it?

As a child, I wanted to be an adult. Every day was gain to me. This has remained the same. The 'deleted' memories are not lost; they are replaced. Something new comes in their stead. I write and chart the course of my life. I am aware of the loss, and it becomes a stimulant to seek replacements. I want to grow old and have sex with my equally old partner, I want to learn about the incapacities of the body. I do not want my organs removed when I die, and I want my integrity and wholeness to be respected. Ageing is why I live, I believe in a process of accrual. Of loss and renewal. I build on the bits that keep being left behind. Life is a test for me – that is what drives me on.

Obliterated by substances during a period of addiction, I was psychologically no age and all ages, my body pre-dating its time. The hourglass was shaken, stirred and turned, repaired in hospital. My spatial coordinates shifted. I was a young child and an old man, sometimes an old woman, or something outside gender. I enjoyed acquiring the ability to disturb the biological clock of my body. It had its consequences, and of course one of the classic signs of ageing is the regret attached to the shortening of one's life by physical abuse. I would like to grow old – now – but do not regret what I did to myself. I regret how it affected others, but do not regret it as a thing-in-itself...

... The introduction of an older person into the equation of the party immediately brought a response. The younger men were jealous of the attention the older man was receiving from the girls of their age, with some of the younger men attracted to him also. Sensing ambivalence in his sexual identity, they were unsure how to critique him. They resorted to his using the benefits of age to exploit the younger. He became, in their words, the proverbial dirty old man. At another location in the city, a younger person visited an aged care home and had men three times her age neglecting their women friends. 'The young hussy', they said, without irony. The men said she made them feel young again ...

... Cycles. Going back to our beginnings. That is the riddle of the Sphinx – the return. But to be alone is not necessarily loneliness. To be old is no more about ageing than being three days old is. Ageing is encoded in our genetic makeup. It is the expansion and collapse of the universe. Had the Steady State Theory proved more likely, then perhaps we would have a different view of it. Perhaps we will anyway. Can you age into reincarnation, or is some other process of change going on? Is change always about time? Duration in narratology: the flashback is longer wordwise than the entire 'now-time' of the story. We are caught in the past moment that brings an inevitable denouement to the present. The end is in the beginning, or beginnings, or past actions. She wrote her best science fiction in her declining years.

A tennis player leaves the pro circuit around thirty, on average. Might join the seniors' or veterans' circuit; probably came out of the juniors. Maturing earlier, she became a professional at fifteen, completing her schooling on the road, beating the older women who remembered what it was to be her age. They are early to mid-twenties now, ageing fast in *their* terms.

Vitus vitalis, the elixir of life. Eternal youth. Paracelsus moved the discourse towards medicine. Simply prolongation of life? They feed on dead corpses, the living. The young as much as the old. The young to grow old and to despise it. The paradox of ageing. One of the paradoxes of ageing?

Cryogenically: the arrested ageing process, hoping to resurrect and cure the ailments that were rapidly leading to death. To the death-state. Risen, Lazarus set foot on earth and felt the cells of an endless number of dead and decayed lifeforms. Out of Hell, Christ rose and walked and rose again, upwards, overlooking. Out of ageing, but waiting out time until tribulation, until the need for time is ended. When ageing ceases. An article of the Anglican church rejects purgatory:

XXII. Of Purgatory

> The Romish Doctrine concerning Purgatory, Pardons, Worshipping and Adoration, as well of Images as of Reliques, and also invocations of Saints, is a fond thing vainly invented, and grounded upon no warranty of Scripture, but repugnant of the Word of God. (*The Book of Common Prayer*, 1969, p. 702)

The teenager worships the pop star, the middle-aged man admires the prime minister, the old woman looks back at Edith Cowan, ignores her faults, and admires her. The first admiration comes with the warmth of the mother, the breast. Or without the mother, the machine or device that facilitates security. Need brings adoration. Adoration, need. A living purgatory? Is ageing our purgatory, that we deny in life?

In *The Book of Common Prayer*, a foundation of my childhood, one might find publick baptism for infants and those who are as of riper years. It is never too late. In the Order of Confirmation, I might have recalled visiting the Flying Angels Club, seeing the old retired sailors, playing snooker, being given a *Wizard of Id* comic, the humour of which was expected to be beyond my years though I found it just right. Is this truth and memory, memory as fact? In these rites of passage, coming of age, I am tolled, am weighed and taken account of.

> So soon as Children are come to a competent age, and can say, in their Mother Tongue, the Creed, the Lord's Prayer, and the Ten Commandments; and also can answer to the other Questions of this short Catechism; they shall be brought to the Bishop. And every one shall have a Godfather, or a Godmother, as a Witness of their Confirmation. (1969, p. 358)

Children adapt to new languages faster. They learn the piano quicker, maybe with more feeling. Or is it age that brings the 'feeling'? The language of God is written in our hearts. Do we learn to translate better as we get older, until it returns to the heart – or some mirrored organ in the imagined body we can no longer feel – or is dulled by the pain of disease?

I had no idea who my godparents were. I still have no idea who my godmother is. I could find out by asking, yet I do not. I do not remember. But I did meet my godfather unexpectedly ...

I was visiting Busselton on the south coast of Western Australia in the company of some American students who had taken my Australian poetry course at Kenyon College. I met them at Busselton jetty, a historic monument stretching a mile out into the ocean. With the others yet to arrive, I visited the ticket office/museum/shop at the entry to the jetty. A man in his sixties asked me if I was X. Saw you down on the shore looking out to sea and knew it was you. Recognised you from the paper. Not being sure what to say, I waited for him to continue. Yes, I thought it was you. Last time I saw you, you were not able to speak. I am your godfather. Overwhelmed, I later introduced him to my students and walked toll-free out to the end of the jetty I had visited a number of times in my childhood. At eighteen, I had tried to reconstruct nine-year-old memories of the place: 'Busselton jetty had stretched to infinity ...' (Kinsella, 1998c, p. 51). I've written this over and over, testing its meaning, the way it changes significance for me as I grow older. Age did not scare me then; neither does it now. Once I was declared clinically dead. When told this had been the case, I smiled. I was older. Experience? Or negation? Or like the existence and presence of my godfather, a confirmation. I was a confirmation for him. He told me how my father had come up to him at work and asked him to be my godfather, out of the blue. 'I've always liked your dad, still see him.'

They tell us this is a society growing older, that its needs are changing. Before, after the baby boom, it was a 'young' society, and facilities and distribution of taxes reflected this. Ageing, political parties of those in their 'twilight' or, rejecting this, retirement or riper years, are established. The needs of the many; this is democracy? In the anarchist communities I envisage, will age be a factor beyond the empirical needs of the body? Of course, the psychological needs change. But change is part of the moment stilled, caught in time as well. Duration. The needs of the one become the needs of the many?

A friend has stopped colouring her hair because now is the time. She will be looked at in a new light. People will treat her differently. More seriously, for her age? My daughter at age ten often grows jealous of the attention that babies and toddlers get. She wraps herself up and says I want to be them, warm and snug and without worries. At other times she reasons like an adult, using complex verbal skills to construct an argument and defend her ground or make a point. She uses her intellect assertively, to control her environment. Mentally, her ages shift. Her body grows in its own way, connects with her mental and spiritual self at various nodal points on the way.

As a poet I watch words age, become anachronistic, then undergo rebirth. Syntax as well. Metaphysical turns of phrase, conceits, artificiality, come into vogue and vanish, or hybridise. Is it happening more rapidly? More words available, change masked by change masked by change. Complementary layers of change, parallel lives of words, expressions? As of the body?

Ejaculation. Sperm count. Diminishing sperm count. Masturbation. Venal sins. Wrong church, but still. Fertility. Eggs. Periods. Cycles. Change of life. Patches to make it easier, like giving up smoking. Viagara like ... drugs. Like drugs? 'Lord, thou hast been our refuge: from one generation to another.'

Across from my room at time of writing is the Kenyon cemetery. John Crowe Ransom is among its dead. He wrote:

> He was pale and little, the foolish neighbours say;
> The first-fruits, saith the Preacher, the Lord hath taken;
> But this was the old tree's late branch wrenched away,
> Grieving the sapless limbs, the shorn and shaken.
>
> (1922)

Taken before the ageing, and so insignificant. Even this last stanza clearly conveys the contradictions. The dead, 'ugly' child ... Time has nothing to do with it? Or am I twisting the meaning to suit my ends? That is, time is eternal in the youthful, childish moment, in old age. The world in a grain of sand ...

The ashes of three generations of my family were transplanted out of the soul of the farm, Wheatlands, and taken to my aunt's new place on the side of Mount Brown. She said she understood for the first time the true displacement of the indigenous people, the annihilation that comes with having to remove the dead, or worse, to lose contact with them. The invasion of indigenous lands in Australia has broken contacts, contacts all of us are obliged to help restore. To be in contact with the dead is to make ageing irrelevant. Ageing stops, and yet is persistent, even eternal. It is about sanctity, of a non-temporal time, a different kind of calibration. Being operated on a few years ago, I recall thinking, before going under anaesthetic: I might not wake up, but in this body I will not know. It was not about the pain I would or would not feel, but how much ageing (for I was certain I would endure spiritually), *would not* be about decay. The body working in a different time scheme, in an entirely different, apposite way. It would still be about growth – a dead heart thick with language. About change. The rotting body as a positive thing, as an increase rather than a residue.

Gender? Will they treat my male body differently? A separate place for males and females in the morgue. A moment's hesitation for the transsexual, the hermaphrodite. Unlikely. All undressed together, medical students playing with our body parts and pretending it is not necrophilia. I have heard the jokes; they are *de rigueur*, I am told. Not many older actresses in Hollywood films – freedom doesn't come with age in that place. And afterwards, Marilyn is digitised and made young again, alive and blooming and gathering no wrinkles. It is virtual, though cut the power and the rules change. Even infinity has its borders, we might guess.

Graphol-age-ia poetica: ageing as confrontation or avoidance of death

From the point of view of this poet, ageing involves a paradoxical relationship between the *loss* of some knowledge and 'experience', and the accumulation, increase, or awareness of other knowledge and experience. In some cases, it is the development of pre-existing, or evolving awarenesses; in others, it is something entirely new, that becomes translatable out of a form of dynamic equivalence – a comparison to what we have known until that point. Poetry, in many ways, exists in this liminal zone of change, in these places of comparison, and in the search for an articulation of the new experience without coordinates in available memory. Instinct, ritual, learned behaviour, commonsense, might help, but essentially we are on our own – take risks, test the waters in different ways.

As a writer, it has always bemused me, when other writers' works are collected, usually after death, that their early child and teenage writings are separated off as 'juvenilia', presented apologetically – or to 'throw light' on the mature, older writer? Is there a point when we cease being child-writers, in the same way that we can officially vote, or drink, or drive a car? Most juvenilia are divided according to both age and level of accomplishment.

Clearly, it cannot be at thirty, but at twenty-two you might have written a poem so critically well-accepted that you have matured enough for subsequent work to be considered non-juvenilia. The line is arbitrary. For me, it is all one and the same line of work: voices change over life, and that is interesting, but the imposed separation is also about control, about not letting the purity of adulthood be tainted by the innocence of childhood.

Arthur Rimbaud, writing his poetry outside of innocence, we are led to believe by Rimbaud himself and by his biographers, is promoted as child-poet-genius – the genius being the reason he wrote poems that appeal to adult sensibilities, more, comes the implication, than any child of the age he was when he wrote them. This is called precocity. Yet at the age of fifteen I was reading Rimbaud and felt he was talking directly to me, as I am sure many other young people have too.

The other argument, which we can share with Rimbaud across the divider of age, is one of the conveniences of packaging. Of course we can, if we are old enough; we have all been children and young people and adults and middle-aged and old. This exploitation of the child-self for the delectation of the older reader is reprehensible in its dishonesty, and in its marketing. I have often wished that poetry would come to us without any biographical reference-points. I could certainly show poems written by my daughter at six that could pass for poems written by an adult.

It is all about content and range: if the emotion is a specific one, and the focus is singular, the utterance of the words itself creates the emotional environment – it translates across age. The more information, the more emotional fracturing, the more clearly it comes out of an emotionally and technically inexperienced voice that has, seemingly, less to offer the adult.

Let us reconsider a poem (in my translation) by Arthur Rimbaud, which I quoted earlier (see p. 13 above: 'Le dormeur du val' ['Sleeper in the Valley'] (1870/1997, p. 105).

Two points leap out. One, that it is a highly sophisticated viewing of death as a child, as an unhealthy infant who can quite look after itself; secondly, that the suggestion of a 'young soldier' brings a sense of witnessing from a point of view that is experienced, and certainly older. What is remarkable is that the dead soldier is certainly no younger than Rimbaud, and probably some years older. Rimbaud casts his voice as a voice of aged authority, even of parental authority, but also allows the luxury of innocent indulgence in the richness of language. He merges the 'pure' and the 'corrupt'. He transgresses the rules of age, of juvenilia.

When I was fourteen, I started working weekends and holidays at Wim Smits Philatelists, in London Court, Perth, Western Australia. With my first pay, I bought a book of Banjo Paterson's verse for my mother. The inscription in it, in my teenage hand, reads: 'To Mum / my first pay Hope you enjoy reading /Love Your Son John / xxxxx Birthday '77'. Now, this might not seem much in itself, but it tells me a few things about my writing practice. The capitalisations were to add gravity to my efforts, to my beneficence, and to my excitement. It was a sign of respect to my mum, but also a sign of respect to myself. The gift was evidence of an independence, a coming of age. The handwriting in that book is the template or core of my handwriting now, though I write faster, with more fluidity, and far less definition of letters. Still, I know that person by his hand. The signature is the signature of a consciousness of maturing, of growth. It is a confrontation with paternity, with a desire to bridge the age gap. My mother was good that way – she allowed us to be *people*, as well as children.

Drafting by hand has always been important to me. The handwritten, even manually typed and hand-corrected poem becomes an engagement with where I am developmentally. The same, but different. To reiterate a fascinating motif: I treasure the knowledge that in banks, those who sign things all day have signatures on record for different points of tiredness. So if someone has been signing for five hours, their signature is compared to the five-hour signature. This change is not only an issue of age and time, but of experience, of emotional and physical tiredness. Being tired has a lot to do with changes we attribute to age. Now, one might feel tiredness more getting older, but as I have already indicated earlier, my grandmother spent her last twenty years wide awake – we have, or had, insomnia in common.

So often when we speak of writing to age, we speak of writing to experience. The younger woman's fascination with the observations, experiences, sufferings, and distillations into poetry of Sylvia Plath are more about associations of feeling and experience, or of the imagination of what that experience might be like, than something solely related to age. People mature at different rates physically, but our emotional needs also have different schedules, and, furthermore, alter. It becomes a question of whom, say, was Plath was writing for? To other young women of a specific social experience and cultural background? Her ventures in form are an illustration of the constraint that young women, especially of the era, faced in terms of sexuality and domestic freedom. This formality is offset by the savagery and haunting physicality of her imagery. There is a tension here. Yet it could speak to an older woman who has lived a life of confinement in all sorts of ways – one can translate across physical age into experience. But the suicidal youthful girl or woman, so often attracted to Plath, is that way for a reason. Like pop music speaking to its generation – but then there are always those who cross the boundaries.

Often the death-poetry of youth comes from a fear of life, of ageing. The rock band The Who says, 'I hope I die before I get old' (1965); the Rolling Stones are notorious for it, and equally notorious for getting old. Do they now play youthful music or have they taken youthful music to all ages, or other ages? When they adapted the blues, were they taking music for an older generation from one culture to the younger generation of another? Of course, the blues know no age, as shown by the apparently possessed and brilliant blues guitarist Robert Johnson (King of the Delta Blues), who died at age twenty-seven. The issues dealt with in the blues – that a woman has left me, or a man has done me wrong, for example – can happen at any time.

So the poetry of death of the young man and young woman reaches across gender divides often to express a fear of ageing, of its inevitable confrontation with mortality. By confronting mortality immediately, a catharsis takes place. Death, as John Donne shows us in his poetry (1977; see for example 'The Flea', pp. 36–37), comes with the act of consummation as much as by being struck down. They are similar moments of climax – and denouement. The poetry of death so common among youthful writers does not go away with the experience of writing; it just becomes wider in its terms of reference, and speaks outside a particular age group. Writers have committed suicide at early ages, and not just from the despairs of youth!

My partner, the poet Tracy Ryan, lost a brother at a young age. In some ways, ageing stopped then for her. In other ways the loss led to its acceleration. Such defining moments in our lives become fulcrums for fears or confrontations with mortality, and so much of ageing is about strategies for negotiating our relationship with our own mortality, that of those around us, and of humanity as a whole.

Here is what Tracy Ryan had to say, first in her youth when writing in her late teens, about age and the issue of death:

> Letting Go
>
> The day the bright balloon slipped from your hand
> There was no sun. The clouds had caught my eye,
> Streamlined hovercraft on unfathomed sky.
> I cried because I could not understand
>
> How something held so tight could still be lost.
> But you let go. I wonder what it saw,
> Trailing its tail above the here and now,
> Tirelessly rising to the uppermost
> World, a giddy angel. Perhaps the light,
> Clouded from vision, somehow warmly called
> To rise and shine, get up and walk, and healed
> The breach between the realms of faith and sight.
>
> It is the star that satellites the heart,
> The final act that tears the spheres apart.
>
> (unpublished ms., 198–?)

I asked Tracy Ryan to comment on how she viewed her subject matter, as far as she can recall, at the age when the poem was composed, and how she views and writes it now:

The main difference in how I treated this subject matter (death) in my teens, and how I approached it later, is that in the earlier writing I used much more formal technique – the poems are stiff, clichéd, metrical. Partly this is because poetry was newer to me (I was still learning how to do those things) but also it's because the main catalyst for my writing poetry – my brother's death – occurred when I was sixteen, and was way too overwhelming for me to deal with directly. The stiff formalism was a means of distancing myself from the experience, trying to 'sort it out', examine it, see what it could tell me. Later on it was the direct emotional aspects of it that interested me – the event, the loss, had retreated or receded with time (though not necessarily the intensity of feeling, which has never been exorcised) and I was more interested in the universal aspect of it – how it was like/unlike what others experienced of death and loss. Distancing still happens through metaphoric treatment, but the voice is more apparently 'immediate'.

In 'Letting Go', that image of the hand letting go of the balloon/the person giving up life, comes from the same fact that is mentioned in the second line of the Wungong poem [below]: Sean's girlfriend said he lifted up one hand and waved at her as he died. (He was a fair way across the water.) For a long time I couldn't deal mentally with the idea that he knew he was going to die, and he chose to 'let go' when he 'should have' hung on. In the early poem, that gets abstracted beyond recognition (only the sky turns into water by implication – the sole remaining trace of the death-place, though I didn't see that at the time). My teacher at school who read this manuscript said that he felt my obsession with ordering and formalising the poems was getting in the way of their energy– back then I thought he was just a 'free-verser', but now I understand what he meant – the imposition of a pattern was constantly leading me away from what I wanted to do. (The poem degenerates into increasingly abstract Biblical and religious imagery.) (Personal communication, 2004)

A horror is implicit in the sign of the hand. It is commonplace, and yet it is invested with an ominous, portentous meaning. A symbol of affirmation and loss: greeting and departure. In Ryan's adult work, 'Wungong Dam' (1999, p. 36), looking back at the death of her brother many years after the incident, it is the hand that ties the loss together. It literally reaches across.

The fact that Stevie Smith's humour in 'Not Waving but Drowning' (1976, p. 303) is being darkly inverted, strengthens our horror. Life goes at any age, and a knowledge of its imminence might be as it happens. The idea that we can know our death, and yet be surprised by it, is where the power of Ryan's poem lies.

We may compare this to poems written over twenty years later, as an adult, and a parent. The parenting experience, more than the age, is probably pivotal to creating a distance of a kind from personal mortality. One's own life becomes a substitute for the child's, which one would readily exchange for the child should it become a choice. Loss of a child, or the loss of someone loved outside the nuclear family before having children of one's own, can, of course, lead to a desire to substitute the self for the dead, but it is less common. The environment of nurturing – and, in the case of women, the extension of the physical self – brings a fear of the mortality of someone else, and not as definitively for the self, unless it be the fear of the child thereby losing protection and care. These are generalisations, but they are certainly patterns we can establish in the poetry of Ryan and many others.

> Wungong Dam
>
> I always dream he is down here
> where he waved one hand and sank
> in the still pool. I forget the real
> dank fistful of dirt and agapanthus
> we threw on him, I forget
> red clods that adhered to
> our soles and dust smeared
> on damp cheeks, the unjust softness
> of kangaroo paws. I forget HE IS RISEN
> clamped over the earth-mouth.
> In dreams I come back for him
> to the one dam you have never
> written of.
>
> (Ryan 1999, p. 36)

Ryan makes an interesting point about the solidity of this later poem. It does not retreat into rhetoric, but still manages to flow and give the sense of the dream it invokes. This is a maturity of technique welded with the learned behaviours of coping with grief. The poem becomes a tool for decoding that grief, but it is also a celebration of her lost brother's memory:

> it's almost entirely concrete. It's about how memory (via dreams) goes looking for the dead brother in the (more spiritual) element of water – even though I know he is buried in the earth, I always dream he is buried in the water. (Private communication, 2003)

In an even later volume, Ryan re-confronts her brother's ghost: her loss is always tinged with a celebration of memory: both its sensual pleasures, and the sense of grief and wastefulness this loss invokes. The flower is fresh and fades fast, as the persona will also fade and in fading join the dead:

> from Hydrangeas
>
> under my brother's window
> as if you knew
> he'd die young and we'd strew
> that pit with just such blue
>
> [... and the petals of that flower, which grew under his window when we were children, are ...]*
>
> like the simple cells
> that form the complex
>
> that is my body
> that will simplify
>
> again, like his, the petals shed
> colourless and drifting.
>
> (2002, p. 46)
>
> *Ryan's interpolation to abridge poem

Finally, Ryan adds:

> As an adult I am more able to recall details from childhood than I was at sixteen and seventeen, to convey the relationship with the dead brother. In the early poem 'Letting Go', everything was filtered through indirect references and symbols unrelated to the core of feeling – kind of abstracted. I didn't have an 'emotional poetic language'. (Personal communication, 2003)

This last comment is vital. Not only is the emotional experience not there, but there is an inexperience in realising how aware the experienced reader will be of literary stock sayings, styles, and clichés. So the use of a symbol or expression or rhetorical device that might seem fresh, or subtextual with a poet from the canon, becomes laboured to the experienced reader, especially the emotionally experienced reader. This does not invalidate the original emotion, or the attempt to express it, and in a sense suggests context *is* relevant.

As part of ageing together, as a couple, Tracy Ryan and I share experience through our work, our children, our veganism, and various other interests and beliefs. But one of the keys to our sharing each other's journey, through reconciling our move towards death, is incorporating each other's sufferings and losses into our own lives. This is a delicate thing – too much burden-bearing can become compromising, crowding – but there has to be some level of attempt at understanding these processes.

Tracy Ryan has moved away from the death of her brother, an event around which all views of relationships were formed (the risk of the most solid ones being 'taken away' without warning, or with warnings we do not know how to read), with one's teenage years being 'deprived' of a belief in the possibility of an immortality – the stuff that makes children think they are Superman. She certainly never felt this. I did feel this, and did things accordingly. Bullying dragged me down – the observation and experience of violence. Drugs and alcohol became a way of short-circuiting the youth I did not want to have. I was always a child who wanted to be an adult because that would give me more freedom, but would also protect me from other children. It seemed to indicate I was mature beyond my years, but I was not: in many ways, I missed out on a part of growing up.

In reconciling ourselves to each other's emotional stultifications, and efforts at ageing mentally, emotionally, and spiritually, as well as physically – or at least to sense the possibilities – we have written into each other's lives. Below is an example of a poem I wrote on visiting Tracy's brother's grave. Both Tracy's 'Wungong Dam' and my poem below refer to kangaroo paws – plants indigenous to Western Australia with red flag-like flowers with green and red stems, yellow anthers – in common, and the plant becomes a way of bridging the gap, of communicating about the idea, and our own mortality. As Tracy Ryan says, she has changed, but her brother in her memory will always be eighteen. It stops her ageing process to some degree as well. I am told I look like him, and am similar in many of my interests. Perhaps subliminally this informed the consolidation of our relationship; perhaps I have become a way of her confronting this mortality. I lost a close friend to suicide when I was in my early twenties, and this loss is something Tracy has been able to understand. The vulnerability of the physical self has united rather than alienated us. We help each other age. Here is my poem:

> Grave
>
> > Serpentine. Tracy asks me to stop
> > at the cemetery – her brother
> > who drowned in Wungong Dam

is buried here. She clears
dry leaves from the framed
blue metal while I think
of Craig whose grave
I've never visited.
It's just something I can't face.
Though I'll wander almost happily
amongst the tombs of those I've
not known. I did not know
Tracy's brother, and it shows.
I set out in search of flowers.
It is autumn and they are scarce.
Behind the cemetery I come across
lines of dead sheep. Wool, red
with raddle paint, hangs
dankly about the carcasses.
I return empty handed.
One can't transfer flowers
from another's grave.
At the right time of year
Tracy says kangaroo paws
are rampant – occasionally
erupting from graves,
bloody windchimes
muttering under their breaths.

(2003, p. 60)

Recently, I found a poem of mine in one of my mother's school poetry books. It is about imprisonment and wears its influence – the Australian poet Judith Wright – loudly. For as far back as I can remember, the issue of imprisonment, especially false imprisonment, has concerned me. The skills one develops as a writer, as much as the perceptions of age, delineate fundamental differences in the poems below which deal with this topic. The first was written at some time during the 1977/78 school holidays when I was fourteen, possibly just fifteen, and having just moved from a city school to a country school. The dislocation was both freeing and imprisoning, so personal experience informs it. For a child who was bullied, new hopes were on offer, but it was not long before it was a case of 'out of the frying pan and into the fire'. I would say I redrafted this in the first few months of 1978. The notion of revenge fascinated me, and here ageing has brought a fundamental difference. I am a pacifist now, but then I played war games, made explosives, and believed in a morality based on 'justice'. 'Justice', to me now, is just another word for violence – psychological and physical.

A Call For 'Freedom'

The silhouetted figures cry for help,
And still the shadows die without a care,
Mournful cries come from within the dead,
Whose shadows wander fluted corridors.

These souls of confined men that call 'Revenge!'
In the face of their oppressors and their guards,
No freedom did they have to call for life . . .
So sought instead the mercy of their death.
(unpublished, 1977/78)

On days when prisoners in the state of Ohio were to be executed, Kenyon College's Episcopalian church, in the American town where I have been teaching as an adult in recent years, would sound its bells as a form of protest. The bells would continue to ring until the protest ate into people's consciences. The death sentence is an appalling hypocrisy and travesty of 'justice', in my mind, so it is not surprising that with the bells ringing through my body I would respond as I did in the poem discussed below. Kenyon College is in an isolated place in mid-Ohio: the village of Gambier, surrounded by woods and cornfields. The management of the lands in relation to the college is distinctly pastoral. The church community's pastoral is of an ecumenical religious form, but the two traditions of pastoral overlap. In this community a few years ago there was an horrific murder. When the murderer was given the death sentence, even the victim's family protested.

With these factors resonating, and given that I write landscape in the same way I write the body, it seemed that there was a violation of both going on with execution. Technically, and certainly in terms of references and nuances in deployment of language, there is 'more to' this poem than the one written out in my mother's poetry book when I was fifteen; yet the concerns are the same. The revenge here is inverted of course, because the implication is that the prisoners (convicts, the results of penal colonialism) were wrongfully or unjustly (in the word of my youth) imprisoned.

The fact that the prisoner being executed in Ohio committed his crime is presumably not in doubt, but the question remains the same: to be murdered for a crime, no matter how grievous, implicates those casting judgement. This entangled issue of ethics crosses over with the first poem. Age has brought extra knowledge, but so-called maturity has brought in many ways no greater insight. Knowledge is relative; the truths we know as children are no less truths for being immature. We might not comprehend a situation, or might not be able to access certain information, but truths are relative to the information we have. A sense of right and wrong is usually instilled at a very young age, and seems often Platonic in its pre-presence. Poetry, the articulation of the inexpressible, becomes the gesture. Audience is the issue – in a sense, both poems are directed towards an unjust and uncaring world.

> Death Sentence in Ohio: epicedium
>
> And yet ... to stay
> and plan this pastoral ...
> families extend in both directions:
> an eclogue of courts and therapy,
> anger and cemeteries,
> default patterns rising
> and closing off the day,
> the emperor's thumbs down –
> all beginnings and endings
> and linking first light
> with total darkness.
>   Blackout,
> as the state you take as host
> executes another – the bell
> keeping steady pace
> for all its heavy going,
> weather dull then bright,
> hardly newsworthy.
> A temporal flexibility,
> aspect of grace ... occasional
> as the angle of script
> on the warrant.
>   You condemn
> the action but live quietly
> in the shadow of *their* gallows –
> dressed as metaphor, half-
> wondering grammatical contexts
> and last meals with their special
> kind of half-life, and what prises
> the soul from the body it makes,
> what takes the place of a face
> to hate, to paint repeatedly
> on paper,
>   electronically.
>
> (Kinsella, 2005b, p. 71)

My daughter and I enjoy going on bush excursions. We both keep field notebooks/journals. Beginnings are so important. My daughter – as I did as a child – keeps a locked diary, and a public diary. As she grows older, I wonder if the private will become more public, as it most certainly has in my case. Our secrets become the stuff of our writing. Georg Lukács begins his 1910 diary with the following:

> 25 April 1910, at night
>
> ... How strange and exciting to begin a diary (even in my current state it affects me). There are questions and suggestions: who among my old friends will reappear? What new names will make me fill these terrifying white pages with my blood? (1995, p. 27)

The point is that the white pages, the unwritten blanks of our lives, are terrifying. We write, we record, to fight ageing, to fight loss. By recording we seem to suggest that we can keep it, that nothing is lost. We see all this in Shakespeare's notion that in writing his lover he gives him or her immortality; in the Egyptians' belief in taking one's earthly goods in the journey across the river of death; in the diary in which teenagers keep secrets from their mothers, only to be traumatised, to be desecrated and feel like part of themselves has been removed on finding that the hair placed acrsoss the pages has been disturbed.

As writers, and writers of all kinds – of emails, tax forms, Christmas or Hanukkah cards, we record where we have been, what we would like to attain. It is all sidestepping mortality. In the *Guardian* newspaper of November 1st there is an article entitled 'World Drowning In a Rising Sea of Information': 'Peter Lyman, one of the leaders of the research team, said the surge in information was due to a new-found desire to document all that happens around us' (McIntosh, 2003). I don't think it is new-found – and numeracy and literacy are not the only ways of recording. When wandering in the bush with my daughter, where I am interested in recording the specific names of things, she makes up for a lack of that knowledge by writing about the moods things create, and drawing pictures of them so she might increase her knowledge. She'll ask me, as someone with more experience, but the process of interest is ageless. In fact, my nine-month-old boy is the most hungry for knowledge of all. He records with plastic cups and the bars of his playpen. We make stories, create narratives and novels out of our lives to show where we've been, and consequently, where we are going. In *Writing Degree Zero*, Roland Barthes says: 'The Novel is a Death; it transforms life into destiny, a memory into a useful act, duration into an orientated and meaningful time.' (1967, p. 39).

He continues to point out that 'society ... imposes the Novel' (1967, p. 39), and, indeed, in the light of the need to control ageing, to categorise and separate our lives' narratives, to profit from them, and for power to be extracted from them, the novel becomes a necessity, as do now the chatroom, the blog.

In creating the time and durational coordinates of a poem, we step outside Genette's (1980) rules. The poem merges in its compaction of the moment, its being stretched out, condensed, recounted, projected, and so on. The poem, as a device, denies age. If Shakespeare is right, poems are a denial of death. However, the use of the sonnet itself, the confinement of language to form, is a recognition of the materiality of the word, and of life. It is like an urn, or the slab of a tombstone. In form, we apply the rules of physics. Tracy Ryan's loss poem juxtaposes the confinement of form with the apparent freedom of the balloon, of life: which the poem suggests is an illusion, a false freedom. It is as trapped as the poem itself.

There's a wonderful quote from A. W. Raitt's 'The Life of Villiers de l'Isle-Adam' (cited in Enright, 1983):

> In 1887, when Villiers de l'Isle-Adam and Léon Bloy were passing the flower-sellers, monumental masons and shops specializing in funeral accessories near the Père Lachaise cemetery, Villiers exclaimed in fury: 'Those are the people who invented death!' (p. 145)

In some ways, literature fetishises and invents death as well.

On one of our outings, my daughter and I explored a piece of reserve bushland near the family home in York, Western Australia. Getting there was an exercise in itself, for though it was easy enough to find the front part of the reserve via the main road down to the city, we wanted to go in from behind, along the extremely potholed gravel roads at the back of Mount Bakewell, where our home is, in the wheatbelt of Western Australia. The actual trail into the reserve is extremely rocky, and we could take the car only so far. My daughter found this exciting, but also slightly threatening. The unknown possibilities of getting stranded bothered her.

On the other hand, she was not really old enough to take this fear into the extreme, though morbid tendencies could potentially evolve later as she fused fiction with reality. At the time, however, the possibility of being shot by a stray bullet from an illegal hunter, or of coming across a drug plantation guarded by underworld figures, were distinct possibilities. The kind of knowledge she had did not lend itself to these possibilities, though if something had happened, then obviously the possibility would have become part of her vocabulary of expectation, on future visits to such places.

Experience told me these were possibilities, so I entertained the thoughts. Our relative experiences of the visit would be coloured by our relative fears and expectations. Though it was mid-winter, she feared a snake might awake and attack her. This was more a phobia than a belief in it actually happening – so more information than necessary would cause cascading fears. We wandered further into the bush, through grevilleas, under the odd jarrah, past York gums and hakeas. As the soil varied, so did the vegetation. We heard kangaroos moving through the bush. It was overcast, and a little humid. Thick clots of sap had dropped from red gums: yes, like blood.

We came across a vast granite outcrop, black, and alive. In a split in the rock, we found bones and skin, probably dropped there by a fox that had captured a native animal. My daughter asked me what it was; a quoll, I thought. We stared at it for a while, lost in our own thoughts, separate, found a place on the rock, and wrote. The poems are below; I have only just seen her poem at time of writing this. Since the outing, I have realised that the skin was that of a brushtail possum, but my daughter has remained confirmed in the unwavering belief that it was a quoll. Still, we both independently sought for more than the death itself. It was symbolic, certainly, but it was more than that. For all my searchings in language, I saw little more than my daughter saw.

It is not a matter of clarity through simplicity, but of choosing the words that work for us at a particular time and place. We are different poets – she is twelve at time of writing, and I am forty – but we were affected by the same sense of the place, the same need for affirmation in a place of death. The fear we have of our mortality is offset by fears of threats even greater than death – loss of soul, pain, loss of loved ones, our sanity – but occasionally the poem lifts out of the referentiality of our vulnerability, and transcends.

If being twelve has anything going for it, it is the ability to do that. We spend our ageing trying to recall it, to escape down its path. The irony is that the twelve-year-old has no more purity of vision than the mature person; it is just a different kind of vision. Once we start talking about the corruption of ageing, we are patronising our earlier selves. Some things are not open to us as children, and neither should they be, but what we did know then was as valid and complex as what we would know later.

Disclosed poetics

Here is my poem:

> Death of a Brushtail Possum
>
> In the valley, on granite faces,
> cosseted by she-oak perimeters,
> lichen, moss, black run-off,
> a brushtail possum broken down,
> strewn over and into cracks –
> a limb, vertebrae, envelope of skin and fur,
> touched by a boot, an undoing
> touching both, that makes the granite
> as overcast as clouds already
> infested by gravity, the pull-down
> levity a host to temperature –
> cold, yet sultry, the ghost-imaging
> it engenders… more blood
> in the emptied body than on
> the distant road, ripping with traffic.
> Yellow robins and dusky wood swallows
> cite a ministry of antithesis over this island
> of all that's been said, plus acacias, flowering dryandra,
> the white-fleshed granite that uncaps
> a grey expression, the blank ink
> they sign in deflection,
> all here with the remains
> of the possum – fox victim.
>
> (2005a, p. 180)

And my daughter's poem:

> Metaphor
> for Daddy, on our excursion to the bush
>
> Having to write about
> the
> latest metaphor in
> mind;
> A granite graveyard
> or
> so it looks
> I
> find a corpse of
> that
> pink gloom, my father

> inspects
> and comes to think it was a quoll
> although
> later knowing it was a
> brush-tailed
> possum, I feel sorry that
> I
> was scared of an animal;
> was it pink
> gloom
> or pink peace?
> I
> think of it now as
> where
> the earth
> is
> the sunset.
>
> (Katherine Kinsella, unpublished, 2003)

In my version, there is a lot of peripheral material, a lot of implied possibilities, a lot of noise coming from without. In Katherine's, there is the honed, unadulterated moment. The rules of the imagist manifestoes are at work. Age brings the trappings, but it does not have to. However, it would be unusual for a child of Katherine's age to include so much distraction to clarify a point. Tangentiality, side-stepping, allusion and avoidance, are the tactics of experience living in a world where responsibility brings its own vulnerability, where one imagines the system will consume the naive. Children learn that, and that is how they age.

A loss of poetics

To write poetry you do not have to like it. I have been increasingly recognising that language and its correlatives in music and art are not the pure coordinates or sole arbiters of poetry. There are two issues evolving out of these comments that seem pivotal to me. The first pertains to the suggestion that poetry might happen either out of necessity, or, paradoxically, incidentally. The second is that poetry does not rely on an aesthetic response to the tensions involved in reconciling interiority and articulation of the external world. These two simple principles are becoming the turning points for a personal re-evaluation of what constitutes the poem for me as a reader, or more precisely 'experiencer', and what it means for me as a maker of poems.

On the surface, I am inclining towards poem as gesture or utterance arising out of the pre-cognitive, or maybe out of the half-realised. I have often used the expressions 'error zones' and 'anchor points' to describe the tautological discomforts that drive the written or spoken poem for me – the error zones being ambiguities that arise out of apparent errors in syntax and form, out of parataxis and enjambment, a disturbing of the rules of prosody, juxtaposed or interacting with 'realisms', points of concrete and external referentiality which clarify and focus perspective – anchor points. This is the hybridising of the unified self and the disrupted or displaced lyrical I.

So in writing poetry I have tried to merge, say, a reference to a specific moment in time – recording with subject–object certainty, and a sense of linearity – with a series of, say, tense-related or syllabic or syntactical disruptions. The wandoo tree covered in pink and grey galahs morphs into an exploration of something metonymically associated with tree or bird that might then evoke a series of historical or etymological associations and so on. In other words, it is a poetry of digressions and associations based largely – though by no means exclusively – in one language, having a point of reference common to the whole work in the epistemology of the language itself. And even should the work digress into other languages, the process of orality becomes the unifying signifier–signified construct. That is how it has been, but it is no longer that way.

Two words best sum up the shift in my poetics. Mimetics and mnemonics. Poetry, in form and in language, in how it is said and why it is being said (which is desirably, at best, at least partially inexplicable on the surface level of 'meaning'), is a process of imitation and reproduction. The word itself derives from the Greek 'mimesis', and in many ways my mimetics is really an adapted and 'personalised' mimesis. Maybe the medical meaning of mimesis is even more relevant: symptoms appearing *without* the actual disease. We might compare the process to watching a mime play, and recalling it later as being rich with language, with voices. We can hear the movements of the players. The same happens for me in the creation of a poem. The poem forms as a series of sounds and images and associations that seemingly have no specific register in language – that is, words do not necessarily correlate to what is being seen or heard; neither is explanation offered. But when it comes to placing them on the page, creating an artefact, or to speaking it aloud – that is, reciting it – language finds its dynamic equivalent, and the poem that was sounds and images becomes an imitation, a mimicry of the original language-less poem.

Sometimes this emerges as the short imagistic poem, distilled, such as my Finch poems:

Finches

Salt Paddocks

Down below the dam
there is nothing but salt,
a slow encroachment.

Fighting back, my cousins
have surrounded it
with a ring of trees.

At its centre
lives a colony of finches,
buried in tamarisks.

Finch Colony

The leaves, like wire, are so tangled
we dare not venture too far into their heart
where flashes of song and dull colour
betray a whole family of finches.

We hold our breath
and become statues.

Is this fear of disturbing their peace
or of a delicate raid from unknown spaces.

Finch Flight

To join the finch
in his tenuous kingdom
amongst tamarisks,
the hot snow of salt

You must gather
trajectory and direction,
sharp summer flights

Exile yourself
from the wind's hand.

Finch Death

The dead finch lies on salt,
tight-winged and stretched.

> The others shimmer
> loosely in heat
>
> the salt's white mystery
> coveting tin cans, skull of sheep.
>
> Slowly, death rides this hot glacier
> further and further away.
>
> (1998c, pp. 84–85)

At others it flows in a more cinematic way, and with less pause or hesitation. It is like too much information trying to distil itself but shifting rapidly from one (often metonymic) connection to another. This is not simply a problem of the synapses, brought about by the excesses of my youth, but a life-issue associated with insomnia, hyperactivity, and a mobile mood register. Poetry becomes tied up with the chemical balance and imbalance of the body.

One of the problems I live with, and which has certainly been compelling my mimicries and their attendant inverted mnemonic transliterations (I write to unremember, not to remember – it is a matter of rearranging the flood of information into art, not into confession or nostalgic reconnection), is the constant interruption of past moments of my life into the present. I can be sitting in a park in St Louis, thinking about an Elizabeth Peyton image, and I am instantly in King's Park in Perth, as a child, with my wooden sailboat, scratching at the rust around the mount for the mast. I can taste the rust, smell the sail that has been soaked and dried dozens of times over in heat that will eventually lead, one day when I am older, to the removal of skin cancers. I can see the '28' parrots exploding emerald and sapphire and yellow in the eucalypts. There are interpolations – a banksia blossom from another time and another place, a heightened emotional moment. There is no biography to this in the strictest sense, the incidents are too fragmentary. But the tactility of the moment is preserved.

A few years ago I wrote an autobiographical or anti-autobiographical work, *Auto* (2001a). The experiences are fragmentary, the narrative shifts around. Issues of duration become pivotal when a brief moment extends into pages, and massive events (on a personal and historic level) are glossed over in a sentence. Time is not as it should be. But then sometimes the words move as they were chronologically enacted. As author, I retell my own story from a variety of points of view, never stable. What is truth – as remembered by whom? My mother's version of events will most often be different; my brother's closer, but still different. And so it goes.

You bypass circadian and diurnal rhythms. The cave is open to light, the Fremantle Doctor fills it with fresh sea air in the late afternoon. You stay in lit places at night. You close your room off to the light in the day. Jet lag kicks in and out. It's midnight and cold out on the hundred acre. The fuel is metal cold as it spills over your hands, the funnel slipping. The heavy soil is sticking to the tines and a fox is barking up towards the Needlings. You grow groggy. The tractors light glow silver and orange. Another two hours at least, the figures of eight that cut out the corners harder and harder to do – the light inadequate, the body hard to steer. Your lift back down to the city arriving at first light. A serepax to link the events ...

... Katherine can't sleep. Think of something nice, you say. Think of Walsingham, of the Shrine of Our Lady. Of the Stations of the Cross. Of the Catholics and Anglicans taking tea together. Can't sleep. Go to sleep. John Kerrigan has invited us to lunch out at the cottage. A vegan feast. Daddy falls to sleep after he's been awake all night. He falls asleep on the couch listening to the stereo and watching the television. He watches the television when he's asleep. Can't sleep. Go to sleep. I can't go to sleep because I'm worried I'll be tired in the morning. I don't want to think, thinking keeps me awake ...

... My head is going fast inside. Go to sleep. Think of the walk to the Slipper Chapel, the fighter jets cutting in over the coast, the ear-tags of cows destined for slaughter as the mist lifts from the field and the thistles dry and the world begins to glow. (2001a, pp. 52–54)

What I did in *Auto* which, like Dante's *La Vita Nuova* in this one respect, searches to understand love – maybe a lack of self-love – with prose commentaries cutting across poetry texts, was to imitate or mimic systematically the experiences of my life as I remembered or re-remembered them. These experiences were presented in different shapes, with different prosodies. A system of mimetics tied them together, but the imitations constantly shifted. As a reversal of Dante's guiding principle, though, I made tangential commentary and illustrated with verse by the object of my subjectivity!:

> Last year I bought my wife a new flute – to replace the one I'd hocked and lost at the beginning of our marriage. As a teenager I'd hated body fluids and dirt and loss of control. I then devoted a dozen years to overcoming these phobias. That's one way of looking at it. Andrew Burke turned up with Tracy at my flat in South Perth near the river. I was pretty far gone. I said something about fucking Tracy and Andrew was disgusted. When I did, or maybe I already had, I burnt the curried vegetables and shaved the hair from around her cunt. She'd written a poem called 'Hair' which I'd published in *Salt* long before I knew her. It went:

> The length
> of my body is an odd
> nudity, what is it
> doing there, how
> did the hair
> get pared down
> to just
> these patches
> we cultivate
> like fetishes
> meant to excite
> when we want
> to play animal
> or we control
> to stress and make
> the difference between sexes
> as if otherwise
> we couldn't find
> ourselves.
> I can't force
> what once was
> to grow now
> in a strange season.
> I'm caught
> between
> the dreams of befores
> that paralyses
> and the need
> of my own nakedness
> which is there,
> which is there.
>
> (2001a, pp. 57–58)

Back to the park. The poem forms between the moment I actually occupy and will occupy, with the short-term past and the imitated (but highly 'real' to me) past that interrupts my thoughts with painful and disturbing clarity. I know every revisiting of this that is foisted on me, though I recall it as being identical to other revisitings, is mediated by the place and context of where it occurs. As with the text read in a different place, or the poem you have read a dozen times, meaning never remains stable or consistent. It shifts.

Perhaps this is why I see the draft as the most relevant part of the poem, why a poem for me is never completed. It is part of an ongoing conversation in which a dialogics forms between the text and the unwritten 'seeing' of what that text might become as conditions of production and reception change.

The mnemonics also has a personal angle. It will not fit the 'poetry definitions' volume. These are associations that assist memory. They are tools of remembering and remembrance. For me, they become tools to lose the moment so that I will not have to revisit it compulsively. Now, I have just said that poetry gives no closure to me, that it is an ongoing series of drafts, a revisiting, a reanimating or mimicry of tensions between the past and present and future, of the real and imagined, of the perceived and conceptualised. All of these. But now I am suggesting that I do not want any of it. And I do not.

I DO NOT WANT TO WRITE OR READ POETRY. I am addicted, compelled. I cannot stop. This is mental illness of a sort, and not inspiration (or delusion of this), but compulsion. What we have tracked so far is the subtext of the poem, the reason it might come into being. Moving along, the process of transcribing or translating or transliterating this compulsion into a form (visual or oral – or never uttered but seen or heard in the head), is a very different process. This is where unmnemonic becomes pivotal for me. I encode my work in traditional ways – often using traditional rhythms which I disrupt with colloquialisms and dialect, using set forms from a variety of cultural spaces (conscious of the appropriative issues therein) – but also encode it with un-mnemonics that cause a disintegration of sense upon rereading, especially as context shifts and changes.

Those points of ambiguity become increasingly larger, and suddenly the anchor points do not hold. The repetitions and patterning of words, which assist us in our ability to recall them, become unstable – an apparent volta is seemingly not where it should have been, a noun is really a verb, and so on. The stock epithet is not quite the same each time. When I read aloud I do so mainly from memory, with the page of the book as a rough guide. No two readings of mine have ever been the same – not only in tone and performance qualities/styles, but in actual textual consistency. I try to be inconsistent. Only slightly. A changed word, a reshaped line.

I can close my eyes and see the poem on the page because I have that kind of memory, but I can also see the drafts that led to that version, and the versions of the poems I should write. They are key points of memory in the poem – specific words that have a texture, a strong form and function association, or that are emotional triggers. Some fit an idiomatic pattern that comes with being brought up in a specific space. The mnemonics are where I try to disrupt, to subvert the poem.

Disclosed poetics

Mnemonic systems can work by abstracted repetitions or patterns of association as much as by, say, a string of music, or a series of visual or verbal prompts. For me, it is a question of disturbing juxtapositions that come out of having witnessed animal cruelty or death, or, for instance, some natural phenomenon that is inexplicable: glowing fields, ball lightning, will-o-the-wisps. Patterns build up in my subconscious, repeat themselves in recreating the poem I have mentally formed onto the page, or in recitation from memory. A chair, a table, a tree might trigger locations and patterns of words, help in the recreation of a poem resembling what I have 'thought'.

Location Triggers

The pillared porch, Corinthian
because it's easiest from books,
plastered, upholding world's ceiling
that goes through to the next story
always colder in winter, maybe cooler in summer,
airflow and loveseat, swinging
where foliage redresses trees
in gendered avenues, sweeping uphill
as around flat fields, the grey rot
of corn stalks, Japanese beetle
driving towards modification, it's said,
avoiding upper rooms where heat unsettles
small windows, vicarious
and remembering a purple rising light,
hillfolds and outcrops bettered
by kites and glider, their freedom
paramount over scrub and small animals
they'd destroy, farmers alarmed
by drop-ins, all land there
like thermals and updrafts, but suddenly
undercut, we resist calling it revenge,
colluding with indifferent Nature,
visa and permit, green card
as crops spread: they won't let me
into their pastoral entirely,
invited to ride the header,
to harvest cobs and interiors
that exchange chemical appearance,
protectionist policies and markets
fill supermarket aisles, fill
hunting and trapping magazines,

fur around collars, covering
cold ears, addressing steers
on Texan clichés, clinging like ideas
of Kansas. We take back leaf-litter
stirring in warmer years, lack of snowdrifts,
birds chopping and changing
or not there at all: correlations so easy,
suppressed to keep mystery
intact . . . or fenceless plurals
full of Wallace Stevens,
growing randomly and imitating
gardens, as if you'd fly straight
from Columbus to Paris, or get diverted
to New Orleans, or Baton Rouge;
I track these infinitudes,
connect nouns from an uncle's paddocks
in places threatened by closure,
by tariffs, sucked into global
silos and temptations,
cantons and guilds and red barns
lit by nuclear light,
as fission is comradeship,
alliance, the blind leading the blind,
and grain swelling on lightless nights,
Biblical texts written with a human hair
on rice, as faith makes cars run
and the fringes shutdown:
deny all access.

(2003, pp. 178–179)

Having spent a lot of my adult life living in various countries other than that of my birth, and being doomed (against my wishes ultimately) to be a perpetual wanderer, memory and the associations of words with a specific place tend to be disrupted. Perhaps that is why I also persistently *write over* the place I come from. That is where most of the flashbacks take me. But it is no longer the story of that place I am telling – that place has changed and become something else – I am telling in poetry the story of hybridisation, of dislocation, loss and disruption. My poetry is full of death, and maybe this is why. It shifts register dramatically. Maybe this is why. I do not feel comfortable in any 'school' or 'camp'. Again, maybe this is why. Poetry, for me, is an eclogic structure: a dialogue between disparate parts of myself, most often centred in the rural, and between conflicting cultural inputs. Characters are speaking through me – sometimes characters close to myself, but they are all mimicking someone from the real world. They are not real. It is all a simulacrum.

I see romanticism in revival. There are obvious cultural-historic reasons for this, and the threat of war (we have been in a state of world war for a number of years now) always brings on a search for a sublime, especially in a world where nature is increasingly being destroyed or disturbed, or can be undone in extreme ways, instantly. The end of Language poetry and the rise of new-lyricists such as Lee Ann Brown, Lisa Jarnot, Lisa Robertson, and Jennifer Moxley, with their strong consciousness of the tensions between deployments of tradition and the fetishisations of linguistic innovation (especially regarding 'class' alienation), illustrates a shift in receptivity not only to environmental and social concerns (also pivotal to language poetry), but to a concern about the ecology of language and meaning. Consider Lee Ann Brown's poem 'No Melpomene':

> No Melpomene
>
> Re: Lone poem, pen nomme
> Pommel pope poop
> Olé, Olé, Ol' Pop Pomp
>
> Pelé mope
> Mono men pole, lop me
> One pen open poem
>
> Peel 'em:
> La Pomme, pome, pommelo
>
> Moon pone molé
>
> (1998)

There is no lyrical self, mediated or otherwise, located textually here, but there is a subjectivity in the texture and immediacy of address. This lyricism locates itself in the implication of song, the implication of self (muse of tragedy becomes muse of poem becomes/IS muse of self and self-devolvement), without being dictated by the unified self. These are poets who do not wish to lose referentiality, or to deny it entirely. Here's the end of Shelley's over-quoted *A Defence of Poetry* (first published 1840):

> It is impossible to read the compositions of the most celebrated writers of the present day without being startled with the electric life which burns within their words. They measure the circumference and sound the depths of human nature with a comprehensive and all-pene-

trating spirit, and they are themselves perhaps the most sincerely astonished at its manifestations; for it is less their spirit than the spirit of the age. Poets are the hierophants of an unapprehended inspiration; the mirrors of the gigantic shadows which futurity casts upon the present; the words which express what they understand not; the trumpets which sing to battle, and feel not what they inspire; the influence which is moved not, but moves. Poets are the unacknowledged legislators of the world. (1988, p. 297)

The abovementioned poets and other innovators, steeped in the historicity of their poetries, the environments their languages arises from, might be forced into this mould. I say *forced*, because their individual intentions and agendas could not be bent in this way. It is the convenience of the overview. There is an emphatic belief that poetry can make a difference. The mere production of it suggests this. Despair has not closed the door to utterance, though, of course, it might in the future. Their significance is in the recognition that the moment of self is undeniable within or outside a political intentionality. Their poetry is a poetry of purpose, they have something to say: it is semantic and linguistic legislation, even if it is a civil or linguistic disobedience.

I would like to consider myself simpatico with them as poets, though more recently my despair has driven me away from cause and effect, and certainly beyond the ironies of engaging with the sublime. Prayer is still poetry for me, and poetry prayer, but nature can't even work as a mimetic construct. The paper I use, the books I read mean suffering for this 'nature'. My existence as a print poet becomes a process of bad legislation, and consequently denial. I wrote a poem when I first became a vegan called 'Of':

> Of emulsifiers and preservatives
> extracted from boiled-down animal,
> of houses with walls of horse hair
> and thongs of leather to restrain
> the tortured awning,
> of feet covered in dead cow,
> kangaroo, crocodile ...
> the business of pig-skin briefcases,
> of those whose guilt lay in fish,
> of those sucking the nectars
> of sacred beasts,
> of the differences between clean and dirty flesh,
> of those who seek truth in the burnt offering,
> of 'perfect and upright' Job, slaughterer
> who sought to appease over and over,

>   of Julius Civilus With A Dead Cock
>   arrogantly accepting what is
>   over and over, back and forth, to and fro.
>
>   (1998c, p. 231)

I do not enjoy polemical poetry, but then I wonder if all poetry is not polemical the moment it is written or sung or spoken. There is another kind of politics when it stays in your head, even if fully realised, but more relevantly, a less explicable politics when it remains half formed. Literally, for me, poems are a series of mime enactments in which characters are never given names. They are dumb eclogues. It is the stone, the leaf, and the made object. That is easy; not original. But it is a truth for me. I wonder what it is I am articulating outside my own chemical disconnections and odd internal wiring. As an anarchist, am I legislating, laying down a series of commands for others to follow? If so, I should stop, stop now. But here is my quandary: I do not want to stop the stone, the leaf. My interpretation of a bird's flight, a baby crying, creates a series of associations that struggle to separate themselves from the thing as thing-in-itself. Past memories burn back. I cannot dispose of the connections. I do not want to be part of a poetic experience, but I am. If there is a 'modern sublime', then maybe therein lies part of the necessity of this contradiction.

Can we reclaim, revamp, and reprise the sublime? Consider it a viable literary tool or mode of expressing a reverence and awe born out of terror for nature. To give an alternative name and face to beauty? Yes, if Burke's 'ocean' (1757/1958, pp. 57–58) with its terror is sublime not only because of tidal waves but because of heavy metal saturation, butchery of its life, oil spills. The sublime of the polluted, the sublime of the greenhouse effect. It is an angry irony. The sublime never worked as more than an idea. An exchange with God or nature that can be transmuted into artistic expression is simply a version of mimicry.

The sublime becomes the space-travel or star-gazing experience in an environment disrupted and destroyed. As a subtext of deep ecology, the sublime may work as an inspiration, but the layers of contaminants and the paucity of wildlife and forests work against it. The mountains become engagements with different kind of contaminants. There was rubbish for Coleridge and Shelley, they were tourists – they made rubbish and were tourists themselves. Nature has overwhelmed me in its infinite complexity in places like Bluff Knoll, or The Gap – both in Western Australia – but simultaneously I feel its loss and destruction.

The sublime is a textual displacement, and divergence, in a cautionary tale of not what will happen, but what is happening and has happened. Time shifts. The duration does not match. We caution in the reading of who we are. That it might not translate into the way we treat each other. But it does. The transcendent that cannot be pinned down in words, despite the movement of the self towards transcendence, the veneration of the path to an unrealisable actuation. Beauty is isolated, and we grapple towards it. The majesty of the sublime remains, necessarily, unobtainable.

I would argue that the sublime has been rendered as trope, as construct that is obtainable insofar as beauty has been forced into subjectivity by modernism, and becomes the ironic footnote in a world perceived in its wholeness as having been made increasingly ugly. The sublime, outside text, rests in the lens of the Hubble, and a cracked mirror is corrected so it can be maintained. The need is there, but it is textually subservient. Maybe it returns to John Dennis, to the 'sublime object' (Burke, 1757/1958, pp. xlvii–xlviii), simply an issue of style. The separation of the sublime and the beautiful is a tension in modern poetry. The beautiful is a fetishised advertising construct that, even in private moments, we are required to question. The sublime suffers the same fate. In isolation they exist per the moment as well, but, constructed in the poem, a consciousness of language and its history renders 'purity' impossible.

Here's an extract from Edmund Burke's essay on the 'Sublime and Beautiful':

> THE passion caused by the great and sublime in *nature*, when those causes operate most powerfully, is Astonishment; and astonishment is that state of the soul, in which all its motions are suspended, with some degree of horror. In this case the mind is so entirely filled with its object, that it cannot entertain any other, nor by consequence reason on that object which employs it. Hence arises the great power of the sublime, that far from being produced by them, it anticipates our reasonings, and hurries us on by an irresistible force. Astonishment, as I have said, is the effect of the sublime in its highest degree; the inferior effects are admiration, reverence, and respect ...
>
> ... No passion so effectually robs the mind of all its powers of acting and reasoning as fear. For fear being an apprehension of pain and death, it operates in a manner that resembles actual pain. Whatever therefore is terrible, with regard to sight, is sublime too, whether this cause of terror, be endued with greatness of dimensions or not; for it is impossible to look on anything as trifling, or contemptible, that may be dangerous. There are many animals, who though far from being large, are yet capable of raising ideas of the sublime, because they are considered as objects of terror. As serpents and poisonous animals of almost all kinds. And to things of great dimensions, if we annex an adventitious idea of

terror, they become without comparison greater. A level plain of a vast extent on land, is certainly no mean idea; the prospect of such a plain may be as extensive as a prospect of the ocean; but can it ever fill the mind with anything so great as the ocean itself? This is owing to several causes, but it is owing to none more than this, that the ocean is an object of no small terror. Indeed terror is in all cases whatsoever, either more openly or latently the ruling principle of the sublime. (1757/1958, pp. 57–58)

And:

> Infinity, though of another kind, causes much of our pleasure in agreeable, as well as of our delight in sublime images. The spring is the pleasantest of the seasons; and the young of most animals, though far from being compleatly fashioned, afford a more agreeable sensation than the full grown; because the imagination is entertained with the promise of something more, and does not acquiesce in the present object of the sense. In unfinished sketches of drawing, I have often seen something which pleased me beyond the best finishing; and this I believe proceeds from the cause I have just now assigned. (p. 77)

The loss of the sublime is in the idea of a universe – expanding but finite in content; but it remains in the idea of the 'unfinished work'. A resistance to closure can be an act of sublimity. I write only drafts, and that is a sublimity. It fits the category of mimetic sublimity. It relies not on nature, but a human construct, or an interpretation of a damaged nature. The ocean is still a place of terror, but we are led to believe it is being controlled. Science works to harness it. It resists, and the sublimity is retained in this. Or a meteorite hitting the planet. The beauty I find in the white wastes of salinity that have destroyed the farm. So it is there, just reconfigured. Consider the sublime in this from Lisa Jarnot's p(r)oems, 'Sea Lyrics':

> I won't go to the waterfront anymore, I am basking on a beach far from the army, I am pointing to a thousand speckled birds, I am watching the salads roll down to the shore, I am on the grounds of Mission High School with the murderers, I am near the edge of all the bungalows, I am reaching toward the pineapples to reach, I am dreaming the dreams I hardly know and know I have tattoos, I am in the ambulance at dawn, I am in this town beneath where you have jumped from bridges row by row, from the midtown light, I am in the dreams Lucretius, I have helped you to assemble all the mammals on the lawn. (1996)

Parataxis, rolled text, and pollution of beauty make the sea-as-sublime terrible before the sea is actually considered. There is a displacement of the sublime by the terror of the incidental, the matter-of-fact. Sublime still, but brought down to ground. The awe has been defamiliarised.

The ur-text of the sublime is now believed to come from the middle of the first century AD, Longinus's (or Pseudo-Longinus's) *On the Sublime*. Here's an extract from Chapter 1:

> [W]riting for a man of such learning and culture as yourself, dear friend, I almost feel freed from the need of a lengthy preface showing how the Sublime consists in a consummate excellence and distinction of language, and that this alone gave to the greatest poets and historians their pre-eminence and clothed them with immortal fame. For the effect of genius is not to persuade the audience but rather to transport them out of themselves. Invariably what inspires wonder casts a spell upon us and is always superior to what is merely convincing and pleasing. For our convictions are usually under our own control, while such passages exercise an irresistible power of mastery and get the upper hand with every member of the audience. (1982, trans. Fyfe, p. 125)

And an extract from Chapter 9:

> Now, since the first, I mean natural genius, plays a greater part than all the others, here too, although it is rather a gift than an acquired quality, we should still do our utmost to train our minds into sympathy with what is noble and, as it were, impregnate them again and again with lofty inspiration. 'How?' you will ask. Well, elsewhere I have written something like this, 'Sublimity is the true ring of a noble mind.' And so even without being spoken the bare idea often of itself wins admiration for its inherent genius. How grand, for instance, is the silence of Ajax in the Summoning of the Ghosts, more sublime than any speech. In the first place, then, it is absolutely necessary to suggest its source and to show that the mind of the genuine orator must be neither small nor ignoble. For it is impossible that those whose thoughts and habits all their lives long are petty and servile should flash out anything wonderful, worthy of immortal life. (pp. 144–145)

It is easy to see how the latter is undermined with every modern irony. Aesthetically, it is the mean and ignoble I search for in language. The Warholian piece of trash, the art that is Cicciolina rather than the Venus or David. These are the contemporary registers of popular culture, of the new sublime. These elements of the 'filthy' sublime, as perhaps we could call them, become codes and triggers in my personal mimetics, another form of mnemonic mapping. My effort at confronting the irreconcilability of the classical and modern, though

Disclosed poetics

the conditions of oppression, and environmental and cultural destruction, share much in common, in 'Bluff Knoll Sublimity', a poem more about language as object and a construct of sublimity, than about the sublime in nature:

> Bluff Knoll Sublimity
>   for Tracy
>
> 1.
>
> The dash to the peak anaesthetizes
> you to the danger of slipping as the clouds
> in their myriad guises wallow about
> the summit. The rocks & ground-cover
> footnotes to the sublime. The moods
> of the mountain are not human
> though pathetic fallacy is the surest
> climber, always willing
> to conquer the snake-breath
> of the wind cutting over
> the polished rockface,
> needling its way through taut
> vocal cords of scrub.
>
> 2.
>
> It's the who you've left behind
> that becomes the concern as distance
> is vertical and therefore less inclined
> to impress itself as separation; it's as if you're
> just hovering in the patriarchy
> of a mountain, surveying
> the tourists – specks on the path
> below. Weather shifts are part of this
> and the cut of sun at lower altitudes
> is as forgiving as the stripped
> plains, refreshingly green at this time
> of year. You have to climb it because it's
> the highest peak in this flat state,
> and the 'you have to' is all you
> can take with you as statement
> against comfort and complacency:
> it's the vulnerability that counts up here.

3.
> You realize that going there to write a poem
> is not going there at all, that it's simply
> a matter of embellishment, adding
> decorations like altitude,
> validating a so so idea
> with the nitty gritty of conquest.
> Within the mountain another
> body evolves – an alternate
> centre of gravity holding
> you close to its face.
> From the peak you discover
> that power is a thick, disorientating
> cloud impaled by obsession, that
> on seeing Mont Blanc – THE POEM –
> and not Mont Blanc – THE MOUNTAIN –
> the surrounding plains
> with their finely etched topography
> can be brought into focus.
>
> (2003, pp. 48–49)

As the horrors of the twentieth century are exacerbated and perpetuated, I am guided by Adorno (1967) in the belief that I cannot but work towards silence. What I am performing is a mime, enacted to a tune in my unconscious, while sublimity raises its polluted head and becomes the acceptable, the desirable awe.

Poetics recidivous and the de-poetics of lightning, herbicides, and pesticides

As stated earlier, Peter Porter said on the televised discussion I had with him some years ago (*Words*, 1999) that *the line* is the basic measure of the poem. I said it was the word, the morpheme, the phoneme ... the letter. And smaller still. The line is an accumulation of other units of measure, and the line hesitates rather than pauses if it carries no punctuation as it ends. And even with punctuation, even if it is the last line of the poem, the line rolls over into something. An abyss of the remaining blank page, if nothing else. The more intact the poem seems, the less it is so for me. A poem is like 360 degrees of activity, and the lines are endless. So, what remains? The line has become distended, dislocated, and working at odds with the expectation of form – and yet it is intended to 'free' itself from the rigours of the form as a whole. Place and the immediate occasion, or recounting something just past – especially a walk, a drive, a visit to another place. The lines, the route, the directions on the map marked out. Observations, but departure points for the seemingly unrelated.

I once wrote to a friend:

> Finished a 'prophetic' poem the other night – a long poem of wild outbursts and crazed (intentionally) lineation. I am about to start a second prophetic poem (they are based on towns). This follows on my 'Perth poem' which has been turned into a radio drama and my 'Cambridge poem' (recently published with some drama of its own!) ...
>
> Anyway, long weird poems are the go. 'The Perth Poem' was published in *The Literary Review* in the US should you wish to read it.
>
> I despair at the 'state of poetry' – an easy and old despair, but one all the same. The desire to enclose poems, to make them orderly and responsible, bores and offends me. What's wrong with having figurative language that merges with the rhetorical, where suddenly something is told or 'explained' only to flash back into metaphoric digression, where a 'cliché' can star (common usage that is) among paratactic obtuseness?! These juxtapositions and shifts are what makes a poem live for me. I don't want to be ruled by taste or good sense. It's got to burn and burn its way out. It need never apologise, it need never excuse itself, it need never explain itself. I am excited that Norton have given me a free hand with my big (I guess it will come in near 250 pages) *The New Arcadia* – hopefully a visionary and digressive journey bound within the five acts of Philip Sidney's arcadia, with the eclogues and 'drives' anchoring the whole thing. The many moods and people and situations of the country touched upon, but not imprisoned by the grand unifying vision. There is not unity. There is no centre. (2004)

This was written in a burst of enthusiasm that was soon defeated by gloom at the increasing strength and damage inflicted by the American military-industrial Christian right and its cronies around the world (Australia as extra state of America, Britain stuck in its fear cycle). A hundred thousand dead in Iraq, at least; no doubt many more. So why do I write poetry? Here are three poems from *Doppler Effect*, which constitutes nearly a collected experimental poems of mine. I originally wrote them out of frustration with the dissolution of the material and spiritual world, and the fact that language – any language – is the captor as much as the liberator. I had been trying to ask a Spanish-speaking poetry email list from Argentina to take me off their books: I was getting massive, unsolicited emails and it was causing problems. I was ignored and ignored. I pasted language together the best I could to make myself understood – using a bit of Spanish I knew from many visits to Spain, French, English, and even Latin. but to no avail. My mood was bad, and my poetry is a direct conduit to my mood; also, a general state of despair with the deceptiveness of poetry, its false claims to agency:

>3 Poems Out of Kilter
>
>I unsubscribe
>
>mis demean our refuse
>topped sub due, a lawn
>and stippled verb, test
>ice-top, signifiosis
>stranger in private proprietory
>cased in language
>replies unrequested,
>requiet paced across
>sharp grassblades,
>hypo, and where locate
>geno flex ion buddings,
>where petit declasse
>testamental cultures,
>columnular scroll, temples
>and feathers parsed
>odour, outré
>
>why write no poetry more
>
>estfavour, pour gramrare
>incur, askew, aka insistentor
>saqueneme est fixator
>in, preser vert er stockist
>clust, awed upclaw
>un apologia, lyris
>instignation, foreclose
>upythesis, gerd luca
>placirds, erd air,
>syrios
>
>& Succor
>
>inist geothemies sistic, treple upclass -ments,
>axiomies, I sest readentary: drinkables, thirst sents
>
>func gigs up crites, less lovely, encircled festeries
>can as can do, fuck hit'n duelists says groups, treez
>
>(2004a, pp. 413–415)

The process was not new to me. I had done this with Portuguese (a language that has long impressed me – sounding like a cross between French and Spanish), and other languages, in an effort to create a hybrid language that refused all certainty. I was not interested in a figurative Esperanto (Srikanth Reddy's excellent poem 'Fundamentals of Esperanto' (2003) with its declining ironies amuses me here – I heard it read in Vancouver in 2004), but in a rebarbative form that sounded lyrical and yet rejected lyrical unity. The language of the fifth person insular! A hermetic, maybe.

Anyway, all this leads me to think of what qualifies the 'cliché' as being something we are supposed to avoid. I have said it before: I have always been fascinated by clichés and at school started an essay secretly during class regarding their complexity and efficacy. I wrote poems consisting entirely of clichés, though I showed them to no one. Clichés in literature seem often to engender a fear of declaration – an emotional or conceptual confrontation is diluted by the 'expected' language. Clichés are debased parables and allegories; they are Fontaine and Aesop rendered to liquidity. And yet they can bite. The claim here is that sudden shifts, sudden highlights, juxtapositions, parataxis (not only linguistic, but conceptual: idea against idea), the casual speech, disrupted syntax, broken rhythm, the 'dull' line among the sparking lines, the pedantic amid the informative, create a generator of possibilities. Inasmuch as the imposition of religion deletes the spirit, as the system controls liberty, so does the poem delete its own possibilities if inflexible. Form and constraint are useful to work against, but they are not an end in themselves. Forcing a poem into a shape can be an important statement, but it is not the only statement. We use Pound's model here, but the model is no more useful than the vase itself: an object used to hold the decoration of death, the severed stems. To glow momentarily, before being lost to atrophy. But all is not lost; through observation we learn from the loss. Rimbaud's faith in the scientific (Steinmetz, 2001), and his declared willingness to do whatever it took to acquire the seer's vision, are paradoxically and inextricably bound in what we now identify as one of the modernist urges. The contradiction holds now as much as then, whatever our views of the engineering and visionary components of the poem.

So, what of grammar? I am told – often – I deny or defy the rules of grammar. Why? And what is grammar to me as poet? The more figurative a poem, the more the poem seems to deny logical progression. The rules of Standard English are the rules that the poem written in English defies. Elizabethan poets composed a poetry without fixed spelling. They heard the words, and the reading in manuscript of these words with their variations still allowed for the metre to be followed: intonation rested in aural interpolation of the visual. When Philip Sidney pushed the trochee he did so against the scribe's transliteration of his text, before destroying the 'foul papers' of his original drafts (Sidney, 1962, p. lxv). The math of the poem was built in the deployment of a language that had as its model ways of reading based in the sciences of rhetoric and oratory derived from a classical education. Sidney rarely used punctuation, though in copying the texts scribes introduced commas and periods and other variant grammars. The grammar was their guide to reading according to their interpretation. In my deployment of grammar I have pursued two outcomes: to strain against 'correct usage' – to find, say, a comma indicating too short or too long a break; to use grammar in the same way as I use shape and form – a vase that holds the 'bright' contents, but also provides a platform for atrophy. Grammar and shape speak against as much as with content.

    Some: an ode to the partitive

Some burn-outs on asphalt stretch outside trig tables
Some galahs refuse to toe the line
Some solar cells gather waving lines of morphemes
Some striated pardalotes nidify just now, some shortly
Some spray booms disassociate, haze painted button quail
Some crop dusters plague the guy waving from his rooftop
Some bush bashers patiently tend some crops-in-the-bush you stay
    away from if you don't want to be shot
Some windmills shake down, rung on rung of saline accumulation
Some hubs on mallees mark driveways
Some samphire is salt bush in some necks of the clear-fell
Some wedgetail eagles harried by crows stay high above pasture
Some laterite conduits are County Peak
Some casuarinas are melaleucas are grevilleas are hakeas are acacias
    are eucalypts if you forget your guide book
Some poddy-dodgers are dodgers of law-makers and indulgers of
    flesh in-takers
Some sandhi are a(n) handy way of vowelling a wheat harvester
Some intermediaries focus specific causes for a decline in yellow
    skink numbers
Some wattles hold back flowering (sometimes)
Some farmers drive past three times in case they've missed catching
    you
Some lives are lost on crossroads
Some parishioners visit other people's churches, temples, mosques

> ...
> Some prayers connect and others don't, all get played back, are held
>   to account
> Some red-capped robins rip into our dark spots and make light of
>   them
> Some polluted places are so beautiful they make you weep buckets
> ...
>
> (Kinsella, 2004b)

Reprise ... re-examination ...
So many of my poems are companion pieces or re-examine the same place at different times, in different seasons. The world is fixed in many ways, but infinitely variable and different in others. As I was obsessed with Rubik's Cube as a teenager, so am I obsessed with the interactions, patterns, and re-arrangements that work around a single plant, or stone, or fence-line. The interconnectedness is my celebration, and the damage to this: the intrusions and profit-driven alterations, the rhetorical jarrings. However, as negative as my work might become, it emits from a celebratory or positive grain, a particle in which all possibilities are present, in which mutuality, as well as uniqueness, emanates.

The project that is forming in my head is the microscopic analysis of five-and-a-half acres of land, divided into a 'house paddock', a 'York gum and granite boulders paddock', and 'the old sheep run'. Across the Thomsonian seasons (Thomson, 1726/1981) lacerated by dispossession and damage to the land, the efforts to heal and let be, to function and be productive as well, the intrusions from outside – the chemical spray from next door, a neighbour's cat hunting robin redbreasts and golden whistlers, planes overhead, the council responding to a 'dobber' to keep dry oats down, warding off the 'keep it down' brigade, the collecting of storm wood from distant properties, the stacking and cutting of wood in winter, the sight of a dugite outside on the drive, the long drive where fieldmice scurry and bobtails move slowly, under the dead York gum where pink and grey galahs sit of an evening and crows surmount them all, '28' parrots around the fruit trees in front of the house, the rain-gauge down the back, the flooded gums working as white-faced heron heronries, and echidna scratchings in the scrubby laneway, music drifting down from the piano, guitar, the drums ... all part of it, but just a glimpse. All companion pieces and the 'rounds' of a very familiar place. Not the farm – not a Wheatlands – but a lot just outside town, below the purple mountain and decayed shoulders of the Dyott Range, right near the horses and haycutters, near where rifles crack and the few kangaroos that come out of the reserves at the top of the hill are shot by spot-lighters on private property. The laments are in so many places, and the small space is weighed down by them.

A pastoral for me is no longer the extreme of a presentation for readers outside that space, nor one purely directed towards those within – in many senses its audience is unknown or shifting. There is no certainty of tenancy or ownership, even if the title deeds and laws of inheritance say so. One can be disinherited, the state can take what is 'yours', a people can be deleted, just like text. You write the land and convince yourself it is an interaction, a mutual inscription. It is not, but the suggestion is there.

The pastoral relies on an idea of what it was, and what it could mean: one writes through and against the discourse, occasionally lapsing into the still authentically inviting smell of the harvest, the early morning heat ... It is a practical pastoral: a pastoral of effect. It is the cliché, the opinion (a lot of that), the observation, the calibration of the rain-gauge, thermometer, and most importantly the barometer. The pastoral has the in-built expectation of disasters because they are part of the cycle, but the counter-pastoral I struggle with is not circular (as per John Barrell discussed by Jonathan Bate [2003, pp. 47–48] regarding the linearity of enclosure and the circular open fields: the block-written poem, maybe, as opposed to the 'round' of the song?), and not geometric: it is delineated and spiralling towards certain dissolution. It ceases to be 'outdoors' the more it is mass and chemical. It is a corrupted biosphere of productivity divorced from the personal and necessary. Ritual has not been supplanted, but relocated and pasteurised. This is obvious. But the need to work to prevent its dissolution, to shatter the spiral is essential. It is a radical pastoral: a pastoral of end results.

John Clare became a pastoral poet the moment he read Thomson's *The Seasons*. Had he not read this or other pastoral poetry, had he based his poetry purely on observation and the oral traditions of the village, then he would have been a poet of place, a rural poet, the ultimate non-pastoral poet. Pastoral is a mediation, and Clare's journey through influence and imitation of pieces composed for a literate and primarily country manor-house and urban audiences, edited and published by a mainstream city publisher, made his work pastoral. Jonathan Bate in his superb Clare biography begins the last chapter, 'The Poet's Poet':

> John Clare called Robert Bloomfield 'the greatest Pastoral Poet England ever gave birth to.' He was wrong: if we take 'pastoral' to mean 'showing a deep knowledge of nature and rural life', then that title belongs to himself. Clare knew his environment with a lived intimacy that sets him apart from well-born pastoral poets ... (2003, p. 545)

Bate's definition of pastoral is a 'throwaway' and 'uncritical' one (in this specific context), one generated from within the privileged pastoral discourse itself. On the other hand, he does recognise the fundamental difference between the genuine peasant (and poverty) 'credentials' of Clare over the socially and often financially better-off composers of pastoralisms. But it is all too neat a model, and the fundamental political conservatism of the pastoral tradition is underplayed. Clare himself was, as Bate identifies, a strange mixture of deep political conservatism and a radicalism sprung from dissenting religious flirtation, as well as a nostalgia and genuine anger over the loss of the open field farming ways and the new surveying and demarcation of enclosure. The pastorality of Clare lies in this friction, and his pastoral legitimacy is undermined by his own refusal to accept change. This is what pastoral analysis has missed in examinations of Clare's poetry: as much as Clare constantly returns to the past, and his celebrations of the past, he has ethically and intellectually evolved within his pastoralising (celebrating, rather than robbing, bird's nests, for example). Clare, always exalting nature and the 'rustic', became a pastoral poet in order to get attention, to get fame. It was an ego urge (and a sexual predator's conflict with the desire not to hurt the living: the irony of the carnivore, the misogyny of the versifying worshipper of women), and this ego-guilt consumed his 'sanity': his identification of himself and 'the self', in his asylum poems, is a recognition of his own pastoral betrayal of the imagined rural 'purity' of his youth. A deeply intelligent poet, he knew his own ironies, and the ironies of what he had done. An ostensibly anti pastoral poet (not an 'anti-pastoral' poet – the hyphen denoting ironic and conscious displacement within practitioners of the actual pastoral model), Clare became the pastoral poet so easily identified with by all others who have sold out to editing, printing, publishing, and the desire for book sales. We are all of the same, be we from the poor or the rich, one locality or another. One's accents and dialects are as legitimate as the standard speech of the metropolis's cultural elites: but those elites will easily fetishise and render them assimilable.

Being a pacifist, I am called 'genial'. But – again – I am angry, and poetry for me is a way of change. Of altering the language of convenience and predictability, of taking the over-used and reinvigorating by shifting context. And regarding Derrida's famous statement that 'Il n'y a pas d'hors-texte', that is that 'there is no outside-of-text' (1987, p. 158), it has always frustrated me that some interpret this as meaning that there is no context – through this window, all has been context for me as a poet. I write because of context. In other words, all thing are contextual because all things are text. You cannot leave the text, though you can, I feel, shift within the text. Preservation comes not through isolation but awareness. We need to be aware of the referents, to respect the signifiers. Clarity is to be found within. That is the spirituality of poetry. It is worth noting that in the wheatbelt of Western Australia, rustic provincialism is informed by the internet and the trappings of the western world.

The more that urban dwellers looking into the rural world would detect such rusticism, the more they should realise that rural people often have a conscious desire to be what the urban are not. Availability of cultural resources is less, but the choice not to connect with them is part of a geographical exclusionism that often rejects the values of the city. The desire for profit is good incentive to be more than familiar with the latest advances in crop science, but not to indulge the protection of the environment for its own sakes: if it is not immediately pragmatic, then it is often rejected. The church as centre of town and centre of selective isolationism is an interesting aside: it is an amplification of intactness, a direct line to the holy verification of presence. If a poetry does not take these possibilities into account, it *will* be stuck in the pastoral tradition, and cease to be radical, cease to stimulate change in the place where change is needed.

The urban has an investment in keeping the rural the way it is: the urban feeds off it literally, and requires the rural as signifier to anchor its own clotted world. The rural is the desirable though mockable other. A counter-pastoral poem must be aware of the ironies of its own production. And to the critic who thought maybe I wasn't aware of the ironies of structure: it is my life's work, and how could I but be, caught in the clearing-zone of contradictory values. There is no absolute, no matter how absolute opinions might seem. And such is the contemporary pastoral poem: it is the paranoid reading *and* hebephrenic satisfaction (Hodge and Mishra, 1991) all in one. Per Hodge and Mishra, certainly, but also within the realm of the pastoral poem's own psychological taxonomy and expediency. The pastoral is about factories and bus lanes as much as about combine harvesters and shearers. They all know each other, even if they disavow the relationships.

I had been thinking that *The New Arcadia* would be – almost had to be – the last of my 'purely' pastoral volumes. It would be the completion of a trilogy that included *The Silo: A Pastoral Symphony* (1995) and *The Hunt* (1998b) – all synergistic books intended to work as single 'discontinuous' poems, as much as individual poems. Most of my other volumes of poetry have been concerned with pastoral issues, and include much rural poetry, but were not formed within the musical and historical literary notion of the pastoral volume in the same way. I certainly wrote and compiled *The New Arcadia* –

drew in its diverse rural pieces – with the idea of it as the third volume of a trilogy in mind. However, I now see a fourth volume, and possibly a fifth. The fourth would be the five-and-a-half acres up close, in micro; the fifth would be the surrounding world, the world of mysticism, and phenomena (lightning, earthquakes, 'ghosts', the church, and so on). It might be that the fourth and fifth belong together, like two symphonic movements working as counterpoint, even as fugue (to mix musical metaphors and notation! note: key to an idea here), within the one volume.

So, in the end: a quartet or a quintet. The process of moving away from the place again and for a considerable period of time, it would seem, has re-ignited the compulsion I thought had been 'spent', or at least closed out. I want to pace this last volume, or last two volumes, to meet the psychological requirement of completeness and order, but at the same time I so strongly reject these that I need to invite an open endedness. There is a plan, a vision, but also a realisation that the obsessive and necessary nature of composition (and experience!) will drive where it will. What is imperative for me is that each unit should have its own shape and structural necessities (even if these are 'deconstructive' – no longer the right word for what I am doing; 'reconstructive' might be more suitable) – and that I should work within the unit of each. That is the 'macro' side of things!

A poetics of being struck by lightning ...

> Struck, was I, not yet by Lightning –
> Lightning – lets away
> Power to perceive His Process
> With Vitality ...
>
> Emily Dickinson (1960, p. 435)

> It struck me – every Day –
> The Lightning was as new
> As if the Cloud that instant slit
> And let the Fire through ...
>
> Emily Dickinson (1960, pp. 171–172)

Lightning is illumination and sickness. Works by John Clare, John Berryman, Emily Dickinson, and many others, have accrued in my reading since I was a child struck by lightning. The lines from Rimbaud's 'Le Bateau ivre' (written in 1871) form a disturbed mantra:

> Je sais les cieux crevant en éclairs, et les trombes
> Et les ressacs et les courants: je sais le soir,
> L'Aube exaltée ainsi qu'un peuple de colombes,
> Et j'ai vu quelquefois ce que l'homme a cru voir!
> (1960, p. 129)

The centrality of personal vision, the ability to see literally what others have imagined they have seen, is at the core of my formative poetic experiences in 'nature'. This (imagined) flash of perception becomes the (real) lightning that struck me as a child, so the visions of nature become a reality that hold one to them, to nature itself. Wandering the farm at ten and quoting Keats, a synthesis took place for me in which language became inseparable from natural surroundings – and the clear alteration of 'nature' – despite the nature of Keats and the other Romantic English and European poets I was reading being so dramatically different. A kind of displaced and grotesque metaphor formed, so that my Claude glass was framed with salinity and erosion, with the blood of rabbits and parrots. I craved it, and yet knew it was its own inferno. A polymorphous perversity crept into visualisation, and a sexuality of the text resulted. Being struck by lightning was physically and mentally horrific, but also ecstatic, and arousing in an unspoken way. I still get aroused during electrical storms.

There's an interesting site on the World Wide Web dedicated to the victims of lightning strikes. Here is an extract from it, that might go part-way to concluding a poetics, or opening a physio-psychological basis for the poetics that I have come to see as my own:

> Early on, survivors may complain of intense headaches, tinnitus (ringing in the ears), dizziness, nausea, vomiting and other 'post-concussion' types of symptoms. Survivors may also experience difficulty sleeping, sometimes sleeping excessively acutely after the injury but changing during the next few weeks to inability to sleep more than two or three hours at a time. A few may develop persistent seizure-like activity several weeks to months after the injury. Unfortunately, standard EEG's do not always pick up injury in the areas that lightning most often affects leading to a diagnosis of 'pseudoseizures'.
>
> Personality Changes / Self-Isolation
>
> Many may suffer personality changes because of frontal lobe damage and become quite irritable and easy to anger. The person who 'wakes up' after the injury often does not have the ability to express what is wrong with them, may not recognize much of it or deny it, becomes embar-

rassed when they cannot carry on a conversation, work at their previous job, or do the same activities that they used to handle. As a result, many self-isolate, withdrawing from church, friends, family and other activities. Friends, family and co-workers who see the same external person, may not understand why the survivor is so different. Friends soon stop coming by or asking them to participate in activities. Families who are not committed to each other break up.

Obviously, depression becomes a big problem for people who have changed so much and lost so much. Suicide is something that almost all severely injured people have thought about at one time or another. Occasionally, those who do not have access to medical care or who do not understand what is happening may self-medicate with alcohol and other drugs, particularly those who have previously sought solace with these compounds. It is very important that the family and friends of the survivor maintain supportive contact even though it requires an adjustment in their relationship with the survivor. An injury such as this is an injury to the family, not just to the person hit. (Cooper, 2005)

I was struck by lightning . . .
When I was about nine or ten I was struck by lightning I was in the passenger seat of a ute driven by my cousin Peter and Ken just a year older than me was in between we'd been at the tip up at Uncle Jack's place empty 44–gallon drums of bottles and setting them up at a distance and smashing them with rocks when the skies which were brooding grew horrifically dark and the exploding glass showered like leaden rain and the confusion of the skies made even the crows swallow their caws and my cousin the cousin driving the oldest cousin by some years said let's go before it really opens up the thunder pealing and the air crackling as you ran through it and dragging the 44s between us and throwing them any which way on the back of the ute slamming the tail-gate shut without really thinking about it and then charging down the track and nearly taking lines of paint off the ute driving so close to the barbed wire the back end sliding out and the wheels spinning and our heads slamming into the roof with every bump then the gate being shut I was sent out to open and shut it and in terror I struggled with the star-picket slung in wire loops and couldn't find the strength to break it open so Ken jumped out and between us we did it and the ute went through over the wire and we pulled it back up and I dropped the loop while Ken held it with his farm-boy strength next to the post and then we were off fishtailing and seeing fork lightning all around doughnutting the crossroads as the salt was etched by electricity and the crystals shot

prismatic rays out through the samphire and the salmon gums so
massive and canopied still on that gravel road wavered in the winds
picking up and distantly explosions of smoke as the day being so hot
and the wind ripping through the stubble we knew fire was on the
world's curve and coming closer and then a crash that was different
from the thunderous crashes all consuming yet this was immediate
and shook us differently the tailgate coming undone and a drum
rolling off and skidding to a halt someone screaming get out get the
drum and without thinking I'm running to the drum trying to look at
the road and the sky lit up and the salt rippling about the gullies and
grabbing the drum to roll to the truck I see a fork of white light come
up from my feet and rise up through me to heaven as if I'm a conduit
from Hell and pyrographed into a purgatory and always welded to
that spot not like some immortal recollection or recollection intimat-
ing immortality but an incendiary reminder of the suffering of
mortality and then being hurled through the air ten or twenty or
thirty feet I don't know but I rolled and Ken said then I think I recall
in the recollection overload that he'd never seen anyone get up like
that and I was into the ute away not really singed but hurting and
getting back to the house my Auntie said and says still my eyes were
out on stalks but there were other things afoot because Uncle Gerry
had been called out with water and wet hessian to fight the storm
fires rolling closer and closer to the farm and what had happened to
my eyes was that they'd become cameras that wouldn't stop photo-
graphing everything at high shutter speed and in quick succession
they saw too much at once flooded by primary colours and polarising
the light of objects and the living so bright that I could see even at
night I thought and the smell of the fire getting closer overwhelmed
me . . .

    Lightning: a parable

    That lightning never strikes twice
    I know is wrong

    a child poet
    my cousin drove madly
    during a storm

    a fire had broken out
    and we could just see
    the flame on the edge
    of the world's curve

> I was shocked to find
> that things burn in the rain –
> maybe it was dry over there?
>
> Thundering home
> a drum dislodged
> from the back
> of the truck
>
> and I was pushed
> into fields of light
> to put things right
>
> lightning struck close by
> and it shook me ...
> and lightning struck again
>
> as if it had chosen me
> as proof of its spontaneity
>
> (Kinsella, 1995c, p. 94)

And other electric shocks ...

> If lightning strikes from the ground up,
> and Heaven is but an irritation
> that prompts its angry spark ...
>
> (Kinsella, 1998c, p. 172)

I have had many electrical shocks and found smaller ones slightly addictive, especially on my tongue which when young I would place across the terminals of a nine-volt battery enjoying the tingle and electric taste though I had two 'throwing' experiences touching generators on car motors and they ripped through me but worst of all and this one re-ignited the lightning memory was when fixing a power-point at my grandparents' house when I was eighteen and down from country Geraldton to the city to start university and someone came in and turned the power back on in the meter box and the jolt threw me so hard against the wall that it almost broke bones and my head literally hummed for a day ...

They say over-stimulated sexuality is possible as a reaction to lightning or electric shock, or no sexuality at all, though in my case all forms of hyperactivity have been the go and an inability to sleep and alcoholism and drug addiction – how much can be drawn back to that lightning throwing me or not at all? It's an obsessive recurrent stimulant in my poetry that links heaven and hell and is the sharp tongue of the prophetic that wins out no matter how bitter or sceptical I am which I have become increasingly as the natural world is ground down to non-existence or at least a contrived nature seems to take its place it is the prayer I make before sleeping the prayers I utter as superstition it is the desire to see my wife and children it is enthusiasm and confidence as well as depression and aloneness it is the manic and the crushed it is the sickness of Berryman and the cold hard practicality of surviving...

I attached myself to a magneto once and cranking the handle tortured my flesh and nerves at school hating school and wanting to be elsewhere or to a Whimhurst generator I preferred the charge coming without external power sources but to be generated locally the light bulb powered by a lemon, which I also wrote secret script with.

Location is paramount in terms of the hermetics of a poem. The codified personal references that have meaning to the creator of the poem, and those intimately connected with its creation. Writing poems takes space from other personal interactions. Tracy tells me she wrote a poem about mirrors being covered up during lightning storms by an old Irish grandmother. Bad luck. I seem to have memories of intentionally watching lightning storms in mirrors. I can't be sure if my memory is Borg-like (as per *Star Trek*), or if this actually happened. But it appeals to me as metaphor, either way. I have a formative book of *Dreams, Superstitions, and Prayers*, which has been cumulatively forming over a number of years. It will probably take many more years to 'complete'. I have superstitious behaviours but no superstitious beliefs. Is that possible? Poems are forms of rituals, wardings-off and interactions with superstitions. All my poems are prayers. The political is inseparable from the utopian *and* dystopian for me.

The poetics of spray

As pesticides and herbicides are absorbed into the soil and the cells of plants and animals – resulting in barrenness, cancer and other terminal illnesses and possibly even altering DNA itself – so the language of poison and spray is absorbed into the poetic language as well. The use of DDT or some other poison in the poem is diluted in its possible protest effect by 'over-usage' and the fact that the social organism has shown a general willingness to replace one banned poison with another. The convenience of usage, the propaganda of the poison companies, dilute the impact of this horror. Poetry is a litmus paper to language in the wider world, and the non-physical impact of something as horrific as, say, the textual nomenclature of DDT or Agent Orange or even Roundup (patented!), means the mind has adjusted, has mutated to a benign acceptance. These words might rouse anger, but it is the idea of the words rather than the visceral quality of the words themselves – they should disturb enough to want to stop the poisoning. As harbingers, the pain they inflict should motivate us to rid the language of their descriptive or signifying necessity. As writing to silence because poetry does not stop or atone for aggression and violence, so too we might write the necessity of these words out of the language. They are not enriching on any level, though they need to exist painfully as long as any of the substances they signify are present or being manufactured.

The fortunes of spray
When I am at 'home' in York, Western Australia, it seems I spend most of my green-season time writing about – that is, against – spray. Last year I was asked to write a general ethics column for a literary journal, and I suggested writing about essays to do with pesticide, herbicide, and even fertiliser spraying. The editor emailed back, pleased, saying she could see a gender angle on the issue: basically along the lines of male occupation of the female earth and so on. While I agree that such a reading could be made, I feel it is ultimately a distraction. Surely it is as much about female abuse of the earth as it is male abuse of the earth. Surely it is people exploiting and fetishising the food and the soil to value-add their eating process, to give it an aesthetic value as well as an increased profit margin as much as anything else. The spray industry is, as with most industries, predominantly run by men, and the farmers who apply the stuff, certainly around our place just outside York, are usually male, but the psychology goes back to the consumer as much as to those providing the 'solution'. The household can of spray, the dabbing of weeds outside along the path with the 'magic wand', are the drivers of an industry that is as much about cosmetics as it is about increasing food production. Blemished and discoloured fruit and vegetables tend not to be bought, and any amount of waxes and chemical agents are deployed to give our vegetables suitable ripening, colour, and zest. In recent years, it has been the new cosmetics industry with its attendant animal abuse, genetic modification. The consumers of this vanity industry are as much female as male, and male as female. The gender codings are obvious already, but so interchangeable that it is almost self-defeating to distract ourselves that much. Getting back to the field: this is the zone where the obvious abuse takes place, though the laboratory is the scene of instigation, as the table is the scene of consumption (and validation).

What is pivotal from a poetics perspective, which for me is inseparable from the ethical and pragmatic implications of this, is the corruption of any pastoral idyll. A negating or negative pastoral is part of late twentieth-century English-language poetry, but the belief that such a negative pastoral is a denial of pastoral mores, should one remove the corrupting elements, is flawed. The model changes not only because the animals are genetically modified, or battery-farmed, or because the land is cleared and drenched in spray, or even (from a vegan perspective) because animals are used and abused, but because of cultural and social templates and flows. John Clare, with his loathing of enclosure, maps an early change in pastoral values, but before that there were numerous shifts in perception of the pastoral, especially whenever one pastoral model was used to fit another: the round peg of Virgil being forced into the square hole of feudal England. The dramatic shifts from country to city that redefine European pastoral are inverted in the Australian case with the 'exploration' and 'settling' of the land.

In more recent decades, the worldwide trend of a move towards cities has evolved, but the weekend farmer market of small lots has meant some movement out to towns at a commutable distance. The pastoral I am interested in here is a pastoral intensivism: an ultra-consciousness of what it means to be country on any level, while accommodating the increasing sins of the country. For example, having your weekender and growing a hand of supposedly organic tomatoes (which die from non-watering during a week of extreme heat), while the larger farms – the real farms – around it pour thousands of litres of spray on their crops. Where I live, weekenders are part of the local economy, but are despised behind closed doors. They are seen as not understanding the reality of living and being brought up in such communities. One's notion of pastoral is different from the other's, and because rural living has a place in the advertisements and literature and film, from *Wake in Fright* (1971) to the local footy team goes country, there is a constructed notion of what pastoral is. One of the arrogances of literature and the arts in general is that it feels the co-ordinates of a discourse belongs only to itself – which is not the case.

To position this argument, I will give a personal history of exposure to spray: Sheltox fly strips in the kitchen – yellow, sticky, and appealing in their skyscraper boxes hanging from the curtain rod. They were certainly post-modern. I tried to unstick a fly once . . . Mortein and Peabeau insecticides floating in clouds down over the Christmas feast, flies thick at the windows . . . down behind the shed spraying the stuff from a pressurised can onto my skin, so cold . . . ice. Or, further back, my grandfather's pump spray bottle that zapped redback spiders, killed aphids . . . . the backpack, the fire-fighter's steel drum curved to fit the back with brass rod and spray nozzle for fighting forest fires ... my paternal grandfather's ... converted to spray the roses ... My uncle spraying on the farm. Other farms used DDT; he probably did as well ... I saw Agent Orange clouding down over the deep green of Vietnam on the television ... farmers drinking beer as the plane returns to the local strip to load up ... a semi-communal effort ... Spray drums dumped in the bush we roll around and make skyscrapers from – 'cities for the country' ... it's endless ...

There is an advertisement on television for rye grass that works on 'flashing' to scare the rye grass to death. The herbicide ... On country television there are many farm-chemical ads as there are home-chemical ads in the city.

I remember an issue of Purnell's *History of World War 2*, which Auntie Jackie bought for me every Saturday, and which she would give me after she finished her stint working in the deli ... pictures of the death camps and the 'showers' with poison gas canisters ...

In searching Iraq for weapons of mass destruction between the two Gulf wars, investigators had a number of false alarms when pesticides were discovered in drums or traces in plants. There is a history of chemical weapons being linked to agricultural production, and it is not surprising. There's not a huge leap between what we intentionally ingest, and what is poured on us in the name of warfare, or for that matter, in the name of purity. *Cleansing* is a common component in both debates. I heard it said that there's a poorly guarded plant in Russia that holds enough stock of smallpox from the cold war days to destroy the earth's population many times over. The fact that small amounts constantly 'disappear' from this stockpile is one thing, but its existence is another. Humanity seems to need to prove its longevity by controlling its destruction. Holding the alpha and omega in both hands. With pesticides and herbicides it is much the same thing – death to bring life. The arguments for safety have about as much ability to break down completely as the chemicals they synthesise and pour on the earth, into the water, the air. DDT is an obvious argument, but there are many. Recently there was a pesticide spill (of a substance banned in many countries) near a school in Welshpool, Western Australia ...

Industries become self-perpetuating – the need is made. Spray is produced because a demand is created. All other solutions to crop growth are subordinated to profit. Genetic modification becomes linked to 'appropriate' chemical use. Symbiotic. Supply and demand. Again and again those verges along country roadsides are sprayed to kill the grass and then cut with a tractor and cutter in any case. The dead grass is cut in any case! Hyper-cyclical ... Repeat.

Alternatives: companion planting, but not pyrethrum because a poison is a poison. Garlic spray works well on vegetables for many 'pests'. Plant what suits the climate, the soil, 'natural predators'. It is a long list. There is a cottage industry of profit-making here as well...

> The Shitheads of Spray: a poetry of abuse
>
> Under-ode, antediluvian reprisal,
> seed vengeance, broad-leaf outrage,
> seed-spray head kick, the pressure point
> rumoured to have dropped Bruce Lee
> in his tracks; haters of weeds,
> haters of any more words
> than needed: say it straight,
> vandals, poofter-bashers, migrant-baiters,
> dead gum lovers, parrot killers,
> worshippers of spray-drenched fruit
> that smiles without blight,
> descendants of those who murdered
> Yagan and chopped his head off,
> sending it to Britain, Queen lovers
> but haters of queens, lizard mockers,
> snake beaters, makers of neat gardens.
> There's no getting away from them.
> Spray-drift sensurround, surround sounds
> but furtively sibilant, odour-ploy.
> Spray objectors have their cups-of-tea
> laced with Antex while the shitheads of spray
> graze sheep on dying grass
> and smile benignly. Residuals denied,
> the global plug: safe as table salt,
> safe as houses, safe as oily rainbows
> in winter light.
>   (Kinsella, forthcoming, *The New Arcadia*)

You can hear the spray planes – slower than the strafing air force trainers' planes, they buzz the fields with a sickly dive into the pit of the stomach, rising out of the throat. They get inside you with their sound, and with the spray drift. Standing outside, the plumes of spray mist across crops of wheat and oats. An electric fog that has the kids in town coughing and sneezing. Conservation and Land Management send you to the Health Department, whose spray-man says that there is not much evidence of spray drift, even in strong winds. And these were strong winds. He said: you can complain, but nothing will happen. He said that you sound like one of these non-spray people. *Too right*. Well, the world can't work like that, denying 5500 years of human 'civilisation'. He does say he will send officers to check out proceedings, that next year they are going to regulate it more: cut down on the 'cowboys'. There is more said in this conversation – it forms a backdrop to this general discussion. Ringing the local shire about the boom-spray that works the sides of roads, dousing standing water for mosquito larvae; they say they do not know much about the health implications but the contractor surely would be putting his own health at risk. He says that occasionally farmers get enthusiastic to 'keep the weeds down', and get out there on the public roads themselves. Chemicals are expensive. They spray rather than plough firebreaks; they spray their gardens.

Roundup has legendary, even mythic, status. The industry has its own lore. One afternoon, driving my daughter home from ballet in Northam, we came across a shire spray vehicle – roundupping or spray-seeding the verges for weeds. The mist was so dense and impenetrable it worked its way through closed windows, ventilators. My daughter felt sick, I had a migraine. This is not a unique occasion, but during the season, a daily occurrence. The armoured planes loop over Mount Bakewell and fly over the house, the spray nozzles leaking objectionably. They are the living dead. The pilot is at their mercy, pulling the levers at their whim. Up close, they look like Valkyries. In fire-danger season they load up with water, bombing fires with water and spray residue. That is never commented on, or even much thought about. If you oppose spray, you are considered weird. It is the fluid that runs through the veins of the community. When he retired from farming, my uncle sub-contracted as a sprayer, his Chamberlain dragging the bubble pod with personal release innovations – he is a true bush mechanic and inventor – over neighbouring properties for barely a profit margin. Respected in the district, he was considered to do a good job. The 'good blokes' spray as well, and see it as a necessary part of modern agriculture. There is also more than an inclination towards genetic farming, and its fetishisation of seed and chemical products. The ownership of growth by chemical companies is the new nationalism, and one that creeps up as surely as war. If you are entirely against spray, you will not be listened to. Half an ear might be cocked if you are for *careful* or *selective* or whatever euphemistic term the health department might deploy in the use of the product. We are for safe usage, sensible usage. Without it, we would be over-run. As with the quarantine laws, there is a fear of impurity. The national good, the national identity is welded to spray. And its makers and purveyors are multinationals that buy disingenuously into the argument.

No gender readings? Then again, there is that 'flasher'. The raincoat and hat and deportment of the body – faceless and fleshless as it is (the zap of the killer supplants the organism) – is clearly male. The growth of the weeds female? Scarily, there might be a case to be made. Does that come from the spraying of seminal fluid, of sperm and semen, or from the male-orientation of the advertising office? Those cowboys would tend that way. Or is the spraying the desire to control the uninhibited growth of the organism, the control of the clichéd feminine, at the forefront of their . . . mind? The penis kills, clearly.

Moving out (a long way out?) from Auden and Empson:

> Spray-o-rama: or a treatise on 20th-century British poetry
>
> On boys on, get that spray flowin',
> gotta get those weeds down,
> gotta get those weeds down.
>
> On boys on, get that spray flowin',
> gotta get those insects out,
> gotta get those insects out.
> On boys on, hitch the boom-spray
> to the tractor,
> hitch the boom spray to the tractor,
> on boys on.
>
> On boys on, the wind is picking up,
> swirling in the paddock,
> rippling through the crop,
> on boys on, the wind is picking up.
>
> On boys on, the chemicals are active,
> bright green crops hungry,
> insects swarming with impunity,
> on boys on.
>
> On boys on, hitch the boom spray
> to the tractor,
> hitch the boom spray to the tractor,
> on boys on.
>
> On boys on, get that spray flowin',
> gotta get those insects out,
> gotta get those insects out.

> On boys on, get that spray flowin',
> gotta get those weeds down,
> gotta get those weeds down.
>
> (Kinsella, 2005c)

The Heroic Versus the Pastoral: a modern slippage ... The heroic pastoral is much the same as the anti-pastoral or any one of its euphemisms. The heroic becomes preservation, protection, and resistance to a pollution both figurative and literal. My book *The New Arcadia* is an epic lyric poem made up of many poems. The heroic most often takes the form of animals or plants; the human figures can be 'heroic', or aspire to the heroic, but are most often its antithesis. The book is really only loosely inspired by Sidney's *The Old Arcadia* (originally completed in 1580/1999), more as a dialogue with pastoral tropes and romantic representations (the ironic in the pastoral, as reflexive against the privileged constructors of pastorality, is rarely appreciated as being historically deconstructive in itself), than with the text itself (though there are some subtextual narrative gestures: the acts, the eclogues, romantic encounters, animals and plants, even the pythia). The essence of my pastoral is a witnessing of the degradation of environments by human exploitation.

My *The New Arcadia* is a book about residues, remnants, and poison, but one that also celebrates the resistance to these things, and even explores the beauty within the most distorted and grotesque. The heroic pastoral is the respect for the land. In an email to my editor Jill Bialosky at W. W. Norton (who are publishing the book), I wrote:

> i often get compared to heaney and murray, even by those who don't like me – but i don't think it's the case. bloom says hart crane, frost, john clare, and wallace stevens. i'd like to think i'm just me, but of course one never is. i suppose i am a large number of poets rolled into one – i have been called wordsworthian, shelleyan, even a follower of dada! and i have called myself one following in the footsteps of william blake. i have been called a formal poet, an experimental poet, language poet, a traditionalist, a pastoral poet, an anti-pastoral poet, an ideas poet, a moral poet, an ironic poet, a didactic poet, a descriptive poet, a painterly poet, a mad poet! etc etc ... this results in the trickster, shaman poet, the shape-changer, poet of the bizarre and weird and unsaid etc etc. but what everyone agrees, myself included, is that i am a poet of the land.
>
> this book was written over a number of years. it's a book full of anecdotes. i have been campaigning to stop pesticide and herbicide spraying in my home district in western australia, and that gets the neighbours hot under the collar. the poem 'mowing' is about a neighbour who

spends most days on his ride on mower (or spraying), actually doing acres and acres – what a tractor should be doing. he just loves to mow and sends me insane should i ever be over near his fence lines. the 'paragliders' poem created a stink recently after being published in the london review of books – hundreds of paragliding people emailed or spoke through a paragliding email list to me protesting about my insulting them. they said it was me that was the pervert, not them. it went on and on and i was asked to respond by a senior paraglider. my reply: 'irony is a beautiful thing . . .' it's still going – so much for metaphor and figurative language. i celebrate old pick-ups and the negatives of place as much as the beautiful. i often find beauty in the grotesque.

in this book i've tried to be with 'nature' – as damaged as it is, but also the people. ALL people. after all, i'm of them and we live locally (when back in oz). (2004)

It is the local I write, no matter how far away I move from it. And every locality I inhabit clarifies another locality. I am left with degraded and resistant lines of prosody, notes to a greater whole that can never been fully realised. 'Form' poems, those written in traditional forms, become a gesture towards a unity that is mythical, and it is in such poems that I find my language most resisting any possible formulas for healing. Struck by lightning, a body now full of spray residues, I am the land as body, walking it and only half belonging.

Afterword to *The New Arcadia*

I worked consciously on this volume for four years, and probably unconsciously for the twenty-five or so years that I have been trying to write a 'new' pastoral, a pastoral that carries with it the ironies and contradictions of any celebration of the rural, a mode of expression that recognises the cultural inheritance as well as the cultural baggage of the bucolic.

The pastoral I have been writing is full of poison and celebration, wheat and salinity, violence and the balminess of a post-harvest evening. The neighbour riding his mower day in day out, cutting the same patch of grass because he laments not working the big tractors any more, is a source of wonder and irritation to me. He sprays poison over the fence-line and has me vigorously protesting and defending our organic lifestyle, though I have no doubt if you were in need he would be ready to lend a hand no matter what. Nothing is straightforward – I never want to write a poetry that says my way is the only way. *The New Arcadia* has bitter poems, but they are as bitter about 'self' as about 'others'. I think I move around among the voices – I do not think my 'character' is fixed anywhere in particular. The anger and irritation are not necessarily, or at least not always, my own!

Fundamentally, however, underlying the work is a recognition that the land I write is not mine, but land stolen from the indigenous people of Australia (the Nyungar people – the Ballardong – in and around York, Western Australia). I have known it since being a small child visiting my uncle's farm; I have known it going to school in the city, going to school in a country town (Geraldton), and living in the country for a great deal of my adult life. I have known it living for nearly a decade outside Australia, in the country and semi-rural places of Cambridgeshire, England and Ohio. It gnaws at me, it speaks through the poison of loss that inhabits any landscape where an exploitation of the land has been inextricable from dispossession. The claim of family being 'early settlers' becomes inadequate and even horrifying in the face of eighty thousand or more years of Aboriginal habitation and custodianship of the land. Since the 1840s when my father's family arrived in the south-west of Western Australia, and began farming there, the bulk of the land has been devastated by European farming practices, logging (my family were and have been foresters – from Ireland – as well), mining, and a reactive attempt to master 'harsh living conditions'. Survival and damage are tragically linked.

In 1995, a book I'd been slowly working on since the early 1980s was published in Australia – *The Silo: A Pastoral Symphony* (1995c). Though declared relatively quietly, these issues rose to the surface in my writing it: they were the reasons for its existence. Against the backdrop of Beethoven's Sixth Symphony (*The Pastoral Symphony*), the paradoxes of beauty and observation and a broader western aesthetic, and the need to *tell*, were formulated into a very different issue of *witness*. A darker book followed in 1998 – *The Hunt* (1998b). Originally called the *Book of Rural Disasters* and divided into a four-part symphony, it became one relentless undivided sonic unit in terms of construction, and hopefully polyphonic in the voices that emerged from this. I envisaged it as the follow-up to *The Silo*. (In 2000, *The Hierarchy of Sheep* appeared [2000a], a hybrid book that pursued the pastoral investigation, with digressions in interest and theme, but it was not a conclusion to a trilogy – it was a crossroads.) And then I imagined a rounding-off to the trilogy with *The New Arcadia*, loosely influenced by, and replying to textualities and tones of, Philip Sidney's brilliant *'Old' Arcadia*. My volume *Peripheral Light: New and Selected Poems* (2003) contained a broad selection of new, separate 'rural' poems that were pivotal in my concurrent thinking and work on *The New*

Arcadia's polyphonic poems and book-poem in its entirety.

In writing *The New Arcadia*, I came to realise that no closure to this pastoral 'life-project' was possible; the larger pastoral project is connected by subliminal and subtextual threads. I would hope that all my 'pastoral' poetry will eventually form one volume as an active record of observation and interaction. It is a single work around which all my other work revolves. If I am living in or staying in the city (in my childhood the corner block was bush, and a few blocks down the road towards the river was a vast amount of bushland ... a little further down was Bateman's farm ... so even within the city, was the rural), I thought and think about the Western Australian wheatbelt. As a child in a Perth suburb, I spent the days waiting to get back up to the farm outside York, the oldest inland town in Western Australia. At high school, I regularly rode my bike out past the town limits of Geraldton (a larger coastal rural town) into the scrub and paddocks; at university down in the city I escaped by working on the wheatbins (places of hyper-violence and macho excess) during my holidays, and ploughed on Wheatlands, my uncle's farm which has been the core of my voice. I wandered the bush as a child quoting Keats – the disjunction probably serving me better than quoting any work praising dispossession and clearing!

A surreal sense of being physically welded to the farm, to the wheatbelt, came when I was struck by lightning as fire raged on the world's curve through summer stubble. Then there was a dejected cloud of dependency for years on a farm called Happy Valley, waiting for my shearer-brother to get home and bring conversation from the shearing shed. My strongest bond is to my mother's home at the base of the 'hill that cries', Walwalinj (Mount Bakewell), that mountain of the central wheatbelt at York, a sacred place of loss and rebirth. It is the place where parrots flock and where deeply painful memories of the many birds and animals I shot in my childhood and youth become almost searing. Memory can be vicious.

I have been literally writing York since my first 'Uncle Jack and the Sheep' poem, drafted when I was thirteen (Uncle Jack did not trust hobby or weekend farmers who neglected their sheep, not watering them and letting them get fly-blown – though he could spend a moment each afternoon shooting the cockatoos off his giant aerial in order to get better reception on his shaky TV screen). It *is* a 'life project' that has different paddocks and fields, different lenses zooming in or out. It is macro and micro and wide-angle, it is snapshot and time-lapse. Sometimes the same piece of dirt is re-examined at different times of year, and the most fixed character changes as the year changes (and the destruction of the atmosphere and physical earth alters the seasons themselves). Scepticism and drop-jaw wonder are mixed.

The New Arcadia may be an end to the trilogy I mentioned, but it is surrounded by other rural work that concentrates on about twenty square miles of wheatbelt Western Australia, with vistas stretching out through the other places I have lived in. I write it *in situ*, I write it in Cambridge, and I write it in Ohio. It is remarkable how similar and different things are in rural Ohio: corn and soy, as opposed to wheat and now canola, 'back home'. Conservative attitudes, 'the church', xenophobia. The list is endless – through the looking-glass we find ourselves. Consciousness of nation, however, is remarkably different. Australians think isolation in a different way. But that is another story. I write intensely about a single region from an often international perspective and geography, but it is no less of that specific place for all this. It is a matter of differing angles.

As an anarchist vegan pacifist, my attitudes to the exploitation of people, animals, and land will not be entirely the same as those of my family and friends, but that makes me no less close to them. I do not believe in nations or countries, but I do believe in communities, even when our individual beliefs are so different. I believe in us having direct say in how we live our lives, and not in others purporting to represent our views. I believe that the natural environment should be protected at all cost. But I know something about growing food – which I have done on a small and a large scale, and I know how much hay itches during hay carting. I also love Dante and Baudelaire and Rimbaud and Whitman and the list is endless: all different coordinates on a language tree at times violent and self-serving, at others linguistically liberating. I believe in peaceful rebellion but no revolution: change comes by example and observation and respect.

The New Arcadia respects its sources, but is its own anti-epic lyrical poem. Many small parts making a whole – almost a discontinuous narrative, it's the story without the explanation. The roads – the journeys – are there, but when and how we take them is up to how we read individually. I hope none of these poems are mere photographs: it is not just a book of memory, though variety and variegations of memory are pivotal, but a living work. I do not want to capture the sound and colours of the bird before it becomes extinct, but help gain recognition for its beauty and necessity and stop the clearing of its habitat, the urge for profit, the indifference. We need to eat, we need 'space', we need our sense of achievement, but not at the expense of all else and all other living things. Space is infinite in a square foot of earth, and by looking close to hand, and inwards, vast horizons present themselves. While the title of the book carries its ironies – there never has been and increasingly never can be an arcadia in a world drowned in pesticide, herbicide, corporate farms, animal abuse, and indifference to indigenous claims to the land, there *can* be arcadias at our feet, at our fingertips. So, start with what we have: the micro can become the macro, then who knows …? For me, it is never too late. Poetry for me is activism.

V

APPENDICES

From Marcus Clarke's 'Preface' to the *Poems* of Adam Lindsay Gordon, 1880/1893

What is the dominant note of Australian scenery? That which is the dominant note of Edgar Allan Poe's poetry – Weird Melancholy. A poem like 'L'Allegro' could never be written by an Australian. It is too airy, too sweet, too freshly happy. The Australian mountain forests are funereal, secret, stern. Their solitude is desolation. They seem to stifle, in their black gorges, a story of sullen despair. No tender sentiment is nourished in their shade. In other lands the dying year is mourned, the falling leaves drop lightly on his bier. In the Australian forests no leaves fall. The savage winds shout among the rock clefts. From the melancholy gums strips of white bark hang and rustle. The very animal life of these frowning hills is either grotesque or ghostly. Great grey kangaroos hop noiselessly over the coarse grass. Flights of white cockatoos stream out, shrieking like evil souls. The sun suddenly sinks, and the mopokes burst out into horrible peals of semi-human laughter. The natives aver that, when night comes, from out the bottomless depth of some lagoon the Bunyip rises, and, in form like monstrous sea-calf, drags his loathsome length from out the ooze. From a corner of the silent forest rises a dismal chant, and around a fire dance natives painted like skeletons. All is fear-inspiring and gloomy. No bright fancies are linked with the memories of the mountains. Hopeless explorers have named them out of their sufferings – Mount Misery, Mount Dreadful, Mount Despair. As when among sylvan scenes in places

> 'Made green with the running of rivers,
> And gracious with temperate air,'

the soul is soothed and satisfied, so, placed before the frightful grandeur of these barren hills, it drinks in their sentiment of defiant ferocity, and is steeped in bitterness.

Australia has rightly been named the Land of the Dawning. Wrapped in the mist of early morning, her history looms vague and gigantic. The lonely horseman riding between the moonlight and the day sees vast shadows creeping across the shelterless and silent plains, hears strange noises in the primeval forest, where flourishes a vegetation long dead in other lands, and feels, despite his fortune, that the trim utilitarian civilisation which bred him shrinks into insignificance beside the contemptuous grandeur of forest and ranges coeval with an age in which European scientists have cradled his own race.

There is a poem in every form of tree or flower, but the poetry which lives in the trees and flowers of Australia differs from those of other countries. Europe is the home of knightly song, of bright deeds and clear morning thought. Asia sinks beneath the weighty recollections of her past magnificence, as the Suttee sinks, jewel burdened, upon the corpse of dread grandeur, destructive even in its death. America swiftly hurries on her way, rapid, glittering, insatiable even as one of her own giant waterfalls. From the jungles of Africa, and the creeper-tangled groves of the Islands of the South, arise, from the glowing hearts of a thousand flowers, heavy and intoxicating odours – the Upas-poison which dwells in barbaric sensuality. In Australia alone is to be found the Grotesque, the Weird, the strange scribblings of Nature learning how to write. Some see no beauty in our trees without shade, our flowers without perfume, our birds who cannot fly, and our beasts who have not yet learned to walk on all fours. But the dweller in the wilderness acknowledges the subtle charm of this fantastic land of monstrosities. He becomes familiar with the beauty of loneliness. Whispered to by the myriad tongues of the wilderness, he learns the language of the barren and the uncouth, and can read the hieroglyphics of haggard gum-trees, blown into odd shapes, distorted with fierce hot winds, or cramped with cold nights, when the Southern Cross freezes in a cloudless sky of icy blue. The phantasmagoria of that wild dreamland termed the Bush interprets itself, and the Poet of our desolation begins to comprehend why free Esau loved his heritage of desert sand better than all the bountiful richness of Egypt.

Windows

In open circle
pass is mustered,
lipid light
of warm day sunset, and there hovers
a quiet, like all birds inhaled,

        portal, east-west

engine

to sun from end to end, sweep the corrugated verandas;

as set to begin / light seeps

sunrise reflected in our opaque
vistas, a smouldering

cold lifts blankets, a walk-by or peering in to wake

as unison / staring illicit
fragmentation,

hopeful, sheer bizarre : real place

        we talk less with manners

                              as cracks,

malleable foundations, *fin de siècle* glass,
a resonating spikiness we darken day too

        turning planetary : our looking into,

Appendices

star chat, or eclipse drawn out /

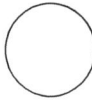

      shock of chart, of chat, of husky
dilation, a burn that blackens
where rods aren't pigmentation,

to angle, make cinders
pack the wound

                            exacting point of ambiguity,
watch crows nightly vanish, no blacker than hot-plate, filaments
of heat stretched to light outside
stress tolerances,
bands linking trees watershed

evenings ago
barely feel them through windows, take the slack, take schema
built to persuade or change

policy : pipe harmonics, percussive front and back, to
                                  resolve in silica;

      a desert pain abjures? a pane teaches shapes,
teaches

<<À gauche des palais d'Hades, tu trouveras la Source ...>>, dare
said who emerges
out of this constellations riveted to the blood-red dirt?

          touch them spread apart our prints, stain electric glass?

Magnesium band underwrites acacias : retinal scan
stretched to refuge, kangaroo trapped in road reserve
too far to be discerned : know it's there

Appendices

vertical blinds have warped the image

    excavated, granite hoardings, lightning

not conducted from wafers of vertical cloud embraced by metal,
earthquake proofed

in regard to view
no less than abolition, wagtails twitch along the ledges,
  insects graphed without the flywire, such narratives,
such transparency of prepositions.

  John Kinsella

Imitation Spatialogue (Sublime)

'I shall not defend Rowleys Pastoral: its merit can stand its own defence –'
  T. Chatterton, To Horace Walpole, 14 April 1769 (First draft)

Some months have passed since the Yenyenning track
proved impassable and I was lucky to get the car
and the kids out of the salty sludge;
      returning,
the ski-boat fraternity has turned out in force,
  and one of the original reasons
for the damnation of the Avon –
      the saline
choke-out of Yenyenning –
      was reiterated.
  Tailgating us in their four-wheel drives,
their inland dry speedboat travesties homed in
on the main lake.

Aim: to rip it up, drink beer.
Depth is not great
but enough to ski
and certainly resplendent to waterbirds
even if the bush in the surrounding reserve
is a villainy of the dead
where polemics accumulate
and some enjoy global warming;
looping
straight back out of there,
also to get the kids out (less so the car), we –
us this time –
want to avoid
confrontation with the vandals
when they've set their scene,
created their combat zone;
the issue
of the lake –
vestigially inherent
but forced into shape
by damming and manipulation,
is one of intrinsic curvature –
otherwise known as Gaussian curvature:
ostensibly,
I feel the strength of *their* –
the skiers and drinkers
and bush bashers –
harnessing the waters of the lake
lies in their confidence
that it is curved in the shape of a bowl,
that the product K
(intrinsic curvature)
is positive
because k_1 and k_2
share a negative sign;
I sense they are wrong,
and that a heavy winter
means the bowl has buckled,
that the floor of the lake has saddled
along the lines of k_1+, k_2-; $K-$,
or, even more extremely
with a monstrousness

      actively preparing
                      to rise up
on the balmy late spring day –
                            a subscription of agency
to the much maligned and abused lake itself –
     $+N$ upwards, k_1-, k_2+; $K-$;
    of course,
          I have the visual representation
in my mind's eye,
    or, if needs be,
    in Graham Nerlich's *The Shape of Space*,
    to fall back on:
        if the ski-boys only knew
    how much
they could get out of considering
the unlimited two-space of the body –
                      Nerlich noting:
    'if we overlook the holes, for the sake of simplicity
and, perhaps, decency)...;
            which leaves you and me and the kids – us –
hightailing it out of there,
    out past the deadly blue of the lake/s,
the crown-of-thorns-work of dead trees –
                  a species lasting longer
dead than alive,
    the warped track and 1–form
      up and down imaging
as the wheels shock-undulate
    across the contours and rides
of the cattle grids;
            and noticing the Gaussian issue
applying to the sky
    which was saddling downwards,
      or maybe breaking out
of this into other spatialities:
                bending into topological meltdown;
holding our hands out against the windscreen,
    a windscreen cracked by stones
      kicked up by tracks and trailers,
star fields not yet linked
           by superstition;

we awaited –
              await and will await –
                            the extrusion
or fold
    that'll absorb our impact:
        we wonder if it's affecting the skiers,
if it's knocked them off their vicarious and rapid perches,
                                    if they'll
even notice it was more than a drop in speed,
            a loss of balance,
    too much to drink;
                warding-off, a branch on the road
brings us to ground –
            we stop, I lift and toss it
to the side of the road,
    collect the fragments,
      drive on
distracted from the sky
    by an old concrete silo on a bare hill,
its vacant bounty,
              and to take it in
        we bend on our seats
as if they were knees
    to look up at an increasing
and past angle –
           in this case,
    though thinking of the Klein bottle,
                    our in actual fact
unmoving knees predicated to the left, and up, and closing, and lost,
are not homomorphic;
            the skiers bend their knees
        in control, or loss,
    edging up,
        especially at take-off,
            the blue salt waters
                washing over the ridge,
into the river system;
            we notice ring-necked parrots
        curving down, grounded, corellas
unable to rise
           more than the height
    of the silo, trees;

                    we surmise
fresh and saltwater aquatic animals
        rising near to the surface –
                            the instabilities
of sky's curvature
        keeping us all close
at hand.

        John Kinsella

Letter from Graham Nerlich

Dear John
It's early days in our dialogue, we stumble towards common ground. Some landmarks loom. Your poetics is founded in ambiguity and stress – of divergent meanings, images and themes. You see this as bending and warping both moral and visual landscapes into new, sometimes literally newly-perceived, shapes. Geometry and sets are somehow basic to this. 'Parrotology' and 'Hyperpoetics' are *approaches* to a new picture of poetics – not just your poetics, but all poetics. But where it counts, each approaches not just a theory of poetry but poetry itself. As you say about poems, those who write them can't write their theory else they'd write prose. Nevertheless, something like a theory is what we are both asking questions about.

Despite my questions and uncertainties, I think we may be close to that common ground.

If set theory is to be a basis, an analogue, a metaphor of the poetic, then I'm puzzled. Do you mean by 'set' what a set theorist would mean? We need to sort this one out. On the face of it, sets look like a wrong turn. Here's a sketch of why.

Sets have a studied austerity: it's called extensionality. Sets inherit it from the rigid emptiness of the logic in which set theory finds its *raison d'être*.

Logic aims to ensure that, when you reason, you can tell whether you are reasoning strictly from your premises or unwittingly smuggling in other peripheral information. That means that the rules by which you reason must, themselves, be utterly devoid of any content or meaning. Only so can invasion by unfocussed information and meaning be fought off. Aristotle gave a first broad hint how to do this by writing familiar syllogistic forms (good or bad) like this:

        All A are B   All A are B
        All B are C   Some B are C

So
All A are C   All A are C

Obviously, these skeletons capture all that counts (for or against) these inferences. 'All' and all other logical particles have no topic, no descriptive force. They crop up in talk on every subject. That washes meaning out of them. Logic is about *form* – patterns of repetition in a structure of logical particles. And absolutely *nothing* else.

Sets need to inherit this same rigid bareness.

Any collection of things of whatever kind and however collected, forms a set. You can collect members under a common description – the set of tigers, say. Or you can list them arbitrarily, writing them between braces {George Bush, the planet Mercury, the number 4}. The random list, as disparate as can be, best captures the essence, since sets *must* ignore every meaningful link between members. Even in a collection by common description, the description drops out of the picture. If all and only animals with hearts are animals with vertebrae then the set of cordates is the set of vertebrates. Just so, the set of leprechauns is the set of griffins, that interesting thing called the null set, the one with no members. It's a set not because 'griffin' has a meaning but because 0 is a number.

This enterprise is through and through *extensional*. Its *whole* point lies in the subtle art of banishing from mathematics any shadow cast by subtlety of meaning. No subtlety of meaning because no meanings at all. Logic stipulates about its target sentences only that they be either true or false, never mind which. Nothing else about them matters apart from internal, meaningless form. So Russell described set theory and logic as the study in which we do not know what we are talking about or care whether what we say is true. That's paradoxical but spot on.

(You might wonder about that great big concept, truth. Don't! Truth is an empty idea, adding precisely nothing to the content of what is true. Maybe that's not quite the last word on truth but it is a splendid first word. If your best pal says 'The earth is round' you needn't say 'That's true'. Simply say again 'The earth is round'. You will do all the work that saying 'true' can do. That holds for a huge swathe of contexts for the word 'true'. So Aristotle told us; it's a shame so few have heeded it, especially the wildly erratic genius Nietzsche. Truth isn't power or knowledge; it's just, trivially, truth.)

Sets were first designed to tell us what numbers are: each is a particular set of sets. So sets *must* be allowed to include sets among their members sometimes. Sets must still remain extensional. All meaning, like sin in purgatory, is burnt and purged away. The light is brilliant, the view austere.

Barren ground for poetry, and any logician would wake in fright to dream of metaphor germinating there. Yet you find in sets not just something poetic, but the essence of poetry, the being of The Poem. At the heart of the problem of poetry for you, I reckon, lie two Russell paradoxes. The first is fecundity in the ultimately lean machine of set theory; the second is your welcoming the set of those sets not members of themselves. In these difficulties, let's hope, lies the charm, the answer.

I have some grasp of what you want; but I'm still guessing why you want it from *sets* and how you think sets can give it. Still, this is an early page in our dialogue. I'm inquisitive, not hostile. Much puzzles me. Hyperpoetics, an *approach* to theory, itself also approaches being a poem. So does much of 'A treatise on rooms and windows' and 'Parrotology'. I'm trying to grasp it as theory, being no kind of poet.

Yet you think that you and I are somehow doing the same thing, and this has something to do with what we are talking about. I'm inclined to agree. I don't want just to explain geometry and the physics that uses it. It's because all that is so elegant and strong and its pioneers had such limpid and penetrating thoughts that I want some small part in it. Its beautifully objectivity is also its exhilarating charm.

In the poems grouped round these essays, you are the poet of one place; the poet of what's in the place and of its geometry. It's about Walwalinj, the wandoo, parrots, Yenyenning, plainly. But it's also about implosions and dynamics of their geometry, about the curvatures and topologies of metaphorical spaces that twist and distort both the visual and the moral. The moral dimension goes together with a literal new perception, seeing anew the shapes of places and things – knees, hands, L-shaped desks, silos, curved rooms.

And there is the circle that figures in the third paragraph of 'Hyperpoetics'?

The circle on the horizon is the precognitive poem. It might bend into itself a theme, a parameter of the poem, but not merely a theme that might persist 'as residue towards the end'. It's a metaphor for any precognitive poem. Its tangents reach into the plane and bend whatever it finds in the infinite plane into itself. Tangents draw in, curve, and bend.

All the imagery of circles, holes, eyes, windows, the enclosing surfaces of rooms and houses and the traverse of the geometry of the mountain through them into the poem – the sense of geometry in so much of the place that is your poetry – that's all wonderful.

Perhaps the circle on the horizon becomes the null set, the empty set. Or so I think. Each is a precognitive poem, indeed, *the* precognitive poem – every poem. The poem is 'the set itself (that is the set of ALL sets) because language contains all possible meanings in the fragment as much as entirely (which is conceivably infinite or at least limitless)'. The role of sets in all this puzzles me, though. Here's more of why.

A set isn't concrete; it suffers no vicissitudes. Like a number, it casts no shadow of meaning round the thing itself. It's not fertile for imagery. Five is prime and odd: five couldn't turn up as even or divisible – not even in some imagined context. Neither can sets turn up as other than extensional, as having just the members they do have. They wouldn't be sets; they couldn't do the work it is their reason of being to do. Most properties of these abstract things are prohibitions – no meanings by demand.

Well, that's dogmatic. There's a lot to be said about sets and even then they are puzzling, almost as bad as numbers, but not quite. It's nearly right to say that sets are defined by what they are required to do and that means by the axioms of, say, Zermelo-Frankel set theory. But I like naïve set theory, and I think you should like it, too. It doesn't involve axioms. That will let you flout the embargo against a set's being a member of itself. You could come within a hair's breadth of Russell's paradox, as you say you want to do. A worry about the foundation axiom, the one that doesn't let you form the Russell set, is that it is a *flat* embargo. It tells you not to do things which it seems you can easily do. It can't explain why, if the set of abstract things is an abstract thing, it isn't also a member of itself.

Compare the barber paradox: a barber in a village shaves all and only those who do not shave themselves. Does he shave himself? If yes, then no; if no, then yes. Here it's easy to say just that there is no such barber. The simplest and oldest of these paradoxes, The Liar, is seen at its simplest in the sentence 'This statement is false'. If it is, it isn't; if it isn't, it is. But we can ask: which statement are we talking about? There isn't one, really. However, there's no such easy way out of Russell: the set of abstract things *is* an abstract thing.

Maybe that is just what you like!

I think I see some of what you want self-membership and self-reference to do. It mimics the way that denying the parrot in our poetry winds up affirming it. That's because 'parrot' has become part of the meaning of 'Nation'. Yet that's a very non-extensional thought. Sets are what they are in order to cancel the sort of link that demands that 'Nation' trail 'parrot' in its wake. If you take extensionality out of sets, I wonder what residue is left – what the idea of a set becomes.

What about Russell's flip side? Would affirming the parrot's role wind up denying it?

It's not easy, in general, to self-refer paradoxically. For Russell, you need self-reference, self-inclusion and negation. That comes by a sort of perverse art. It's usually innocent to make comments in a poem on that very poem or essay. Self-reference has to be tight to be troublesome. An image *in* a poem can well be an image *of* the poem or of all poetry. Witness your nice circle. But you can't use the end joint of your index finger to point at that finger joint itself. At best it can draw attention to itself (by wiggling, say). You can think about your own mind, and think that you've been arguing well, say, but no thought can think about its own semantics. An Escher drawing can be of *two* hands, each drawing the *other* and neither complete. A main part of the famous Gödel theorem on the incompleteness of arithmetic is an elaborate construction whereby arithmetic can be read as talking about itself – but only about its syntax (its proof strings) not its semantics. None of these is like a set's self-membership. Yet we don't quite know why that leads to disaster.

Extensionality might help with what you say about the null set. No set is a member of the null set. But the null set is a subset of every set. Is that good or bad?

In point set topology, the null set is both open and closed, as you say. Perhaps that mimics the way the circle reaches out into the plane with its tangents to touch what is outside the circle and yet be bent into it. Nothing is yet inside the circle, or inside the braces that denote the null set. Yet much might be there metaphorically, in a sort of tension, in the circle and the braces themselves. (Is that how the poem-set contains all possibilities of language?) Strictly, the null set doesn't qualify as being either open or closed by containing either its boundary or its interior points: it contains nothing at all. My little topology book says that the null set is classified as both open and closed for *convenience* (it's non-extensional to have a set that doesn't meet either a definition or its contrary. In general you want all sets to have each relevant property or its contrary). But it's not actually mere convenience, but another aspect of extensionality. To say a set S is open means 'For all points p, *if p is in* S then some neighbourhood of p is wholly in the set. 'S is closed' means 'For all points p, *if p is in* S then p has no neighbourhood wholly in S'. But since set theory uses extensional (truth functional) logic, the conditional '*if p is in* S, then p has a neighbourhood in S' will be true *just because* the (italicised) conditional clause is *false* for all p. The extensional conditional 'if p then q' is true just if p is false or if q is true. So the truth of the conditional does not imply the truth of the clause in the consequent. The null set doesn't contain any points of any kind. So its being closed doesn't imply that the null set fulfils the condition of main interest – that it contains its limit points. Thus being open and being closed are *trivial* properties of the null set.

It's a bit like 'If there are honest politicians then I'm a Dutchman'. If that were true (and it does often seem that bad), it wouldn't be saying that I'm a Dutchman but that there are no honest politicians.

I'll end with some questions. Is Hyperpoetics a theory or a developing imagery for poetics, or both? That would clarify what sort of challenges (you say you love a challenge) have a point. Are sets *images* of poems and poetics, and the accumulation of poetry? 'Accumulation' sounds nicely extensional. Or are poems, precognitive or other, *literally* sets?

Best
Graham

BIBLIOGRAPHY

Adams, C. J. (2001) *The sexual politics of meat: A feminist-vegetarian critical theory*. New York: Continuum.

Adamson, R. and Kinsella, J. (1997) 'Interview with Robert Adamson by John Kinsella', www.johnkinsella.org/interviews/adamson.html (accessed 2005).

Adorno, T. W. (1967) *Prisms* (S. and S. Weber, trans.). Cambridge, MA: MIT Press.

Agenda (2005) Vol. 41, Nos. 1–2 (Weymouth).

Allen, C. (2005) 'Animal Consciousness', *The Stanford Encyclopedia of Philosophy* (winter 2004 edition), Edward N. Zalta (ed.), http://plato.stanford.edu/entries/consciousness-animal (accessed September 2005).

Andrews, B. (ed.) (1984) *The language book: Poetics of the new*. Carbondale: Southern Illinois University Press.

Arnold, M. (1969) *Poetical works*. London: Oxford University Press.

Ashbery, J. (1985) *Selected poems*. New York: Viking.

Bachelard, G. (1994) *The poetics of space* (Maria Jolas, trans., rev. edn). Boston: Beacon Press.

Bakhtin, M. (1984) *Problems of Dostoevsky's poetics* (C. Emerson, trans.). Minneapolis: University of Minnesota Press.

Barr, J. (1968) *Comparative philology and the text of the Old Testament*. Oxford: Oxford University Press.

Barthes, R. (1967) *Writing degree zero* (A. Lavers and C. Smith, trans.). Boston: Beacon Press.

Bate, J. (2003) *John Clare: A biography*. New York: Farrar, Straus, & Giroux.

Blanchot, M. (1995) *The writing of the disaster* (A. Smock, trans.).

Lincoln and London: University of Nebraska Press.
Bloom, H. (1973) *The anxiety of influence: A theory of poetry* (second edition, 1997). Oxford: Oxford University Press.
The Book of Common Prayer (1969). Oxford: Oxford University Press.
Borges, J. L. (1962) 'Pierre Menard, author of the *Quixote*' (A. Bonner, trans.). In J. L. Borges, *Ficciones* (pp. 45–55). New York: Grove Press.
Brockman, E. (1870) *The writings of Elizabeth Deborah Brockman* (forthcoming edition, 2006). Great Wilbraham, England: Salt.
Brown, L. A. (1998) 'No Melpomene'. In *The Boston Review*, www.bostonreview.net/BR23.5/Equi.html#No%20Melpomene (accessed 10 March 2005).
Buckley, C. (1999) 'Made in patriarchy: Theories of women and design – a reworking'. In J. Rothschild and A. Cheng (eds), *Design and feminism: Re-visioning spaces, places, and everyday things* (pp. 109–118). New Brunswick: Rutgers University Press.
Bunce, P. (1988) *The Cocos (Keeling) Islands: Australian atolls in the Indian Ocean*. Milton: Jacaranda.
Burgess, C. V. (1967) *Speech training*. London: The English Universities Press.
Burke, E. (1757) *A philosophical enquiry into the origin of our ideas of the sublime and beautiful* (reprinted 1958, J. T. Boulton, ed.). London: Routledge & Kegan Paul.
Burns, J. (1999) 'Statement'. In J. Kinsella (ed.), *Landbridge: Contemporary Australian poetry* (p. 73). Fremantle: Fremantle Arts Centre Press.
Caddel, R. (1998) *Subject line unknown*. Message posted to electronic mailing list, archived at www.jiscmail.ac.uk/lists/british-poets.html (accessed January 2005).
Cixous, H. (1994) *The Hélène Cixous reader* (S. Sellers, ed.). London: Routledge.
Clarke, M. (1876) 'An Australian paean – 1876'. In M. Pizer (ed.), *Freedom on the wallaby* (pp. 48–50). Sydney: Pinchgut Press.
Clarke, M. (1880/1893) 'Preface' to the *Poems* of Adam Lindsay Gordon. Transcribed from an 1893 edition published in Melbourne, http://download.franklin.com/cgi-bin/franklin/ebookman_free_preview?agord10 (accessed 26 June 2001).
Coleridge, S. T. (1798) 'The rime of the ancient mariner'. In M. Ferguson, M. J. Salter and J. Stallworthy (eds), *The Norton anthology of poetry* (4th edn, 1996, p. 744). New York: Norton.
Cooper, M. A. (2005) *Lightning injury research program*, www.uic.edu/labs/lightninginjury (accessed 10 March 2005).

Crystal, D. (1995) *The Cambridge encyclopaedia of language*. Cambridge: Cambridge University Press.
Dale, Ensign (1830) *Journal of an expedition whilst exploring the country eastward of the Darling Range*. (p. 7 of Battye Library transcription, provided to author in 2004).
Darwin, C. (1846) *Coral reefs*, http://charles-darwin.classic-literature.co.uk/coral-reefs/ebook-page-09.asp (accessed 10 March 2005).
Davers, J. M. (1975) *Architecture as a home for man*. New York: Architectural Record.
Deleuze, G. and Guattari, F. (1977) *Anti-Oedipus: Capitalism and schizophrenia*. (R. Hurley, M. Seem and H. R. Lane, trans.). New York: Viking.
Derrida, J. (1981) *Dissemination*. Chicago: University of Chicago Press.
Derrida, J. (1987) *Of grammatology* (G. C. Spivak, trans.). Baltimore and London: Johns Hopkins University Press.
Derrida, J. (1992) *Given time: 1. Counterfeit money* (P. Kamuf, trans.). Chicago: University of Chicago Press.
Descartes, R. (1637) *Discourse on Method for Reasoning Well and for Seeking Truth in the Sciences* (Ian Johnston, trans.), www.mala.bc.ca/~johnstoi/descartes/descartes1.htm (accessed 10 March 2005)
Dickinson, E. (1960) *The complete poems of Emily Dickinson* (T. H. Johnson, ed.). Boston: Little, Brown.
Donne, J. (1977) *Complete English poems*. London: Penguin.
Duncan, A. (2001) *Anxiety before entering a room: Selected poems 1977–99*. Great Wilbraham, England: Salt.
Eliot, T. S. (1922) *The sacred wood: essays on poetry and criticism*. London: Methuen; Bartleby.com, 1996, www.bartleby.com/200 (accessed 10 March 2005).
Eliot, T. S. (1979) *On poetry and poets*. New York: Farrar.
Eliot, T. S. (1990) *Selected Poems*. London: Faber and Faber
Enright, D. J. (ed.) (1983) *The Oxford book of death*. Oxford and New York: Oxford University Press.
Forbes, J. (2001) *Collected poems 1970–1998*. Rose Bay: Brandl & Schlesinger.
Foucault, M. (1977) *Discipline and punish: The birth of the prison* (A. Sheridan, trans.). New York: Pantheon.
Fraser, G. S. (1970) *Metre, rhyme and free verse*. London and New York: Methuen.
Fromm, E. (1969) *Escape from freedom*. New York: Avon.
Fussell, P. (1965) *Poetic meter and poetic form* (revised edn, 1979). New York: Random House.

Gellert, L. (1917) *Songs of a campaign*. Sydney: Angus & Robertson.
Genette, G. (1980) *Narrative discourse: An essay in method* (J. E. Lewin, trans.). Ithaca: Cornell University Press.
Goeje, C. H. de (1951) *Space, Time and Life*. Leiden: E. J. Brill.
Green, N. (1994) *Broken spears: Aborigines and Europeans in the south-west of Australia*. Perth: Focus Education Services.
Groser, T. S. (1927) *The lure of the golden west: experiences and adventures in a bush brotherhood of Western Australia: early problems and conquests: all about group settlements of the west: the land of sunshine & opportunity*. London: Alexander-Ouseley.
Hall, D. (1992). *Their ancient glittering eyes: Remembering poets and more poets*. Boston: Ticknor & Fields.
Hampton, S. and Llewellyn, K. (eds) (1988) *The Penguin book of Australian women poets*. Ringwood: Penguin.
Han-Shan (1990) *The poetry of Han-Shan: A complete, annotated translation of 'Cold Mountain'* (R. G. Henricks, ed.). Albany: State University of New York Press.
Hardy, T. (1898) *Wessex poems and other verses*. New York: Harper; Bartleby.com, 1999, www.bartleby.com, (accessed 10 March 2005).
Harford, L. (1941) 'Pruning flowering gums'. In *The poems of Lesbia Harford*. SETIS: The Scholarly Electronic Text and Image Service, http://setis.library.usyd.edu.au/pubotbin/toccer-new?id+har.v00033.sgml&images=acdp/gifs&data=/usr/ot&tag=ozlit&part=68&division=div1 (accessed 26 June 2001).
Hejinian, L. (1991) *Oxota: A short Russian novel*. Great Barrington: Figures.
Hesiod (ca. 750 BC–675 BC) 'Works and days'. In Hesiod, *Theogony, Works and days* (M. L. West, trans., 1999, pp. 35–62). Oxford: Oxford University Press.
Hewett, D. (1995) *Collected poems 1940–1995*. Fremantle: Fremantle Arts Centre Press.
Hinckfuss, I. (1975) *The existence of space and time*. Oxford: Clarendon Press.
Hodge, B. and Mishra, V. (1991) *The dark side of the dream: Australian literature and the postcolonial mind*. Sydney: Allen & Unwin.
Hogarth, W. (1997) *The analysis of beauty*. New Haven, CT, and London: Yale University Press.
Hull, C. and Kinsella, J. (2000) *Zoo*. Sydney: Paper Bark Press.
Jakobson, R. (2004) 'Closing statement: Linguistics and poetics'. In Jon Cook (ed.), *Poetry in Theory: An Anthology 1900–2000* (p. 356). Oxford: Blackwell.
Jarnot, L. (1996) 'Five prose pieces from *Sea Lyrics*, 1996', http://jack-

etmagazine.com/02/jarnot02.html (accessed 10 March 2005).
Johnson, S. (1750/2000) *Samuel Johnson: The major works*. Oxford: Oxford University Press.
Joyce, J. (1961) *Ulysses*. New York: The Modern Library.
Joyce, J. (1975) *Finnegans Wake*. London: Faber and Faber.
Kachru, B. B. (1986) *The alchemy of English: The spread, functions and models of non-native Englishes*. Oxford: Pergamon.
The Kenyon Review (2003) Special issue: Culture and place. Vol. 25, Nos. 3/4.
Khlebnikov, V. (1997) *Collected works of Velimir Khlebnikov, volume III: Selected poems* (P. Schmidt, trans.). Cambridge, MA, and London: Harvard University Press.
Kinsella, J. (1989) *Night parrots*. Fremantle: Fremantle Arts Centre Press.
Kinsella, J. (1993) *Full fathom five*. Fremantle: Fremantle Arts Centre Press.
Kinsella, J. (1995a) 'Dissertation on a dysfunctional personality'. *Mattoid*, Vol. 49, p. 109.
Kinsella, J. (1995b) *Erratum/frame[d]*. Fremantle: Fremantle Arts Centre Press, and Folio (Salt).
Kinsella, J. (1995c) *The silo: A pastoral symphony*. Fremantle: Fremantle Arts Centre Press.
Kinsella, J. (1996) *The Radnoti poems*. Cambridge: Equipage.
Kinsella, J. (1997a) *Genre*. Fremantle: Fremantle Arts Centre Press.
Kinsella, J. (1997b) *Graphology*. Cambridge: Equipage.
Kinsella, J. (1998a) *Grappling Eros*. Fremantle: Fremantle Arts Centre Press.
Kinsella, J. (1998b) *The hunt*. Newcastle upon Tyne: Bloodaxe Books.
Kinsella, J. (1998c) *Poems 1980–1994*. Newcastle upon Tyne: Bloodaxe Books.
Kinsella, J. (ed.) (1999a) *Landbridge: Contemporary Australian poetry*. Fremantle: Fremantle Arts Centre Press.
Kinsella, J. (1999b) *Visitants*. Newcastle upon Tyne: Bloodaxe Books.
Kinsella, J. (2000a) *The hierarchy of sheep*. Fremantle: Fremantle Arts Centre Press.
Kinsella, J. (2000b) 'Sounds like the future of English poetry'. *The Observer* (2 January), http://books.guardian.co.uk/reviews/poetry/0,,118626,00.html (accessed 10 March 2005).
Kinsella, J. (2000c) 'And Everyone Gathered In Objection yet Again', http://jacketmagazine.com/06/kins.html (accessed 10 March 2005).
Kinsella, J. (2001a) *Auto*. Great Wilbraham: Salt.

Kinsella, J. (2001b) 'Hay-baling in the early morning: late spring'. In *Diagnostics* (a Web Del Sol chapbook), http://webdelsol.com/LITARTS/John_Kinsella/hay_baling.html (accessed 10 March 2005).
Kinsella, J. (2001c) 'Infra Red'. In *Diagnostics* (a Web Del Sol chapbook), http://webdelsol.com/LITARTS/John_Kinsella/infra-red.html (accessed 10 March 2005).
Kinsella, J. (2001d) 'Alternative spaces'. *The literary review*, Vol. 45, No. 1, pp. 7–10.
Kinsella, J. (2003) *Peripheral light: selected and new poems* (Harold Bloom, ed.). New York: W. W. Norton.
Kinsella, J. (2004a) *Doppler effect*. Great Wilbraham: Salt.
Kinsella, J. (2004b) 'Some: an ode to the partitive'. *The Iowa review*, Vol. 34, No. 2, p. 48.
Kinsella, J. (2005a) *The New Arcadia*. New York: W. W. Norton.
Kinsella, J. (2005b) 'Death sentence in Ohio: epicedium', *The Yale Review*, Vol. 93, No. 2, p. 71.
Kinsella, J. (2005c) 'Spray-o-rama: or a treatise on 20th-century British poetry'. *The Idaho Review*, Vol. 7.
Kinsella, J. (ed.) (forthcoming) *Anthology of Australian Poetry to 1930*. Nedlands: UWA Press.
Lamont, D. (2005) 'Farmnote'. Department of Conservation and Land Management and Marion Massam, Department of Agriculture, http://agspsrv38.agric.wa.gov.au/pls/portal30/docs/folder/ikmp/pw/vp/bird/fn008_2002.pdf (accessed 10 March 2005).
Larkin, P. (2001) *Terrain seed scarcity*. Great Wilbraham: Salt.
'Longinus' or Pseudo-Longinus (AD 1st century) 'On the sublime'. In *Aristotle – the poetics; 'Longinus' on the sublime; Demetrius on style* (W. H. Fyfe, trans., 1982, pp. 119–254). Cambridge, MA: Harvard University Press; London: William Heinemann.
Lucas, J. R. (1973) *Treatise on Time and Space*. London: Methuen.
Lukács, G. (1995) *The Lukács reader* (A. Kadarkay, ed.). Oxford and Cambridge, MA: Blackwell.
Lynn, D. and Kinsella, J. (2001) *The House*. Unpublished.
Lyotard, P. (1984) *The postmodern condition: A report on knowledge* (G. Bennington and B. Massumi, trans.). Minneapolis: University of Minnesota Press.
McAdams, J. (2000) *The island of lost luggage*. Tucson: University of Arizona Press.
McAdams, J. (2003) 'Ghost ranch'. *TriQuarterly*, Vol. 116, pp. 188–189.
McAuley, J. (1966) *A primer of English versification*. Sydney: Sydney University Press.

McCaffery, S. (2003) 'Some versions of pastoral'. *TriQuarterly*, Vol. 116, pp. 50–56.

Macey, R. (2004) 'Party in the botanic gardens'. *Sydney Morning Herald*, Sydney, http://www.smh.com.au/articles/2004/10/28/1098667910200.html?oneclick=true (accessed 10 March 2005).

McIntosh, N. (2003) 'World drowning in a rising sea of information'. *The Guardian* (1 November), www.guardian.co.uk/international/story/0,,1075449,00.html (accessed 10 March 2005).

MacNamara, F. ('Frank the Poet') (1979) 'Labouring with the hoe'. In J. Meredith and R. Whalan (eds), *Frank the Poet: The life and works of Francis Macnamara* (p. 39). Melbourne: Red Rooster Press.

Mariani, P. (1998) *The broken tower: The life of Hart Crane*. New York: W. W. Norton.

Marx, K. (1867) *Capital: A critique of political economy, Volume one* (B. Fowkes, trans., 1977). New York: Vintage.

Microsoft Help and Support (2005) http://support.microsoft.com/default.aspx?scid=kb;EN-US;q287816 (accessed 2005).

Mitchell, A. G. (1970) 'The Australian accent'. In W. S. Ransom (ed.), *English transported: Essays on Australasian English*. Canberra: Australian National University Press.

Mitchell, R. L. (1976) *The poetic voice of Charles Cros: A centennial study of his songs*. University of Mississippi: Romance Monographs, Inc.

Murray, L. (1998) *Collected Poems*. Manchester: Carcanet.

Nerlich, G. (1994) *The shape of space*. Cambridge: Cambridge University Press.

Olson, C. (1997) *Collected prose* (D. Allen and B. Friedlander, eds). Berkeley: University of California Press.

Ouyang Yu, private email correspondence, August 2005.

Paulin, T. (1999) *The wind dog*. London: Faber and Faber.

Perloff, M. (2001a) 'After free verse: The new non-linear poetries'. Electronic Poetry Center, http://wings.buffalo.edu/epc/authors/perloff/free/html (accessed 15 January 2001).

Perloff, M. (2001b). 'Language poetry and the lyric subject'. Electronic Poetry Center, 15 January 2001, from http://wings.buffalo.edu/epc/authors/perloff/langpo/html.

Platt, J., Weber, H. and Ho, M. L. (1984) *The new Englishes*. London: Routledge & Kegan Paul.

Poetryetc. (1998) Electronic mailing list, which does not contain earliest material from the list's beginning, archived at www.jiscmail.ac.uk/lists/poetryetc.html

Portoghesi, P. (ed.) (1983) *Postmodern: The architecture of the postindustrial society*. New York: Rizzoli.

Radnóti, M. (2003) *Forced march* (G. Gömöri and C. Wilmer, trans.). London: Enitharmon.
Ransom, J. C. (1922) 'Dead boy', www.theotherpages.org/poems/poem-qr.html#r (accessed 12 March 2005).
Ransom, J. C. (1941) *The new criticism*. Norfolk: New Directions.
Ransom, W. S. (ed.) (1970) *English transported: Essays on Australasian English*. Canberra: Australian National University Press.
Reddy, S. (2003) 'Fundamentals of Esperanto', www.aprweb.org/issues/july03/reddy.html (accessed 12 March 2005).
Rimbaud, [J.-N.-]A. (1960) *Oeuvres*. Paris: Garnier-Frères.
Rimbaud, [J.-N.-]A. (1997) *Collected poems* (O. Bernard, trans.). London: Penguin.
Robertson, L. (1993) *XEclogue*. Vancouver: Tsunami Editions.
Rodriguez, J. (1994) 'Nasturtium scanned'. In J. Tranter and P. Mead (eds), *The Bloodaxe book of modern Australian poetry* (p. 210). Newcastle upon Tyne: Bloodaxe.
Russ, J. (1983) *How to suppress women's writing*. London: The Women's Press.
Ryan, T. (1999) *The willing eye*. Fremantle: Fremantle Arts Centre Press.
Ryan, T. (2002) *Hothouse*. Fremantle: Fremantle Arts Centre Press.
Ryan, T. (forthcoming, 2007) *bloc-notes*. Cambridge: Equipage.
Rykwert, J. (1982) *The necessity of artifice*. New York: Rizzola.
Salmon, W.C. (1975) *Space, Time and Motion: A Philosophical Introduction*. California: Dickenson.
Sardello, R. (ed.) (1995) *The angels*. New York: Continuum.
Shakespeare, W. (1977) *The tempest*. Cambridge: Cambridge University Press.
Short Cuts [Film] (1993) Robert Altman, dir., USA.
Shelley, P. B. (1988) *Shelley's prose, or the trumpet of a prophecy* (D. L. Clark, ed.). New York: New Amsterdam.
Sidney, P. (1580) *The Countess of Pembroke's Arcadia (The Old Arcadia)* (K. Duncan-Jones, ed., reprinted 1999). Oxford: Oxford University Press.
Sidney, P. (1962) *The poems of Sir Philip Sidney* (W. A. Ringler, ed.). Oxford: Clarendon.
Skelton, J. (1983) *The complete English poems* (J. Scattergood, ed.). New Haven, CT: Yale University Press.
Skrzynecki, P. (1970) *There, Behind the Lids*. Sydney, NSW: Lyre-Bird Writers.
Smith, S. (1976) *The collected poems of Stevie Smith*. New York: Oxford University Press.
Spenser, E. (1987) *The faerie queene*. London: Penguin.

Stein, G. (1936) *The geographical history of America, or the relation of human nature to the human mind*. New York: Random House.
Stein, G. (1994) *Stanzas in meditation*. Los Angeles: Sun & Moon.
Steinmetz, J.-L. (2001) *Arthur Rimbaud: Presence of an enigma* (J. Graham, trans.). New York: Welcome Rain Publishers.
Stevens, W. (1982) *The collected poems of Wallace Stevens*. New York: Random House.
Stevens, W. (1997) *Collected poetry and prose*. Washington: Library of America.
Storr, G. M. and Johnstone, R. E. (2001) *A field guide to the birds of Western Australia*. Perth: Western Australian Museum.
Thomson, J. (1726) *The seasons* (J. Sambrook, ed., 1981). Oxford: Clarendon.
Toy, M. (1994) *Architecture and film*. New York: Architectural Design.
Tranter, J. (1998) *Late night radio*. Edinburgh: Polygon.
TriQuarterly (2003) Pastoral issue, Vol. 116.
Ueda, M. (1982) *Haiku poet Matsuo Basho*. Tokyo: Kodansha.
Virgil (1st century BC). *Eclogues. Georgics. Aeneid I–VI* (H. R. Fairclough, trans.). Cambridge, MA and London: Harvard University Press.
Vitruvius (1st century BC) *The ten books on architecture*. (M. H. Morgan, trans., 1960). New York: Dover.
Wake in Fright [Film] (1971) Ted Kotcheff, dir., Australia.
Walwicz, A. (1994) 'Wonderful'. In *The Bloodaxe book of modern Australian poetry* (J. Tranter and P. Mead, eds, p. 416). Newcastle upon Tyne: Bloodaxe.
Wark, M. (1994) *Virtual geography*. Bloomington and Indianapolis: Indiana University Press.
Whitman, W. (1968) *A choice of Whitman's verse*. London: Faber and Faber.
Wikipedia (2005) 'Russell's Paradox', from http://en.wikipedia.org/wiki/Russell's_paradox (accessed 2005)
Williams, R. (1973) *The country and the city*. New York: Oxford University Press.
Winmar, E. (1999) *The legend of Mount Bakewell and Mount Brown* www.yorkwa.com.au/york/History_MtBakewellBrown.htm (accessed 10 March 2005).
Winmar, R. (1997) *Walwalinj: the hill that cries – Nyungar language and culture*. Manning, WA: Dorothy Winmar.
Wittgenstein, L. (1999) *Tractatus logico-philosophicus* (D. F. Pears and B. F. McGuinness, trans.). London and New York: Routledge.
Words (1999) Television programme hosted by James Griffin.

Australian Broadcasting Commission.

Wordsworth, W. (1800) 'Michael'. In *William Wordsworth* (S. Gill, ed., 1984, pp. 224–236). New York: Oxford University Press.

Wyatt, T. (1988) *The complete poems* (R. A. Rebholz, ed.). Harmondsworth: Penguin.

Yeats, W. (1962) *Selected poetry*. London: Pan.

Zawacki, A. (2000) 'Review of *Zoo*'. In *Australian Book Review*, November, Issue 226.

Note

I have found the Wikipedia sites on Set Theory and related issues to be useful, if unstable and unreliable. They have been utilised, but only so far as they might be before one has to journey into the generics, vagaries and eccentricities of set theory manifested in numerous zones across the net. Wiki sites are a form of netdeath before one even opens a link: now you see it, now you don't. Interesting, but dubious bibliographical use. Still, a rolling and sometimes participatory (even indirectly) recognition and acknowledgement needs to be made.

EU authorised representative for GPSR:
Easy Access System Europe, Mustamäe tee 50,
10621 Tallinn, Estonia
gpsr.requests@easproject.com

www.ingramcontent.com/pod-product-compliance
Ingram Content Group UK Ltd.
Pitfield, Milton Keynes, MK11 3LW, UK
UKHW021832140426
5217IPUK00021B/1399